It Happened to Me

Series Editor: Arlene Hirschfelder

Books in the It Happened to Me series are designed for inquisitive teens digging for answers about certain illnesses, social issues, or lifestyle interests. Whether you are deep into your teen years or just entering them, these books are gold mines of up-to-date information, riveting teen views, and great visuals to help you figure out stuff. Besides special boxes highlighting singular facts, each book is enhanced with the latest reading lists, Web sites, and an index. Perfect for browsing, these books contain loads of expert information by acclaimed writers to help parents, guardians, and librarians understand teen illness, tough situations, and lifestyle choices.

1. *Epilepsy: The Ultimate Teen Guide*, by Kathlyn Gay and Sean McGarrahan, 2002.
2. *Stress Relief: The Ultimate Teen Guide*, by Mark Powell, 2002.
3. *Learning Disabilities: The Ultimate Teen Guide*, by Penny Hutchins Paquette and Cheryl Gerson Tuttle, 2003.
4. *Making Sexual Decisions: The Ultimate Teen Guide*, by L. Kris Gowen, 2003.
5. *Asthma: The Ultimate Teen Guide*, by Penny Hutchins Paquette, 2003.
6. *Cultural Diversity—Conflicts and Challenges: The Ultimate Teen Guide*, by Kathlyn Gay, 2003.
7. *Diabetes: The Ultimate Teen Guide*, by Katherine J. Moran, 2004.
8. *When Will I Stop Hurting? Teens, Loss, and Grief: The Ultimate Teen Guide to Dealing with Grief*, by Ed Myers, 2004.
9. *Volunteering: The Ultimate Teen Guide*, by Kathlyn Gay, 2004.
10. *Organ Transplants—A Survival Guide for the Entire Family: The Ultimate Teen Guide*, by Tina P. Schwartz, 2005.

11. *Medications: The Ultimate Teen Guide*, by Cheryl Gerson Tuttle, 2005.

12. *Image and Identity—Becoming the Person You Are: The Ultimate Teen Guide*, by L. Kris Gowen and Molly C. McKenna, 2005.

13. *Apprenticeship: The Ultimate Teen Guide*, by Penny Hutchins Paquette, 2005.

14. *Cystic Fibrosis: The Ultimate Teen Guide*, by Melanie Ann Apel, 2006.

15. *Religion and Spirituality in America: The Ultimate Teen Guide*, by Kathlyn Gay, 2006.

16. *Gender Identity: The Ultimate Teen Guide*, by Cynthia L. Winfield, 2007.

17. *Physical Disabilities: The Ultimate Teen Guide*, by Denise Thornton, 2007.

18. *Money—Getting It, Using It, and Avoiding the Traps: The Ultimate Teen Guide*, by Robin F. Brancato, 2007.

19. *Self-Advocacy: The Ultimate Teen Guide*, by Cheryl Gerson Tuttle and JoAnn Augeri Silva, 2007.

20. *Adopted: The Ultimate Teen Guide*, by Suzanne Buckingham Slade, 2007.

21. *The Military and Teens: The Ultimate Teen Guide*, by Kathlyn Gay, 2008.

22. *Animals and Teens: The Ultimate Teen Guide*, by Gail Green, 2009.

23. *Reaching Your Goals: The Ultimate Teen Guide*, by Anne E. Courtright, 2009.

24. *Juvenile Arthritis: The Ultimate Teen Guide*, by Kelly Rouba, 2009.

Juvenile Arthritis

The Ultimate Teen Guide

KELLY ROUBA

Illustrations by Geoffrey Trapp

It Happened to Me, No. 24

The Scarecrow Press, Inc.
Lanham, Maryland • Toronto • Plymouth, UK
2009

SCARECROW PRESS, INC.

Published in the United States of America
by Scarecrow Press, Inc.
A wholly owned subsidiary of
The Rowman & Littlefield Publishing Group, Inc.
4501 Forbes Boulevard, Suite 200, Lanham, Maryland 20706
www.scarecrowpress.com

Estover Road
Plymouth PL6 7PY
United Kingdom

Copyright © 2009 by Kelly Rouba

British Library Cataloguing in Publication Information Available

Library of Congress Cataloging-in-Publication Data

Rouba, Kelly, 1980–
  Juvenile arthritis : the ultimate teen guide / Kelly Rouba.
    p. cm. — (It happened to me ; no. 24)
  Includes bibliographical references and index.
  ISBN-13: 978-0-8108-6055-1 (cloth : alk. paper)
  ISBN-10: 0-8108-6055-4 (cloth : alk. paper)
  ISBN-13: 978-0-8108-6715-4 (ebook)
  ISBN-10: 0-8108-6715-X (ebook)
  1. Rheumatoid arthritis in children—Popular works. 2. Rheumatism in children—
Popular works. I. Title.
  RJ482.A77R68 2009
  618.92'7227—dc22   2008042317

♾™ The paper used in this publication meets the minimum requirements of
American National Standard for Information Sciences—Permanence of Paper
for Printed Library Materials, ANSI/NISO Z39.48-1992.
Manufactured in the United States of America.

Contents

Acknowledgments   vii

Introduction   ix

1 The Personal Side of Juvenile Arthritis   1

2 What Is Juvenile Arthritis?   9

3 The Bigger Picture: Arthritis-Related and
       Secondary Conditions   31

4 Treatment Options: From Medicine to Surgery   55

5 Exercising and Maintaining a Proper Diet   91

6 Physical Therapy and Occupational Therapy   127

7 Managing Your Physical and Mental Health   155

8 Moving Forward: Adapting Your Life   193

9 Looking Toward the Future   231

Appendix A: Assistive Devices   247

Appendix B: Research Initiatives   255

Bibliography   273

Index   281

About the Author and Illustrator   287

Acknowledgments

Thank you to:

- ◎ My parents, Kerry and Frank, and my brother, Kevin, for their support and encouragement of all my endeavors.

- ◎ Sally Jones, Alana Wallace, and Diane and Amanda White for inspiring me during this process.

- ◎ Geoff Trapp for creating the marvelous illustrations seen throughout this book. I am so glad we finally had the chance to collaborate together and look forward to more opportunities in the future.

- ◎ Lynn Rich, English and gifted & talented teacher at Nottingham High School in Hamilton, New Jersey, for guiding me through the citation process. You taught me so much when I was in your class and I am glad that you are still willing to teach me today.

- ◎ All the rheumatologists I interviewed. I appreciate you taking time out of your busy schedules to share your expertise. And a special thank-you to Dr. Randy Cron for becoming my "go-to" person on medical questions and helping to proofread.

- ◎ Helene Belisle, Morrie Granger, Marla Brodsky, Kristen McCosh, Jacqueline Kuhns, Javier Robles, and Carolyn Hayer for sharing your knowledge and helping to proofread. Thank you also to Stephen Alexander and Ferne Allen for proofreading.

- ◎ The countless people I interviewed for this book. I cannot thank you enough for sharing your stories or professional expertise.

Acknowledgments

Also, thank you to the following for providing me with information and/or setting up interviews:

- The Arthritis Foundation (national headquarters and local chapters), especially Kim Thompson-Almanzor and Peggy Lotkowictz from the New Jersey Chapter.
- Juliann Walsh at the Children's Hospital of Philadelphia.
- Rob Black of the American Occupational Therapy Association.
- Erin Latimer of the American College of Rheumatology.

Introduction

Although it has been said that L. Frank Baum, author of the Oz book series, created the Tin Man character based on a lifelike metal figure he created for the window display of a small hardware store, it wouldn't be too far-fetched to think that the rusty woodsman was actually modeled after someone with arthritis.

Each day, more than 46 million Americans with arthritis struggle to overcome their limited range of mobility. For them, swollen joints and stiffness can make even the simplest tasks difficult to complete.

Although many people commonly associate arthritis with aging, there are close to three hundred thousand children and teens now living with the disease nationwide. According to Poonam Balani, communications and events manager for the

TEENS, THIS MEANS YOU!

Even though you may not consider yourself a juvenile, the Arthritis Foundation states that juvenile arthritis (JA) refers to any form of arthritis or arthritis-related condition that develops in individuals who are younger than eighteen years of age.

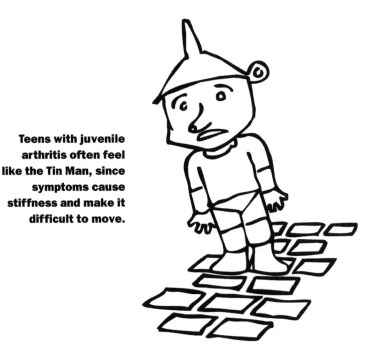

Teens with juvenile arthritis often feel like the Tin Man, since symptoms cause stiffness and make it difficult to move.

New Jersey Chapter of the Arthritis Foundation, "The number of children living with arthritis in the United States is more than muscular dystrophy, hemophilia, and cystic fibrosis combined."

While this statistic may be surprising, children and their families can find comfort in knowing there is hope. Just like the Tin Man was able to continue down the yellow brick road after finding relief in an oilcan, numerous medical treatments and wellness programs (which are mentioned throughout this book) are now available to help young people with juvenile arthritis lead fulfilling lives so that they, too, can continue to pursue their own journeys.

The Personal Side of Juvenile Arthritis

Seventeen-year-old competitive figure skater Amanda White has had her fair share of sports-related injuries since she first began hitting the ice in the fourth grade. And while some injuries have left her sidelined for a few weeks at a time, Amanda has always remained devoted to the sport and works hard to regain any lost ground in time for the next competition.

But in the summer of 2004, Amanda's determination to become a top skater at the sport's novice level was put to the test more than ever before. Conditioned to skate five or six days a week, Amanda was bewildered when her entire body began aching with pain, on and off the ice. "It is really common for skaters to be hurt and injured all the time," Amanda admits. However, it is considered unusual to have pain in multiple areas at once, since most skating mishaps result in damage to either the ankles, the knees, or the spine—not all of the above.

Amanda White is an avid ice skater when her arthritis is under control.

Concerned over her daughter's health, Diane White took Amanda to a pediatrician, a podiatrist, physical therapists, and several orthopedists, who ordered numerous MRIs and X-rays. After test results proved inconclusive, the doctors and Diane determined that it was most likely the rigors of competitive skating that had taken a toll on Amanda's body. "I thought this [pain] was caused by her ice skating," Diane affirms. "I thought she wasn't built for it."

As the condition of her knees, feet, and back worsened, Amanda started going to physical therapy for some relief. Fighting through the pain, Amanda continued to skate competitively for almost a year, until Diane noticed that her daughter's hands had become quite swollen. "It was weird, because I don't use my fingers in skating," Amanda remarks.

As the severe pain and swelling in her hands persisted, Amanda underwent more medical tests in hopes of finding the cause of her condition. A neighbor even suggested she get tested for Lyme disease, because her swollen fingers appeared to be a symptom of the illness. This advice proved futile; the tests were negative.

Still at a loss as to what could be at the root of Amanda's problem, Diane reached out to a friend for help. Her friend, a rheumatologist who treats adults, recommended that Amanda see a pediatric rheumatologist so she could be tested for arthritis. "And it turns out she was right," Amanda says.

Only fourteen years old at the time, Amanda was shocked when doctors diagnosed her with juvenile rheumatoid arthritis (JRA)—the disease is now referred to as juvenile

"I went through a week where I just didn't believe it."—Amanda, age seventeen

idiopathic arthritis (JIA)—in June of 2005. "It never occurred to me what it was," Diane says, adding, "I was convinced it was Lyme disease."

With no history of arthritis in their family, the diagnosis was surprising, and Amanda and Diane were just as surprised to learn that children, like adults, could get arthritis.

Faced with a severe case of JRA that had progressed to her knees, feet, toes, fingers, wrists, ankles, and back, Amanda often struggled with pain during the onset of the disease. She received several injections of cortisone in her back and wrists to help alleviate some of the pressure.

As her freshman year in high school came to a close, Amanda also found herself wrapping up her skating career—temporarily, at least—on the advice of her doctor. "After I was first diagnosed, the doctor wasn't sure if I would be able to keep up with the pace I was skating," she explains. "Skating had taken such a toll on my body. And just with the medicine, I was getting sick."

Reflecting back on the early stages of Amanda's diagnosis, Diane says, "It's amazing what happened to her in such a short amount of time."

There were many nights when Amanda's hands were so swollen that it prevented her from sleeping, Diane recalls. And in the mornings, Amanda often had difficulty making it from her second-floor bedroom to the kitchen downstairs because of the stiff joints in her legs. In fact, sometimes she could not even make it down the stairs.

"I used to listen to her come downstairs in the morning so I could tell if she was going to have a good or a bad day," Diane recalls.

Some days, the pain was so intense that Amanda even stayed home from school. "I was really devastated when I first got arthritis and I thought it would ruin my life. The really ironic thing is it didn't ruin my life," she says. "It almost changed my life for the better."

During her hiatus from skating, Amanda began reevaluating her lifestyle and made a conscious decision to make her health and well-being a priority. She also worked with doctors in order

Figure 1.1.   Amanda White participating in the Moran Memorial Championship skating competition in Hackensack, New Jersey, in August 2004. "This was a pretty emotional time," her mother, Diane, says. "Amanda accepted that competing was going to be a problem because of her RA."

to find a treatment plan that would enable her to live life as pain-free as possible.

"At the beginning, we had a hard time finding the right medicines for me," Amanda says. According to Diane, doctors put Amanda on several strong anti-inflammatory medications, including prednisone, to help reduce the inflammation. She also started taking Ultram to help relieve the pain.

Later, doctors switched Amanda to a new regimen of medicine, including a combination of methotrexate pills, which double as an anticancer drug, and Humira injections to slow the progression of the disease and provide pain relief.

Today, Amanda still receives injections of Humira. She also takes Celebrex each day to alleviate her joint pain and swelling, and she gets weekly injections of methotrexate, since the pill form of the medication made her sick to her stomach. "I refused to take the [methotrexate] shot last year, so I would take it orally and I got so sick." But now, she says, "I really haven't been getting as sick from [the injectable form], I guess because it doesn't pass through your stomach."

In addition to taking medications, Amanda also works with a personal trainer at her local gym in an effort to keep her body in shape. "I have an exercise routine that I do," she says, adding that she learned the stretching exercises when she went to physical therapy.

Although there are still times when the disease flares up, Amanda says she has learned how to manage the condition when that happens. "I know my body more and I know not to push myself through things."

Amanda has also resumed skating competitively, but she no longer allows the demands of the sport to run her life. "In the beginning, I was allowed to skate once a week, but it was almost too hard [emotionally] because I'd get a taste of it and want to come back," she says.

But by September 2006, she did just that. Having found a drug therapy treatment plan that aided in stabilizing her condition, Amanda was able to return to skating on a competitive level and now practices four or five days a week for a couple of hours at a time.

Although skating is a big part of her life, Amanda also devotes much of her time to schoolwork. Preparing to enter college at the University of Richmond as a freshman in the fall of 2008, Amanda was confident that she would be able to adapt to her new surroundings just as she had in high school. Although the workload was overwhelming at times, Amanda's high school teachers were aware of her physical limitations. Discussing her situation with her teachers helped them to understand that there are days when she tires easily because her joints ache and many responded positively to accommodating her needs.

"If I was having a bad day or something, most of them were extremely understanding," Amanda says. "I had extended time on tests, which was a big help. I [also] brought a voice recorder to school sometimes, and that helped when it was a class with a lot of note taking."

"I was also extremely close to the nurse at school," she adds. "Every time I ever had a problem, I could go see her, which is really great."

Although she was initially worried that having arthritis would make her stand out among her peers, Amanda says that most of her classmates were very supportive after she was diagnosed.

"She developed a chronic disease at a difficult age," Diane remarks. "As a freshman in high school, everybody's already uncomfortable with themselves and worried about how they'll fit in."

"I've learned through this [experience] that you need to pick the right friends," Amanda adds. Outside of school, Amanda's friends still include her in social activities and have rallied to support her efforts as a volunteer with the Arthritis Foundation, a national nonprofit organization dedicated to eradicating arthritis.

To help the foundation promote awareness of arthritis and raise funds for research initiatives, Amanda served as youth chair of the 2007 Mercer County Arthritis Walk in New Jersey. "[My friends] know that I'm involved in the Arthritis Foundation and they think it's really cool," Amanda says, noting that several of them even participated in the walk.

Diane, who is aiding Amanda in her mission, says, "People just have to be more aware of this disease with kids. So many people have asked me if Amanda developed this disease because of all the time she spent ice skating. You want people not to think it's just an old person's disease. I have a whole new appreciation for children and young people with arthritis, or any chronic disease."

"[Having a disease] gives you the chance to reevaluate your life and what you really want to do. You can live a very normal life and still do the things that you love to do."—Amanda, age seventeen

As Amanda continues to adjust to life with arthritis, she is glad to know that her family is there beside her, every step of the way. "I'm really close to my family," she says. "They are really supportive. I think that is a huge, huge help."

Amanda was devastated when she was first diagnosed, but her family helped her to get her life back in order, and now she has a different attitude toward life. "Her life is just much more fulfilled now. Before, skating was her life, and because of this disease, she's had a chance to learn there's a lot of other things out there," Diane says.

2

What Is Juvenile Arthritis?

Imagine waking up every morning so stiff from joint pain that you are barely able to crawl out of bed. You hobble your way to the tub to fix a hot bath—after all, it's the only thing that will help your joints to loosen up. After taking a bath, your stiffness has lessened, leaving you with just the normal aches and pains you're faced with daily. Today the pain may not be so severe, but tomorrow it could be much worse. It's the type of pain that makes everyday tasks quite difficult—sometimes even impossible. All you want to do is escape. Going to bed has become your favorite "activity," just as long as you don't lie there thinking about the day ahead.

The situation I just described might sound like the life of someone in his or her golden years—perhaps even your own grandmother or grandfather—but it's not. It is the life of more than three hundred thousand children and teens living with juvenile arthritis.

JUVENILE ARTHRITIS DEFINED

It's no secret that arthritis often comes with aging. In fact, more than 46 million adults have some form of the disease. But 8.4 million young adults between the ages of eighteen and forty-four also have the disease.[1] "Rheumatoid arthritis affects one in every one hundred people, but [studies or surveys] in the workforce estimate as high as one in three people are affected by arthritis related issues at work," says Dr. Randy Cron, director of the Division of Pediatric Rheumatology at

Children's Hospital of Alabama/University of Alabama at Birmingham.

Moreover, "arthritis is the leading cause of disability in the United States among those over sixteen," adds Kristen Delaney, a seventeen-year-old from Fort Dodge, Iowa, who has juvenile idiopathic arthritis.

At last count, there are more than one hundred different types of arthritis found in adults. You might be surprised to learn that Lyme disease, carpal tunnel syndrome, and systemic lupus erythematosus all fall into this category.

As you know by now, arthritis also affects children and young adults. Arthritis that affects children under the age of sixteen is called juvenile or childhood arthritis. And like its adult counterpart, juvenile arthritis is also an umbrella term for multiple forms of arthritis, although there are far fewer types found in children. These range from juvenile idiopathic (or rheumatoid) arthritis to juvenile psoriatic arthritis. In most cases, juvenile arthritis often remains in a person's body for months or years; therefore, it is considered to be a chronic illness.

The word "arthritis" was created from the Greek roots *arthr* and *itis*, meaning "joint" and "inflammation," respectively. Put simply, arthritis means inflammation of the joints.

"Arthritis is defined as swollen joints or loss of the normal range of motion [along] with pain," said Dr. Marisa Klein-Gitelman, head of the Division of Rheumatology at Children's Memorial Hospital in Chicago, Illinois. Children who have

COMMON FORMS OF JUVENILE ARTHRITIS FOUND IN YOUTH

Juvenile Idiopathic Arthritis
Juvenile Spondyloarthropies
Juvenile Psoriatic Arthritis
Juvenile Dermatomyositis
Juvenile Systemic Lupus Erythematosus
Juvenile Vasculitis

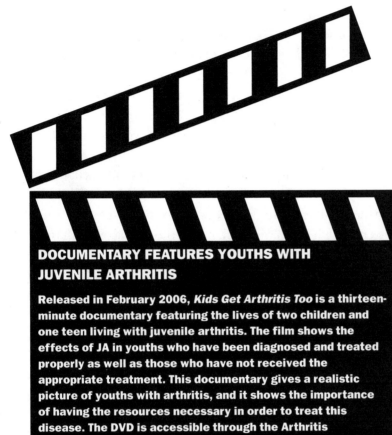

DOCUMENTARY FEATURES YOUTHS WITH JUVENILE ARTHRITIS

Released in February 2006, *Kids Get Arthritis Too* is a thirteen-minute documentary featuring the lives of two children and one teen living with juvenile arthritis. The film shows the effects of JA in youths who have been diagnosed and treated properly as well as those who have not received the appropriate treatment. This documentary gives a realistic picture of youths with arthritis, and it shows the importance of having the resources necessary in order to treat this disease. The DVD is accessible through the Arthritis Foundation Alabama Chapter. Send DVD requests to the chapter at: 2700 Highway 280 East, Suite 180, Birmingham, AL 35223, or e-mail info.al@arthritis.org. For more information, call (205) 979–5700.

juvenile arthritis experience pain, stiffness, and swelling in at least one joint.

In order to better understand arthritis, let's take a look at the function of joints. You probably already know that your knees, wrists, elbows, and hips are all joints. So are your knuckles, shoulders, and even your jaw—to name just a few more. Simply put, joints are the parts of your body that move by connecting two or more bones.

"Around the bones are tissues connected together to make a joint capsule. Inside the joint capsule is a lining called the synovium (or synovium membrane). The synovium makes synovial fluid."[2] According to information published by Penn

State Children's Hospital, it is synovial fluid that keeps the joints lubricated and helps bones to move more easily.

People who have arthritis will notice that their joints feel swollen or hot in a way that is often painful. "The swelling comes from having a thick synovium and too much synovial fluid inside your joints. This causes them to hurt. You also get more blood going to the area around your joint, making it feel warm."[3]

"When the synovial membrane becomes inflamed, it stiffens and thickens, making it difficult to move the joint. This constant inflammation damages protective tissue that covers the end of a bone in the joint, called the cartilage. With time, the joint can become deformed, the cartilage can be destroyed, and the unprotected bone can begin to wear away."[4] This can lead to significant damage to the body.

The amount of swelling seen in children varies depending on the individual. Children who do not have much swelling may still experience extreme stiffness, however.

Overall, though, "it's hard to have a general definition for arthritis because there are so many variables. Every person with

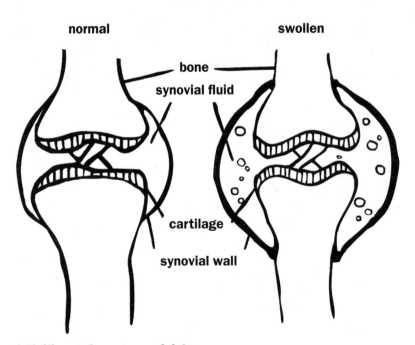

Arthritis can damage your joints.

HISTORY OF JUVENILE ARTHRITIS

According to Dr. Patience White, chief public health officer for the National Arthritis Foundation, "Juvenile arthritis was discovered by [Sir] George Frederic Still." More specifically, Still is actually credited with discovering a form of juvenile arthritis that is known as systemic juvenile idiopathic arthritis, or Still's disease.

While working at a children's hospital in Cambridge during the late 1800s, Still, who was a medical student at the time, reported twenty-two cases of children who showed signs of having a form of arthritis.[5] Still found that the condition had caused their joints to become stiff and in some cases even enlarged. Still also noticed that the children's glands and spleen seemed to be enlarged as well. In addition, he stated that the disease caused "a general arrest of physical development, a slow disease course and progression to a condition of general joint disease."[6]

"In 1897, he published his results in a paper entitled *On a form of chronic joint disease in children*. It was also the subject of his MD thesis and introduced a previously unrecognizable disease, known, as it is today, as Still's Disease (or systemic juvenile idiopathic arthritis)."[7]

Still reported that the disease seemed to occur more often in girls than in boys. He also noted that the disease is typically not considered fatal, even though some children did die due to complications.

arthritis is so individual. Somebody may have it in one joint and somebody, like me, may have it in multiple joints. And some people's pain is more severe," says Kristen.

DIAGNOSING JUVENILE ARTHRITIS

There is no one specific test that determines whether or not an individual has juvenile arthritis. Instead, doctors must go through a variety of measures to make a diagnosis. And "most doctors, unless they have a specific interest [in juvenile arthritis] don't know how to do a specific exam," says Dr. Harry L. Gewanter, a pediatric rheumatologist from Richmond, Virginia. Because of this, doctors sometimes miss telltale signs of the disease and consequently mistake symptoms for those of other conditions, like Lyme disease or even just normal wear and tear of the body.

"Juvenile arthritis is a fairly uncommon illness, even despite the numbers," says Dr. Gewanter, who is also a clinical associate professor of pediatrics, physical medicine, and rehabilitation at Virginia Commonwealth University School of Medicine. For that reason, juvenile arthritis isn't typically something doctors think of first when a young patient complains of joint pain. For instance, in Amanda White's case, doctors simply mistook her pain as injuries caused by her involvement in competitive ice skating.

Kristen, who was diagnosed with juvenile idiopathic arthritis at the age of two, says that just like the Whites, her family also had a difficult time getting doctors to realize the constant pain in her ankle wasn't caused by an injury. "My mom really went through a tough time because a lot of people kept saying, 'Were you abusive to your daughter? Did you push her down the stairs?' A lot of doctors and nurses have to ask that. They don't think about kids having arthritis," says Kristen.

Shaun-Marie Robbins, a twenty-eight-year-old from Hamilton, New Jersey, says her mother also had a rough time convincing doctors that she was seriously ill when she began experiencing symptoms of juvenile idiopathic arthritis at the age of one and a half. "It may have been closer to age two [when I was diagnosed] since the doctors were having a hard time trying to find out what was wrong. My mom had the worst time trying to tell them that something was even wrong to begin with," she says.

Making an official diagnosis of juvenile arthritis can be difficult because "there are lots of things that make you hurt and not all the things that make you hurt are arthritis," says Dr. Gewanter.

"To diagnose juvenile arthritis, although [the] systemic [form] is a little different, we are talking about it lasting at least six weeks without any other cause," says Dr. Klein-Gitelman. As part of their examination, doctors look to confirm whether the child has severe joint pain. Since arthritis causes

Figure 2.1.   Shaun-Marie Robbins (on left) with cousin Heather Olex in Florida. Shaun-Marie was diagnosed with juvenile rheumatoid arthritis as a baby.

inflammation in the lining of the joints, the result is joint pain, swelling, stiffness, and restricted mobility. Most children who have juvenile arthritis shy away from using a particular limb because of the stress on their joints. Some even limp or overcompensate by changing the way they move a particular limb in an effort to avoid pain. "How the child moves and how they sit and all those other nonverbal cues are extremely important [when making a diagnosis]," says Dr. Gewanter.

When conducting a complete physical exam, Dr. Gewanter looks to discover swollen or warm joints on the patient and to determine exactly where and why the patient is experiencing pain in his or her body. He also looks to answer questions like: Are the muscles surrounding that joint smaller because they haven't been used as much? How does the person move?

This routine is fairly commonplace among doctors. Aside from looking for joint inflammation, doctors also want to see if a patient has any rashes, skin conditions, eye problems, or nodules—all signs of juvenile arthritis. In addition, children often experience high fevers at the onset of juvenile arthritis.

And, among other symptoms, children may feel fatigued when the disease first comes on.

Ten-year-old Eric Terry of Woodbridge, Virginia, was only two years old when he was diagnosed with juvenile idiopathic arthritis. Although he is young, Eric is wise beyond his years and often shares advice on coping with JA to older audiences at events hosted by area chapters of the Arthritis Foundation. He was even featured in the National Arthritis Foundation's video campaign in 2007.

Eric's mother, Cynthia Terry, is also an advocate for those living with juvenile arthritis and will never forget when her son first became ill. "I was giving him a bath and I noticed that his knee kept swelling and I didn't remember him falling," Cynthia says. Not long after noticing her son's swollen knee, Cynthia took Eric to be examined by their doctor. The diagnosis was polyarticular juvenile idiopathic arthritis, which means that the disease had invaded five or more joints.

Cynthia believes it's possible that Eric acquired juvenile arthritis quite a while before he was diagnosed. "As a baby, he would get these fevers, and we didn't know what was going on. [My husband and I] took him to the emergency room about three or four times. Looking back, I really just think he had [juvenile arthritis] as an infant," Cynthia says.

Although there are still times when doctors don't pick up on the symptoms of juvenile arthritis right away, Dr. Gewanter thinks these instances are not as common nowadays. "I have a sense it's happening less frequently or it's not taking quite as long [to diagnose], but it still takes a while," he says.

Still, says Dr. Gewanter, "we don't have any single test to diagnose [juvenile arthritis]." Instead, doctors must consider a multitude of factors before they can diagnose someone with juvenile arthritis. X-rays and several specific blood tests—including a complete blood count, erythrocyte sedimentation rate (ESR), rheumatoid factor (RF), and antinuclear antibody (ANA)—are usually necessary to help doctors make a determination, since the disease affects the body's blood cells. Doctors also test the patient's blood to see if there is a high white blood cell count and to see whether the individual has

Routine blood tests are often required when taking medicine for juvenile arthritis.

"a marker called C-reactive protein in their blood, which measures the amount of inflammation." Some individuals with juvenile arthritis also have anemia, which means their red blood count is low.[8]

To further aid in the diagnostic process, doctors like to get a complete medical history on the patient. This includes asking

COMMON DIAGNOSTIC BLOOD TESTS

The following is a quick look at some of the blood tests doctors usually order when determining whether an individual has juvenile arthritis.

- *Rheumatoid factor (RF).* Although it is not found in everyone with juvenile idiopathic arthritis, some individuals will test positive for rheumatoid factor. Basically, rheumatoid factor is a protein (or antibody) found in the blood. "In patients with symptoms and clinical signs of rheumatoid arthritis, the presence of significant concentrations of RF indicates that it is likely that they have RA."[9]
- *Complete blood count.* This test is both a count and assessment of the various types of red blood cells, white blood cells, and platelets in a person's blood. Depending on the results, it can indicate that an illness is present.
- *Erythrocyte sedimentation rate (ESR).* An ESR measures the rate of fall (or sedimentation) of red blood cells (erythrocytes) in order to detect and monitor inflammation levels.
- *Antinuclear antibody (ANA).* Some individuals with JIA have a protein in their blood known as an antinuclear antibody. This blood test is done to determine whether ANA is present in the bloodstream.

whether family members have had any similar health conditions. To make a proper diagnosis, "for me, it's really [about] sitting down and talking to people for a long time," Dr. Gewanter says.

Once the doctor suspects arthritis, he will refer the patient to a rheumatologist, a doctor who specializes in treating arthritis. Individuals who are experiencing symptoms of arthritis are encouraged to visit their doctor as soon as possible, since an early diagnosis, along with proper treatment, can slow or prevent further joint and tissue damage.[10]

EXPLORING JUVENILE IDIOPATHIC ARTHRITIS

Juvenile arthritis is the number one cause of acquired disability in young people. Also, it "is the sixth most common childhood disease, following asthma, congenital heart disease, cerebral palsy, diabetes, and epilepsy."[11] Furthermore, juvenile idiopathic arthritis is the most common form of juvenile arthritis, affecting nearly fifty thousand children in the United States.[12] JIA is one of the most prevalent chronic childhood illnesses.

Symptoms of JIA generally include swollen joints, stiffness or pain, and fatigue. As a result, children experience joint tenderness and their range of motion becomes limited. Rheumatoid nodules, which are bumps under the skin, can also be found on some children with JIA. "Typically, [they occur] over the elbows—sort of on the back of the forearm between the elbow and the pinky," says Dr. Ilona S. Szer, chief of allergy, immunology, and rheumatology at Rady Children's Hospital in San Diego, California. According to Dr. Szer, who is also a professor of clinical pediatrics at the University of California, San Diego School of Medicine, the nodules resemble a "bump" that would occur if you hit yourself badly—however, they are the same color as your skin, and not purplish in color. "It's extra tissue that develops, and really it only occurs in less than three percent of children. They are about half an inch round. [They are] not tender and they only occur in older adolescent girls who have JIA," Dr. Szer adds. Nodules may hurt for a while, but they will eventually go away.

Each case of JIA is unique, however, and not every individual who has the disease will experience the same type of symptoms. It's also important to note that juvenile idiopathic (or rheumatoid) arthritis is quite different from the adult form of rheumatoid arthritis. In fact, according to Dr. Szer, some forms of JIA are not present in adults. Adults with arthritis also typically have rheumatoid factor present in their blood, which isn't always the case in children. Furthermore, arthritis can affect a child's growth and the disease may go into remission after a number of years, which isn't true for adults.

It is important to note that juvenile idiopathic arthritis was referred to as juvenile rheumatoid arthritis and sometimes even juvenile chronic arthritis (JCA) until recently.

"A few years back, the classification for juvenile idiopathic arthritis was revamped and will likely be revamped again in the future," says Dr. Cron. According to Dr. Cron, the cause of JIA is unknown, and by definition, it's not associated with any other underlying disease, like lupus.

Presently, there are several forms of JIA. "Ultimately, genetics will probably assist in the most appropriate classification of the subtypes of childhood arthritis. The current system lumps what used to be called juvenile rheumatoid arthritis with the spondyloarthropathies—HLA-B27-associated diseases that frequently have enthesitis [inflammation of the point where a bone connects with a tendon or ligament] in addition to arthritis. These subcategories were developed in part because the course and outcome somewhat differ between the subgroups, and for research purposes it is usually important to compare apples to apples and not to oranges."

Subgroups of Juvenile Idiopathic Arthritis

According to Dr. Randy Cron and Dr. Harry Gewanter, the following are the current subgroupings of juvenile idiopathic arthritis:

- ◎ *Systemic JIA* (formerly systemic onset JRA).
- ◎ *Oligoarticular JIA* (formerly pauciarticular JRA). This subgroup is further divided into *persistent* (meaning after six months of

having the disease, four joints or less are affected) and *extended* (meaning after six months, more than four joints are affected).

◎ *Polyarticular JIA.* This subgroup is also divided into those who are rheumatoid factor negative or rheumatoid factor positive.

◎ *Enthesitis-related arthritis/Juvenile Spondyloarthropathies* (formerly SEA or seronegative enthesopathy and arthropathy syndrome).

◎ *Psoriatic arthritis.*

◎ *Other JIA cases* (meaning those that do not fit any of the above criteria or those that fit in more than one category).

Each JIA subgroup has varying degrees of severity in terms of how individuals with the illness are affected. Here is a look at what to expect with each condition.

Systemic JIA

Also known as Still's disease, systemic JIA affects the entire body. Aside from severe joint inflammation that occurs throughout the body, teens with systemic JIA may also have inflammation of the outer lining of the heart and lungs. Or the heart and lungs themselves may also become inflamed. Teens with systemic JIA may also have anemia, and their lymph nodes, liver, or even their spleen may become enlarged.

Other symptoms include dramatic fevers of 103 degrees or higher that can last for several weeks or months and usually occur at the onset of systemic JIA. Rashes may also develop on the patient's body, most often appearing on his or her chest or thighs. Typically, the rashes consist of pale red spots that seem to come and go at times.

To date, systemic JIA is the least common form of JIA and affects boys about as equally as girls.[13] "A number of them will have one episode and it goes away for whatever reason," Dr. Gewanter says. Others may no longer experience most symptoms of the disease, but will find that the arthritis remains in their body. In order to monitor the disease, doctors will routinely request blood work.

Oligoarticular JIA

This is the most common form of JIA. Teens with oligoarticular JIA may experience inflammation in up to four of their joints. In fact, it's possible that only a couple of joints will become inflamed as a result of the disease. Generally, larger joints like the knees are affected most by this form of JIA. When joints become inflamed, it often causes an individual to experience pain, stiffness, swelling, and can restrict his or her mobility.

Although it may sound odd, the iris (the colored part of the eye) may also become inflamed in those who have oligoarticular JIA. This condition, known as uveitis or iritis, can also occur in teens who have other forms of JIA. "[Children with oligoarticular JIA] have the risk of eye inflammation more than other groups," Dr. Klein-Gitelman notes.

Polyarticular JIA

Polyarticular JIA affects five or more joints. "It's like a painful disease that nobody likes that keeps you away from doing things, and it's something that you don't really want to have," Eric says.

"It's a much more aggressive arthritis," agrees Dr. Gewanter. He says that this form of JIA can be likened to an adult onset that starts before age sixteen. This is significant because JIA is not usually as severe as the adult form of the disease.

Polyarticular JIA "usually affects the small joints of the fingers and hands, but it also can affect weight-bearing joints, such as the knees, hips, ankles, and feet" in young people.[14] And, in most cases, the same joints are affected on each side of the body, which is known as symmetrical arthritis. This is not the case in individuals who have oligoarticular JIA.

Cynthia says her son has arthritis in his ankles, knees, shoulders, hips, wrists, and right ring fingers. "He complains a lot about his back too," she says. Sometimes he still experiences fevers and headaches as well.

In 1990, eighteen-month-old Stefanie Tepley of Culver City, California, was diagnosed with polyarticular JIA and Lyme disease. Dr. Cron notes that JIA has no real known cause, whereas Lyme disease is triggered by a spirochete (a kind of bacteria) infection. In her case, the infection was brought on by a deer tick bite. Unfortunately, both diseases can be agonizing. "I just basically grew [up] into knowing that I was in pain and that I had a lot of limitations that the kids in school didn't have," says Stefanie.

At the onset of her condition, Stefanie was very sick. She had strep throat, ear infections, pneumonia, and was even having trouble walking. "She had been sick from six months to eighteen months," says Kathy Tepley, Stefanie's mother.

Typical signs of polyarticular JIA, however, include a low-grade fever at the onset of the disease, along with joint pain or swelling. Doctors will request several blood tests to look for other indications of the disease. Teens who have polyarticular JIA will be rheumatoid factor positive or negative, which can be determined by a blood test.

"Rheumatoid factor is an immunoglobulin [antibody] which can bind to other antibodies. Antibodies are normal proteins found in the blood which function within the immune system."[15] According to Dr. Klein-Gitelman, "With the factor being negative, those patients tend to have a better outcome." Those who do test positive for rheumatoid factor will likely have a more severe form of the disease. Doctors also test to see if patients have anemia, or low red blood cell counts.

According to information released by the Arthritis Foundation, polyarticular JIA is found more often in girls than in boys. "Primarily, it's teenage girls who fall into the subtype," Dr. Gewanter adds.

Both Amanda and Kristen have polyarticular JIA. Kristen's condition first began in her ankle, and she complained so much while walking in the mall one day that her parents took her to the pediatrician. Her pediatrician sent her to a rheumatologist, who confirmed she had arthritis.

At first, "my ankle was hurting me, and as I got older they started finding it in other places," Kristen says. Today, she has arthritis in both of her ankles, knees, wrists, and all of her knuckles.

It's important to remember that not everyone with polyarticular JIA is affected in the same way. Some teens with polyarticular JIA also have problems with their neck. Others may have it in their temporomandibular joint, which is "the joint in front of the ears where the lower jaw connects to the base of the skull."[16] This condition, known as TMJ arthritis, is known to limit jaw movement and can even affect growth.

Teens who have arthritis in their neck, or cervical spine, are vulnerable to spinal cord injuries because the connections between the vertebrae become unstable. If doctors feel a child is at risk for injury, routine exams and X-rays will be required to monitor the activity of the disease.

Psoriatic Arthritis

Psoriasis is a skin condition that causes a scaly red rash to form on much of the patient's body, including the elbows, eyelids, knees, scalp line, belly button, buttocks, and even behind the ears. In some cases, patients also have pitting, ridging, or yellowing of their fingernails.

Approximately 12 to 14 percent of people with psoriasis will develop psoriatic arthritis.[17] Sometimes the psoriasis begins quite a few years before or after the onset of arthritis. Young people who have psoriatic arthritis may experience problems with larger joints, like their hips. Sometimes the same joint on both sides of the body may have arthritis. The sacroiliac joints, which are located at the bottom of the back, may also be affected.

Another symptom of psoriatic arthritis is swelling of the fingers and toes, which often become so swollen that they seem to resemble sausages. This is known as dactylitis. Inflammation of the eye or eyes also occurs in 10 to 20 percent of youth living with this condition.[18]

Enthesitis-Related Arthritis/ Juvenile Spondyloarthropathies

Certain types of arthritic-related diseases affect the spine as well as tendons. They specifically target the areas where the tendons attach to the bone. These forms of arthritis are classified as seronegative spondyloarthropathies. "When seen in children, they are referred to as juvenile spondyloarthropathies."[19]

There are several different forms of juvenile spondyloarthropathies (JSp). These include reactive arthritis, enteropathogenic arthritis (which is arthritis associated with inflammatory bowel disease), juvenile ankylosing spondylitis (AS), and seronegative enthesopathy and arthropathy (SEA) syndrome.

"The spondyloarthropathies are a group of diseases that may involve the spine or sacroiliac joints, and the joints of the lower extremities, most commonly the hips and knees."[20] Often the diseases only affect particular joints (usually the larger ones) on one side of the body. In addition, eye inflammation is also likely.

Those who have juvenile ankylosing spondylitis are highly likely to develop arthritis in larger joints in the lower half of the body as well as the axial skeleton, which are the bones that make up the head and trunk of the body. It is especially known to cause arthritis along the spine and joints located at the bottom of the back. Individuals who have AS will find that their joints and spine are very stiff. Loss of motion and deformity also occur over the years. In addition, AS can "cause inflammation of the eyes, lungs, and heart valves."[21]

At the onset of AS, it may be thought that the patient solely has a problem with his spine. However, one of the first signs of AS is that it causes a significant "loss of flexibility in the lumbar spine."[22] Eventually, the disease progresses to the upper back and neck areas; arthritis may also affect the patient's hips, feet, and shoulders. Other signs of AS include fever, fatigue, and weight loss. Additionally, patients may become anemic or develop inflammatory bowel disease, which are described further in chapter 3.

Unlike some other forms of JIA, spondyloarthropathies occur more often in boys than girls.[23] Typically, the onset is during the adolescent years. It is also commonly found in children with a certain "gene, called HLA-B27, which is present in about 8 percent of Caucasians in the United States," Dr. Cron notes. Therefore, when making their diagnosis, doctors will test the child's blood to look for HLA-B27.

However, "there are not really any [specific diagnostic] tests, so it was really hard to find out what I had," says Allyson Shapiro, who was diagnosed with JSp in 2003, at ten years of age. Allyson, now fifteen, resides in Manhattan, New York, and discusses her struggles with the disease regularly on Bravo's reality show *The Real Housewives of New York City*. "It hurts the most in my neck and shoulders," Allyson says. "Sometimes, it could be [more painful in] my knees, but not every day."

Figure 2.2.   Allyson Shapiro (right) and her mother, Jill Zarin. Both talk about Allyson's struggles with juvenile spondyloarthropathy on Bravo's reality show *The Real Housewives of New York City*.

Because there is no single test used to diagnose JSp, a variety of tests may be necessary to come to a firm diagnosis. Doctors also look to confirm that all symptoms of JSp are persistent for at least six weeks before diagnosing a patient with a form of juvenile spondyloarthropathy.[24] In Allyson's case, she experienced symptoms for quite a while before being diagnosed. "Over about one year, I just started [feeling] really weird and had a lot of different pains all over my body," she says. After she saw several different specialists, a doctor finally made the diagnosis.

FLARES IN PATIENTS WITH ARTHRITIS

Teens with juvenile arthritis find that their symptoms are not always the same from day to day. Some days they might feel better, and some days they feel worse. As long as the arthritis is present in at least one joint, it is considered to be active. At times when the arthritis is more active than usual, it's referred to as a flare, flare-up, or exacerbation.

Aside from causing intense joint pain and stiffness, flares can also cause fatigue or general weakness. When Eric was about five, he had a bad flare. At the time, his father, Reggie, was serving in Iraq. "They had to get the Red Cross to send [Reggie] home because of Eric's condition," Cynthia says. Eventually, doctors stabilized Eric's condition with additional medication. Getting plenty of rest is also important during times when the arthritis is flaring up.

When experiencing a flare, it's important to inform your doctor so he or she can determine whether additional or alternative medications are needed to stabilize the disease. "Flares can happen for a lot of reasons," Dr. Klein-Gitelman says, adding that even bad weather or other illnesses can trigger a flare. "Some people are bothered by wet weather and cold weather and other people aren't." Allyson definitely notices a difference in her condition when temperatures drop. "It hurts more in the winter," she says.

Doctors may also run tests to see if the flare is an indication of increased inflammation. Morning stiffness is also an indicator of active arthritis. The longer the child remains stiff, the more active the arthritis is.[25] Increased inflammation can create further joint damage or the erosion of joint surfaces. Inflammation can also alter growth, since it can advance or impede the process that occurs in the growth centers in bones. "Almost all growth plates near joints with arthritis overgrow," Dr. Cron says. "One exception is TMJ, which results in smaller jaw bones. [In addition], steroids can stunt overall body growth, but uncontrolled disease activity can also suppress overall growth. So, the goal is to shut down the disease inflammation with drugs other than steroids for the longer term."

Depending on the type of arthritis a child has, flares often come and go for many years. "Fortunately for most children, these flares tend to become less severe and occur less often with time."[26]

REMISSION

Just as the number and severity of flares tend to lessen over time, so too can symptoms of juvenile arthritis. Symptoms of JA can also simply disappear altogether. In fact, studies have shown that JA symptoms in particular disappear in more than half of all affected children and teens by the time they reach adulthood.[27]

When symptoms subside or simply go away, it means the individual has gone into remission. Doctors can confirm this by running various tests. It is important to remember that even though a teen may enter remission, it is possible that the disease will become active again. Also, even if the arthritis has quieted down or gone away, it still may have caused permanent damage to the body while it was active. In this case, surgery or other treatments may be needed. (We'll discuss this in greater detail in chapter 4.)

WHAT CAUSES JUVENILE ARTHRITIS?

"I actually have no family history of arthritis. How and why I got arthritis, I still have no idea to this day," Kristen says. Nor do rheumatologists or scientific researchers, for that matter. In fact, the cause of juvenile arthritis is still unknown.

What doctors do know is that juvenile arthritis is an autoimmune disease, which means that the body's white blood cells are unable to determine the difference between healthy cells and "invaders," like bacteria or viruses. So the immune system releases chemicals that damage healthy tissues.

No one knows why this happens, but "when immune cells and proteins, called antibodies, crowd into the joints, the joint lining becomes inflamed," and it causes swelling and stiffness. In most cases, inflammation ceases after the body has fought off unwanted viruses or bacteria. But the opposite is true in patients with juvenile arthritis, which is what makes it qualify as a chronic condition.[28]

Scientists are still working hard to find a definitive answer as to what causes or triggers juvenile arthritis. To date, there is no definitive evidence that food, toxins, allergies, or vitamin deficiencies are causes of juvenile arthritis. We also know that the disease is not contagious. "Current research indicates that there may be a genetic predisposition to juvenile arthritis." It appears that certain environmental factors, when combined with these particular genes, contribute to the development of the disease.[29] (To learn more about ongoing research, see chapter 9.)

WEB SITES WORTH CHECKING OUT

- *Arthritis Foundation.* To find more information pertaining to juvenile arthritis and related conditions, visit www.arthritis.org.
- *Health Talk.* For more information on juvenile arthritis and related conditions, visit www.healthtalk.com.
- *Arthritis Chat.* To participate in an arthritis chat room or to learn more about arthritis, related conditions, and alternative treatments, visit www.arthritischat.com.

NOTES

1. Arthritis Foundation, "Arthritis in Children, Teens and Young Adults," www.arthritis.org/juvenile-arthritis.php.

2. Joyce L. Falco et al., *JRA & Me: A Fun Workbook* (Denver, CO: Rocky Mountain Juvenile Arthritis Center at the National Jewish Center and the Arthritis Foundation, 1987), 18.

3. Ibid., 19.

4. Penn State Children's Hospital, "Health & Disease Information: Juvenile Arthritis," www.hmc.psu.edu/childrens/healthinfo/jkl/juvenilearthritis.htm.

5. Who Named It? "Sir George Frederick Still," www.whonamedit.com/doctor.cfm/1671.html.

6. S. J. Farrow, "Sir George Frederick Still (1868–1941)," *Rheumatology* (2006): 777–78.

7. Ibid.

8. Penn State Children's Hospital, "Health & Disease Information: Juvenile Arthritis."

9. Lab Tests Online, "Rheumatoid Factor," www.labtestsonline.org/understanding/analytes/rheumatoid/test.html.

10. Arthritis Foundation, "Arthritis in Children, Teens and Young Adults."

11. Childhood Arthritis and Rheumatology Research Alliance, "Fact Sheet," www.carragroup.org/content_dsp.do?pc=fact.

12. Nemours Foundation, "Juvenile Rheumatoid Arthritis," KidsHealth, www.kidshealth.org/parent/medical/arthritis/jra.html.

13. Arthritis Foundation, *Arthritis in Children* (pamphlet, 2004), 5.

14. Ibid., 4.

15. Carol Eustice and Richard Eustice, "What Is Rheumatoid Factor?" About.com, http://arthritis.about.com/od/radiagnosis/a/rheumfactor.htm.

16. Arthritis Foundation, *Arthritis in Children*, 5.

17. Arthritis Foundation, "Juvenile Psoriatic Arthritis," http://ww2.arthritis.org/conditions/DiseaseCenter/juvenilepsoriaticarthritis.asp.

18. Ibid.

19. Arthritis Foundation, "Juvenile Spondyloarthopathy," http://ww2.arthritis.org/conditions/DiseaseCenter/juvenilespondyloarthopathy.asp.

20. Arthritis Foundation, *Arthritis in Children*, 6.

21. Ibid., 7.

22. Ibid.

23. Ibid.

24. Arthritis Foundation, "Juvenile Spondyloarthopathy."

25. Arthritis Foundation, *Arthritis in Children*, 19.

26. Arthritis Society of Canada, "Juvenile Arthritis," www
.arthritis.ca/types%20of%20arthritis/childhood/default.asp?s=1.

27. Consumer Health Information Network, "Juvenile Arthritis
Symptoms," http://arthritis-symptom.com/Juvenile-Arthritis-Symptoms/
index.htm.

28. Penn State Children's Hospital, "Health & Disease
Information: Juvenile Arthritis."

29. Arthritis Foundation, *Arthritis in Children*, 2.

The Bigger Picture: Arthritis-Related and Secondary Conditions

Chapter 2 summarized many of the various forms of juvenile arthritis that young people may experience. Here is a look at a few others: juvenile dermatomyositis, juvenile systemic lupus erythematosus, and juvenile vasculitis. In addition, there are quite a few related conditions that have also been known to cause arthritis in a number of cases. In the first part of this chapter, we will explore those conditions that are most likely to trigger arthritis in young people.

And—as if dealing with juvenile arthritis or a related condition isn't enough for anyone to handle—sometimes the

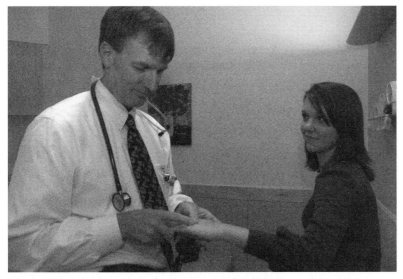

Figure 3.1. Dr. Randy Cron, director of the Division of Pediatric Rheumatology at Children's Hospital of Alabama/University of Alabama at Birmingham, examining a patient.

31

disease can bring about even more health problems, known as secondary conditions. "The subtype of arthritis the child has dictates the secondary conditions the child with JIA may get," says Dr. Randy Cron. This chapter will also explore a few of the more common secondary conditions found in those with juvenile idiopathic arthritis, and several individuals will share their experiences in dealing with these conditions.

RELATED CONDITIONS AND DISEASES

Arthritis can develop as result of a number of conditions and diseases. Here are a few of the more common ones.

Sjögren's Syndrome

Sjögren's syndrome is an autoimmune disease that is considered to be arthritis related; it can occur as a primary or secondary condition. The disease is present in several million Americans whose bodies are unable to tell the difference between healthy cells and foreign substances. As a result, lymphocytes (a type of white blood cell) attack "moisture-producing glands, such as tear and salivary glands, and in some cases the lungs, kidneys, liver, skin, nerves or joints."[1]

According to the Arthritis Foundation's Web site, symptoms can include:

- Dryness of the eyes, throat, mouth, and vaginal area
- Cavities from lack of saliva
- Joint pain, stiffness, and swelling
- Enlarged glands near the jaw
- Fatigue
- Rashes
- Numbness
- Inflammation of the lungs, kidneys, or liver[2]

To diagnose Sjögren's syndrome, doctors conduct a physical exam to look for relevant symptoms. An eye exam is also needed to determine the degree of dryness and whether the disease has caused any damage to the eyes. In addition, a lip biopsy is performed to see whether the salivary glands are inflamed. Blood will also be drawn to see if antibodies, like ANA or anti-SSA, are present.

Fibromyalgia

Individuals who have fibromyalgia experience chronic pain in their joints and muscles. They also typically feel achy and stiff, and often have severe fatigue and difficulty sleeping. Sometimes individuals with fibromyalgia suffer from depression or anxiety. According to the Fibromyalgia Network's Web site, other symptoms include:

- Jaw discomfort
- Painful periods
- Chest pain
- General swelling and morning stiffness
- Cognitive or memory impairment
- Numbness and tingling sensations
- Twitching
- Irritable bladder
- Sensitive skin
- Dry eyes and mouth
- Dizziness and impaired coordination[3]

To diagnose fibromyalgia, doctors typically conduct a palpation exam to determine if there is muscle pain present in

"My doctor was doing his routine checkup and he asked me if a few things hurt and I said, 'Yeah, actually it does hurt there.'"—Kristen, age seventeen

the neck, shoulder, chest, hip, knee, and elbow regions by applying pressure with his or her fingers. It was the winter of 2006 when Kristen Delaney found out she also has fibromyalgia in addition to arthritis.

At the time, Kristen didn't realize something else was wrong with her body. "I was every day with pain. I'm kind of used to the pain so any other bodily pain that I have I hadn't noticed because the pain in my joints was so overwhelming," she says.

Treatments for fibromyalgia typically include medication, massage, physical and occupational therapy, trigger point injections, acupuncture, biofeedback techniques, and chiropractic care. Most of these options will be discussed in the upcoming chapters. However, "although these types of therapies are used in adults, they are really ineffective in childhood fibromyalgia, which responds to intensive aerobic exercise and psychological counseling," Dr. Cron notes.

Lyme Disease

While the severity of symptoms caused by Lyme disease varies, the joints, nervous system, organs, and skin can all be affected. According to the Nemours Foundation's KidsHealth Web site, these are a few of the possible symptoms:

- **Facial paralysis**
- **Tingling or numbness in the arms and legs**
- **Irregular heart rhythm or chest pain**
- **Headaches and neck stiffness**
- **Swelling and pain in the large joints**[4]

"Lyme disease is an infection caused by the bacterium *Borrelia burgdorferi*," which is typically found in mice and deer. "Ixodes ticks can pick up the bacteria when they bite an infected animal, then transmit it to a person, which can lead to Lyme disease." Initial signs of Lyme disease often involve flulike symptoms, including headaches and muscle aches, swollen lymph nodes, and fatigue. A circular rash that looks similar to a bull's-eye often appears on the skin and may be warm to the touch. If Lyme disease is not treated quickly or properly, it can lead to cognitive deterioration and chronic arthritis. These symptoms can show up anywhere from just a few weeks to years after the onset of the disease.[5]

"I got bit by a deer tick at six months old," says Stefanie Tepley, adding that she visited several doctors before she was diagnosed with Lyme disease and JIA at eighteen months old. "The knowledge of the doctors where we were from in Minnesota, there wasn't really any cases like mine that they were used to."

"Finally, because her walking wasn't getting any better, [doctors] sent her down to the University of Minnesota, where they found the Lyme disease and the JRA at the same time," Stefanie's mother, Kathy, adds. "We didn't know if the Lyme disease had been so rampant in her system that it caused the JRA, but at that point on, they treated the Lyme disease with high doses of antibiotics and then were trying to keep the inflammation down, thinking that she would grow out of it. They feel the juvenile rheumatoid arthritis was secondary to the Lyme disease because it just wasn't treated immediately."

Inflammatory Bowel Disease

Inflammatory bowel disease (IBD) encompasses a group of disorders that cause inflammation in the intestinal tract. Often ulcers also occur, which means there are "tears or breaks in the lining of the intestines that can cause pain or bleeding."[6] Arthritis of the joints and spine result in about 25 percent of people who have IBD.[7]

Crohn's disease and ulcerative colitis are two of the most common forms of IBD and can cause ongoing inflammation for years. Stefanie also has Crohn's disease. "Crohn's disease most often develops where the small and large intestines meet and usually causes all layers of the intestinal wall to become sore, inflamed, and swollen. Crohn's disease can affect any part of the digestive tract, including the mouth, esophagus, stomach, small intestines, large intestines, and anus." Ulcerative colitis, however, only causes inflammation of the inner lining of all or part of the colon and rectum. In some cases, only the rectum is inflamed.[8]

Common symptoms of IBD include:

- ◎ **Repeated diarrhea**
- ◎ **Rectal bleeding**
- ◎ **Significant weight loss in a short amount of time**
- ◎ **Fatigue**
- ◎ **Cramps or abdominal pain**
- ◎ **Delayed growth and development[9]**

IBD usually affects individuals between the ages of fifteen and thirty-five, but it can occur in children as young as eighteen months old. Overall, close to one hundred thousand children under the age of eighteen living in the United States have IBD. Although the cause is unknown, researchers suspect it may be due in part to genetics as well as a defect in the immune system.[10]

Sarcoidosis

Individuals with sarcoidosis have inflammation that "produces tiny lumps of cells in various organs [of their] body" called granulomas. Granulomas, which resemble grains of sand, are known to expand and clump together, which can create problems if they are present in organs.[11]

Often, granulomas originally form in the lungs or lymph nodes, but they can develop in the liver, eyes, skin, brain, heart, and bones, among other areas. Many times, symptoms of sarcoidosis are not apparent. According to the National Heart, Lung, and Blood Institute, they can include, but are not limited to, the following:

- ◎ **Joint and muscle pain, stiffness, or swelling**
- ◎ **Arthritis in the ankles**
- ◎ **Shortness of breath**
- ◎ **Wheezing**
- ◎ **Chest pain**
- ◎ **Enlarged or tender lymph nodes**

- ◎ **Bumps on the skin**
- ◎ **Changes in vision**
- ◎ **Red, burning, itchy, or teary eyes**
- ◎ **Anemia**
- ◎ **Fever**
- ◎ **Fatigue[12]**

Sarcoidosis affects thousands of Americans. It can be found in both adults and children, although it is rare in young people. In order to make a proper diagnosis, doctors conduct a physical exam, and may order a variety of tests. These tests may include blood tests, chest X-rays, an electrocardiogram, computerized tomography (CT) scans, and magnetic resonance (MR) scans, among others.

Juvenile Vasculitis

Simply put, vasculitis is an inflammation of the blood vessels. It can be a primary childhood disease or a symptom of dermatomyositis or lupus.

There are several types of juvenile vasculitis, including Henoch-Schönlein purpura (HSP), Kawasaki disease, cutaneous polyarteritis nodosa (PAN), Behçet's disease, giant cell arteritis, and Wegener's granulomatosis. Individuals who have any of these conditions may develop arthritis. Below is a brief look at each condition.

Variations of Juvenile Vasculitis

Henoch-Schönlein purpura. This type of vasculitis is one of the most common forms of juvenile vasculitis found in children. It typically affects children between the ages of two and ten, and it's found in boys more often than girls.[13]

Symptoms may last for several days or weeks and include abdominal pain, renal dysfunction, and arthritis. Arthritis is found in about 75 percent of cases and involves one to four joints, most often occurring in the ankles and knees.[14]

Children who have HSP also develop a rash on their buttocks or lower extremities that turns from red to purple to brown. About half of children diagnosed with HSP also have kidney problems.

Before these symptoms occur, children commonly have fevers, headaches, or muscle and joint pain for two to three weeks. When diagnosing HSP, doctors will run a blood and urine test in order to look at kidney function. A skin biopsy may also be needed to confirm whether a child has HSP.

Kawasaki disease. This illness is another common form of juvenile vasculitis. According to the Nemours Foundation's KidsHealth Web site, symptoms of Kawasaki disease occur in phases and initially include fevers, red eyes, enlarged lymph glands, swelling of the feet and hands, and a rash that makes the lips become bright red and swollen, which often causes them to crack and bleed. Later on, children will experience peeling of their hands and feet. They may also have joint and abdominal pain, along with diarrhea and vomiting.

Kawasaki disease usually occurs in very young children, especially those under the age of five, and it affects boys more often than girls. It is treatable and typically resolves in four to eight weeks.[15] However, while it runs its course, children are vulnerable to arthritis and even heart problems that can be long lasting.

Since there is no specific test to diagnose Kawasaki disease, doctors look for a multitude of factors when making their diagnosis. More specifically, most children have a fever that lasts one to two weeks or more and is not responsive to antibiotics, in addition to the symptoms described above.

Cutaneous polyarteritis nodosa. Also known as periarteritis nodosa, PAN is a form of vasculitis that is rarely found in children. It is a condition that causes inflammation to the small and medium-sized arteries of the skin. It can also affect any of the organs, but most often attacks the kidneys and intestines, as well as skin and joints.

When diagnosing PAN, doctors look for tender lumps under the skin that are between 4 and 15 mm in diameter. Skin may also blister or have purple or black patches. Lesions can be found on the legs or feet, as well as other areas of the body. Other symptoms include fevers, sore throat, joint and muscle pain, numbness, tingling, and general weakness.

Behçet's disease. Although this disease occurs most often in people in their twenties or thirties, Behçet's can also affect teens and children.[16]

Certain symptoms are specific to Behçet's disease, including sores on the mouth, genitals, and skin; inflammation of the eye; and loss of vision. It's important to note that the disease is not contagious and that most of these symptoms are believed to be caused by inflammation of the blood vessels. Arthritis is also a common symptom of the disease and can cause pain, swelling, stiffness, and redness of the joints.

As with all forms of juvenile arthritis, there is no single test to diagnose Behçet's disease. A positive response to a skin prick test, after which small red bumps arise, is one indication of the disease. Behçet's is also difficult to diagnose because symptoms traditionally do not appear all at once and they can resemble symptoms of other illnesses. It can take months or even years for all the symptoms to appear.

Wegener's granulomatosis. This type of juvenile vasculitis causes certain blood vessels to swell and become inflamed, restricting the flow of blood. In most cases, the blood vessels in the nose, sinuses, ears, kidneys, and lungs are affected. Because of this, many children experience sinusitis. In addition, children may get nosebleeds and sores around the nose. Fevers are also common as well as fatigue, night sweats, loss of appetite, and skin lesions.

"Arthritis occurs in about half of all those with this disease." Some children may also develop kidney problems or have swelling of their eyes. Other symptoms include ear infections, chest pain, coughing, rashes, trouble breathing, and general weakness.[17]

Although this condition is considered to be rare in children, it can be found in those as young as three months old. To diagnose Wegener's granulomatosis, doctors may request a urinalysis in order to detect signs of kidney disease, which is a strong indicator of the condition. Blood tests are also requested so doctors can see whether proteins called antineutrophil cytoplasmic antibodies—another indicator of the disease—are present in the system.

Finally, a biopsy is required to confirm whether the illness is actually Wegener's granulomatosis. "The exact type of biopsy depends on which area of the body the doctor wants to look at." It is also possible that the doctor will order a chest X-ray, CT scan, or bone marrow aspiration.[18]

Juvenile Dermatomyositis

Juvenile dermatomyositis (JDMS) is an inflammatory disease that causes muscle weakness. It's usually the muscles of the trunk, shoulders, and upper legs that are most affected. Because of their muscle weakness, teens with JDMS may have difficulty with physical activities like running, going up and down stairs, and even walking. Additionally, about 20 percent of children or teens with JDMS have arthritis. Some will also develop vasculitis.[19]

Teens or children with JDMS also get rashes that appear on the eyelids, cheeks, interior chest, and knuckles. "It's a very, very specific rash. [For] JDMS, it is how we diagnose the disease," Dr. Szer says, noting that tiny papules also appear on the knuckles. Furthermore, "the children develop very ragged and yucky looking cuticles." Weight loss is another indicator of the disease.

When making a diagnosis, doctors may conduct strength tests and order MRIs of truncal muscles. Doctors will also look to see if "liver function tests, lactic acid dehydrogenase (LDH), creatine phosphokinase (CPK), and aldolase" blood tests come back abnormal.[20]

Most individuals are between the ages of five and fourteen when diagnosed with the disease.[21] Like JIA, juvenile dermatomyositis occurs more frequently in girls than boys.

Juvenile Systemic Lupus Erythematosus (SLE)

Systemic lupus erythematosus (SLE) is a chronic, inflammatory autoimmune disorder that affects more than one organ system in the body. The muscles, joints, stomach, kidneys, lungs, blood vessels, eyes, and brain can all be affected. SLE may initially affect only one organ or body system and then progress to other areas later. If left untreated, SLE leads to renal disease.

Most teens who are diagnosed with SLE experience joint pain, and many get arthritis. Typically, the arthritis can be found in the knees, hands, wrists, and fingers.

"SLE is an episodic disease with a history of symptoms that come and go."[22] General symptoms experienced include fever, fatigue, rashes on the skin, sensitivity to light, joint and muscle pain, nausea, and seizures, among others.

According to the Arthritis Foundation, when determining whether a patient has SLE, doctors must find at least four of the following symptoms:

- **Arthritis**
- **Inflammation of the heart and lungs**
- **Pleuritic chest pain (a common symptom among children)**
- **Malar rash**
- **Discoid lupus (which affects only the skin)**
- **Skin reactions to ultra violet light**
- **Oral or nasal ulcers**
- **Neurologic symptoms (psychosis or convulsions)**
- **Protein in urine**
- **Abnormal blood tests (detecting anemia, leukopenia, or thrombocytopenia)**
- **Positive blood tests (indicating anti-native DNA antibodies, anti-SLE antibodies, antiphospholipid antibodies, or false-positive syphilis test)**
- **Positive antinuclear antibody (ANA) blood test**
- **A form of renal disease. Central nervous system involvement and cognitive disturbance may be subtle.[23]**

SLE usually develops between the ages of ten and fifty, and it affects nine times more females than males. In addition, the disease is found more often in Asians and African

Americans.[24] Most children who get SLE are stricken with the disease during their adolescent years. It is rare to find anyone under five who has the disease, but newborn babies can get neonatal lupus syndrome.[25]

Juvenile Scleroderma

Juvenile scleroderma is a connective tissue disease that involves the skin, blood vessels, and immune system. In some cases, the muscles, tendons, joints, and bones are also affected, causing severe growth abnormalities.

Literally, scleroderma means "hard skin." It is believed that an inflammatory disorder causes a buildup of certain proteins, including collagen, which leads to the thickening and tightening of the skin. This is known as dermal fibrosis. As a result, "this widespread, uncontrolled production of scar tissue not only results in cosmetic disfigurement, but may severely limit daily activity."[26]

Although juvenile scleroderma is rare, "the disease affects approximately 5,000 to 7,000 children." However, juvenile scleroderma, like many forms of juvenile arthritis, is commonly misdiagnosed or, in some cases, goes undiagnosed. Therefore, the number of children who actually have the disease may be higher than reported.[27]

Those who do have the disease have either localized or systemic juvenile scleroderma. The following is a description of each condition.

Localized Juvenile Scleroderma

The localized form of scleroderma is more commonly found in children than adults. This condition does not involve internal body systems, but it does cause skin lesions. According to the Juvenile Scleroderma Network, skin lesions found on young people with juvenile scleroderma are classified as follows:

◉ *Morphea.* This type of lesion looks like thickened, waxy, ivory, or yellowish-white shiny patches on the skin.

- *Linear.* Here, thickened skin runs down a child's legs or arms in the form of a line. "Pigment changes both dark skin and patchy areas of lighter skin." These lesions can also cause atrophy (or wasting away of muscles) and therefore inhibit growth.

- *Generalized morphea.* These lesions cover most of the body and are a combination of both morphea and linear conditions.

- *En coupe de sabre.* Individuals with this form of lesion have an indentation on their forehead or near the frontal hairline. Also, thickened skin can cover the entire face and cause atrophy to the lower part of the face, a condition called Parry-Romberg syndrome.

- *Eosinophilic fasciitis (EF).* Considered to be a "scleroderma-like disorder," eosinophilic fasciitis occurs when the white blood cells attack the fascia, which is a thin sheet of tissue that separates muscles from the fat and skin above them. The fascia can become inflamed. Eosinophilic fasciitis is known to affect the legs, arms, and trunk.[28]

Systemic

The systemic version of juvenile scleroderma can involve the internal organs. This condition appears less often in children and teens than the localized version; however, symptoms mimic those experienced by adults. There are two types of systemic juvenile scleroderma found in young people:

- *Limited (or CREST syndrome).* According to the Juvenile Scleroderma Network, CREST stands for:

  Calcinosis, meaning there are calcium deposits in the skin

  Raynaud's phenomenon, a condition that causes fingers and toes to turn white, blue/purple, and red when exposed to cold temperature or stress

  Esophageal dysmotility, meaning frequent heartburn or difficulty swallowing

  Sclerodactyly, which is thickening of the skin of the fingers that can cause fingers to remain in a bent position

  Telangiectasias, dilated small blood vessels that appear red[29]

◎ *Diffuse (or progressive systemic sclerosis).* **This condition can cause thickening of the skin or loss of skin elasticity. It can also affect organs, like the heart, lungs, or kidneys. Poor food absorption, constipation, and esophageal dysmotility are also symptoms. Raynaud's is common in youth who have diffuse. The joints can also be affected, since "contractures can develop by having the thickened skin pass over the joints," Dr. Cron says.**

Mixed Connective Tissue Disease (MCTD)

Teens who have MCTD experience a combination of symptoms caused by juvenile idiopathic arthritis, scleroderma, juvenile dermatomyositis, and systemic lupus erythematosus. In most cases, children have fevers at the onset of MCTD and feel weak or fatigued.

Symptoms vary from case to case, but arthritis occurs in 93 percent of young people with MCTD. Many teens also get Raynaud's phenomenon, muscle disease, and thickened skin. Dry eyes, dry mouth, and rashes are also seen in quite a few cases.

MCTD is considered to be very rare, but can be found in children of all ages and is referred to as pediatric MCTD in those under sixteen years old. The disease is also more commonly found in girls than in boys.[30]

When diagnosing MCTD, doctors conduct a thorough exam and test patients for, among other things, RNP antibodies. "RNP is a nuclear protein in the blood that some scientists believe could be involved in causing the disease."[31] Those who have MCTD will test positive for RNP antibodies.

Chronic Regional Pain Syndrome

Formerly known as reflex sympathetic dystrophy (RSD), chronic regional pain syndrome (CRPS) causes constant pain, which can worsen after even mild activity. It can also trigger swelling and cause the area to be tender to the touch. Skin may also be blotchy or feel cool. "[CRPS], like fibromyalgia in kids, is usually psychologically stress related and not usually related to injury," says Dr. Cron. However, as individuals age, CRPS may occur as a result of an injury to one or more of their extremities.

SECONDARY CONDITIONS

When it comes to secondary conditions, "if arthritis is undertreated or very difficult to treat, bony erosions or ankylosis of joints can occur [which means] joints can fuse leading to decreased or absent range of motion, and contractures of joints can also occur," Dr. Cron says. "Micrognathia [meaning "small jaw"] frequently occurs from lack of detection and treatment of TMJ arthritis, which is very common in children with all types of JIA." Micrognathia can cause teeth to misalign, which can make eating difficult.

Unfortunately, however, those are just a few of the secondary conditions that can arise in a person with juvenile arthritis. The following are brief summaries of some of the other common secondary conditions individuals with JA may experience.

Uveitis (or Iritis)

Youth who have pauciarticular JIA are at especially high risk for developing uveitis, which is also sometimes referred to as iritis.[32] The iris is the colored part of your eye, and everyone has fluid that is located in the frontal portion of the eye; it is this fluid that becomes inflamed. Therefore, the condition is called iritis or uveitis because it causes chronic inflammation of the iris.

Uveitis occurs most often in girls who have a protein called antinuclear antibody (ANA) in their blood. However, it can still affect those who do not have ANA in their blood.[33]

Although uveitis typically occurs within three to five years after a person is diagnosed with arthritis, it can develop up to thirty years later. In most cases, there are no symptoms of uveitis. Therefore, individuals with arthritis need to visit their eye doctor (or ophthalmologist) regularly so he or she can

Teens who have uveitis might be prescribed mydriatic eyedrops.

detect whether the condition is present and begin immediate treatment in the event it should occur.

"Uveitis, if untreated, can lead to blindness," says Dr. Cron. "It is typically treated with topical corticosteroid drops. Prolonged use of these drops can lead to glaucoma and cataracts, so most of us are quick to add methotrexate, which works well for uveitis. In addition, one of the TNF inhibitors, infliximab [also called Remicade], works rather well for uveitis." Individuals with uveitis are also usually prescribed mydriatic eye drops, which make the pupil open wider.

Anemia

Individuals with a low red blood count have a condition called anemia. Those who have a low level of hemoglobin, a protein that exists in red blood cells and carries oxygen, are also considered anemic.

Typically, anemia is caused when an individual isn't getting enough iron. As a result, the body cannot produce hemoglobin. "Anemia also can develop if the bone marrow is not working properly. This may be because of an infection or a chronic illness, such as arthritis or kidney disease."[34] According to Dr. Ilona S. Szer, anemia "is very common" in children with polyarticular and systemic arthritis. Uncontrolled inflammation can also lead to anemia.

According to the Nemours Foundation, symptoms of anemia include:

⦿ Paleness because "there is less blood flowing through the blood vessels in the skin"

⦿ A fast heartbeat, because "the heart has to work harder to get the same amount of blood and oxygen to the body"

⦿ Weakness or fatigue[35]

To confirm diagnosis of anemia, doctors may run a blood test called a hematocrit. If an individual tests positive for anemia, he or she might need to take iron supplements so that the body produces more red blood cells. It's also beneficial for individuals with anemia to eat iron-rich foods, like meat, beans, tofu, and grains. In addition, the body also requires "vitamins B_{12} and folic acid to make red blood cells." Vitamin B_{12} can be obtained from meat, eggs, and dairy, while folic acid comes from citrus fruits and green vegetables.[36] If taking supplements or adding more iron to the individual's diet doesn't help, a blood transfusion may be needed in dire situations.

Thyroid Disorders

Hyperthyroidism and hypothyroidism are considered to be the most prevalent thyroid disorders or diseases. Hyperthyroidism means "the thyroid is too active and releases too much thyroid hormone into the blood." Hypothyroidism, on the other hand, means "the thyroid isn't active enough, so not enough thyroid hormone is being made."[37]

According to the Nemours Foundation, symptoms of hyperthyroidism include:

⦿ Difficulty concentrating

⦿ Faster heartbeat

⦿ Trembling

- Sweating
- Trouble sleeping
- Weight loss (even though appetite may increase)
- Bulging eyes[38]

Symptoms of hypothyroidism include:

- Feeling fatigued or lethargic
- Slower heartbeat
- Feeling cold
- Brittle hair
- Skin is dry and pale or slightly yellow
- Constipation
- Slow growth[39]

In addition, individuals who have thyroid disorders may get nodules (or lumps) on their thyroid gland. Others may develop a goiter, meaning the neck swells because the thyroid gland is enlarged.

Another type of thyroid disorder is Hashimoto's thyroiditis (or Hashimoto's disease), which Allyson Shapiro was diagnosed with. It is also sometimes referred to as autoimmune thyroiditis or chronic lymphocytic thyroiditis. An autoimmune disease, Hashimoto's thyroiditis causes antibodies to "react against proteins in the thyroid gland, causing gradual destruction of the gland itself, and making the gland unable to produce the thyroid hormones the body needs."[40]

Symptoms of Hashimoto's thyroiditis include:

- Goiters
- Anxiety
- Difficulty sleeping and fatigue
- Weight fluctuation
- Depression
- Hair loss
- Muscle and joint pain
- May lead to hypothyroidism[41]

To make a diagnosis, doctors may order several blood tests. An ultrasound, radioactive uptake scan, and/or a fine needle aspiration may also be requested by the doctor.

Depending on the type of thyroid disorder, it can be caused by a number of things. In some cases it's inherited, while in others it is triggered by medications that block the thyroid from producing enough of the hormone. Other times, the disorder occurs because an individual does not consume enough iodine, a mineral derived from seafood or milk that's needed to produce the thyroid hormone, in his or her diet.

When making a diagnosis, doctors also conduct a physical exam. An ultrasound or thyroid scan may also be needed. If a disorder is present, treatment usually entails taking daily medication. In extreme cases and depending on the disorder, surgery may be required to remove all or part of the thyroid or nodules.

Osteoporosis

Osteoporosis means that an individual's bones are more fragile and therefore at a greater risk of breaking. Like arthritis, osteoporosis is often thought of as an "old person's disease," but it can affect people of any age. In fact, about 10 million people in the United States are living with the disease.[42]

Osteoporosis can affect any bone in the body, especially the hips and spine. If the disease is left untreated, it will continue to progress, causing bones to become more brittle. Those with severe osteoporosis are more likely to suffer fractures of their wrists, hips, and spine. Unfortunately, most people are unaware they have osteoporosis until they break a bone.

However, certain people are more at risk than others, and they should discuss the possibility with their doctor. According to the National Osteoporosis Foundation, these risk factors include:

- Being female
- Having a family history of osteoporosis or broken bones
- Being small and thin

- Low sex hormones. This includes: low estrogen levels in women, including menopause; missing periods (amenorrhea); and low levels of testosterone and estrogen in men
- Diet concerns—low calcium and vitamin D intake, as well as excessive intake of protein, sodium, and caffeine
- Inactive lifestyle
- Smoking
- Alcohol abuse
- Certain medications, such as steroid medications and anticonvulsants
- Certain diseases and conditions, including anorexia nervosa and asthma[43]

To diagnose osteoporosis, doctors order bone mineral density (BMD) tests that measure bone density. One such test is a dual energy X-ray absorptiometry (DXA) scan, a scan of the body that takes only a few moments. Although there is no cure for osteoporosis, the doctor might prescribe medications like Fosamax (depending on the patient's age and condition) to help prevent further bone damage.

The National Osteoporosis Foundation lists steps you can take to "optimize bone health and help prevent osteoporosis." They are:

1. Getting the daily recommended amounts of calcium and vitamin D
2. Engaging in regular weight-bearing and muscle-strengthening exercise
3. Not smoking and not drinking excessive alcohol
4. Talking to your health-care provider about bone health
5. Having a bone density test and taking medication when appropriate[44]

Heart Conditions

Pericarditis

Juvenile idiopathic arthritis, systemic lupus erythematosus, sarcoidosis, and scleroderma, among other conditions, have been known to cause pericarditis. Simply put, pericarditis means that the tissue layers surrounding the heart have become inflamed.

Individuals with pericarditis experience sharp and stabbing chest pain that can worsen when breathing deeply. Other symptoms include shortness of breath when doing tasks or exercising.

To diagnose pericarditis, doctors may order a chest X-ray as well as an echocardiograph (or ultrasound) of the heart. In addition, an electrocardiogram (EKG) may be performed so doctors can see the "electrical activity of the heart." First and foremost, however, doctors will listen to the heart with a stethoscope to determine whether fluid and inflammation are present. Depending on the amount of fluid, it may put "pressure on the outside of the heart to prevent it from beating adequately [in order] to push blood to the body and lungs"—which can be a serious problem.[45]

Ventricular Tachycardia

Although not something traditionally associated with JIA, Stefanie's doctors found she had supraventricular tachycardia (SVT) about two years ago. SVT is a rapid heart rhythm that originates from the atria or the AV node. "She can lose her breath, kind of like an asthma attack. It can cause pain, and it can make her light-headed," her mother, Kathy, says. "They told us it's not life threatening (in her case). It's more frightening than anything."

Similarly, "ventricular tachycardia is a rapid heartbeat initiated within the ventricles, characterized by three or more consecutive premature ventricular beats. [Furthermore, it] is a potentially lethal disruption of normal heartbeat that may cause the heart to become unable to pump adequate blood through the body."[46]

Symptoms of ventricular tachycardia include:

- Chest pain
- Heart palpitations
- Feeling dizzy or light-headed
- Shortness of breath
- Fainting[47]

Ventricular tachycardia can stem from other heart conditions or it may "result from anti-arrhythmic medications or from altered blood chemistries (such as a low potassium level), pH (acid-base) changes, or insufficient oxygenation."[48]

Treatment of ventricular tachycardia may require the use of oral antiarrhythmic medications. In extreme cases, implantable cardioverter defibrillators (which are like pacemakers) may be implanted in the chest and connected with the heart.

NOTES

1. Arthritis Foundation, "Sjögren's Syndrome," *Arthritis Today*, July/August 2007, www.arthritis.org/sjogrens-syndrome.php.

2. Ibid.

3. Fibromyalgia Network, "Symptoms," www.fmnetnews .com/basics-symptoms.php.

4. Nemours Foundation, "Lyme Disease," KidsHealth, www.kidshealth.org/parent/infections/bacterial_viral/lyme.html.

5. Ibid.

6. Nemours Foundation, "Inflammatory Bowel Disease," KidsHealth, www.kidshealth.org/kid/health_problems/ stomach/IBD.html.

7. About.com, "Arthritis and IBD," http://ibdcrohns.about.com/ cs/relatedconditions/a/arthritisibd.hem.

8. Ibid.

9. Ibid.

10. Ibid.

11. National Heart Lung and Blood Institute, "What Is Sarcoidosis?" www.nhlbi.nih.gov/health/dci/Diseases/sarc/ sar_whatis.html.

12. Ibid.

13. Alan Greene, "Henoch-Schonlein Purpura," www.drgreene .org/body.cfm?id=21&action=detail&ref=842.

14. New Zealand Dermatological Society, Inc., "Henoch-Schönlein Purpura," www.dermnetnz.org/vascular/hsp.html.

15. New Zealand Dermatological Society, Inc., "Kawaski Disease," www.dermnetnz.org/vascular/polyarteritis-nodosa.html; Nemours Foundation, "Kawasaki Disease," KidsHealth, www.kidshealth.org/parent/medical/heart/kawasaki.html.

16. National Institute of Arthritis and Musculoskeletal Diseases, "Behçet's Disease," www.niams.nih.gov/Health_Info/Behcets_Disease/behcets_disease_ff.asp.

17. U.S. National Library of Medicine & the National Institutes of Health, "Wegener's Granulomatosis," MedlinePlus, www.nlm.nih.gov/medlineplus/ency/article/000135.htm.

18. Ibid.

19. Arthritis Foundation, *Arthritis in Children* (pamphlet, 2004), 7–8.

20. Brandie J. Roberts, "Conference Report: Highlights of the Society for Pediatric Dermatology Annual Meeting," *Medscape Dermatology*, 2005, www.medscape.com/viewarticle/512426_5.

21. Arthritis Foundation, *Arthritis in Children*, 7.

22. Arthritis Foundation, "Juvenile Arthritis—Other Types and Related Conditions," http://ww2.arthritis.org/conditions/DiseaseCenter/ja_other.asp#JPA.

23. Ibid.

24. U.S. National Library of Medicine & the National Institutes of Health, "Systemic Lupus Erythematosus," MedlinePlus, www.nlm.nih.gov/medlineplus/ency/article/000435.htm.

25. Arthritis Foundation, "Juvenile Arthritis—Other Types and Related Conditions."

26. Arthritis National Research Foundation, "Studies May Yield New, Better Therapies," press release, October 2007.

27. Juvenile Scleroderma Network, "What Is Juvenile Scleroderma?" www.jsdn.org/whatisjsd.htm.

28. Ibid.

29. Ibid.

30. Cincinnati Children's Hospital Medical Center, "Mixed Connective Tissue Disease," Arthritis and Rheumatology Conditions and Diagnoses, www.cincinnatichildrens.org/health/info/rheumatology/diagnose/mctd.htm.

31. Ibid.

32. Arthritis Foundation, *Arthritis in Children*, 5.

33. Ibid., 20.

34. Nemours Foundation, "About Anemia," KidsHealth, www.kidshealth.org/kid/health_problems/blood/anemia.html.

35. Ibid.

36. Ibid.

37. Nemours Foundation, "Thyroid Disorders," KidsHealth, www.kidshealth.org/kid/health_problems/glandshoromones/thyroid.html.

38. Ibid.

39. Ibid.

40. Mary Shomon, "Hashimoto's vs. Hypothyroidism: What's the Difference?" About.com, http://thyroid.about.com/cs/hypothyroidism/a/hashivshypo.htm.

41. Ibid.

42. National Osteoporosis Foundation, "Fast Facts on Osteoporosis," www.nof.org/osteoporosis/diseasefacts.htm.

43. Ibid.

44. Ibid.

45. Benjamin C. Wedro, "Pericarditis," MedicineNet, www.medicinenet.com/pericarditis/article.htm.

46. U.S. National Library of Medicine & the National Institutes of Health, "Ventricular Tachycardia," MedlinePlus, www.nlm.nih.gov/medlineplus/ency/article/000187.htm.

47. Ibid.

48. Ibid.

Treatment Options: From Medicine to Surgery

Even after an official diagnosis is made, treating juvenile arthritis can be tricky. Arthritis tends to affect people in different ways, and not everyone responds well to the same type of medication. In fact, it usually takes more than one type of medicine to get the disease under control. Furthermore, like in Amanda White's case, sometimes it can take quite a while before you and your doctor find a treatment plan that is right for you. Admittedly, the onset of juvenile arthritis can be very painful, especially during the weeks or even months it takes for the medicine to take effect. But hang in there! Eventually, your body will respond and begin to feel better.

In order to make this process easier for you and your doctor, it is strongly recommended that you keep a record of how you are feeling at certain points throughout the day in a special journal. During the initial phases of your diagnosis, you will be visiting your doctor more often. Make sure to bring the journal with you to each visit so the doctor can get a clearer picture of when the disease is more active and what medications may or may not be working. It will also help your doctor to determine whether any of the medications are causing adverse side effects. As a result, your doctor may substitute a new medication for any treatments that are not working or seem to be causing problems. Also, if you notice anything unusual before your next doctor's visit, don't hesitate to call to let him or her know. Your doctor may be able to provide a solution over the phone or move your appointment up so that he or she can make adjustments to your treatment plan sooner than later.

PERSONAL STORY

By Alexander Fernandez, age twelve, Littleton, Colorado

Figure 4.1.   Alexander Fernandez
was diagnosed with juvenile
rheumatoid arthritis
at the age of eight.

I was diagnosed with juvenile rheumatoid arthritis when I was eight years old. My story begins over four years ago, when I broke the heel of my left foot. I had gone to the orthopedic doctor to have a cast put on my leg. But during this time, I started feeling a lot of pain and stiffness in my legs, feet, and back—some of which started before the injury. My symptoms kept getting worse and they weren't going away with over-the-counter medicine.

After having the cast for six weeks and then having it removed, we went back to the orthopedic doctors to see why I was feeling so bad all the time. I was run-down and had no energy, and it was starting to get difficult to get out of bed. I also had a lot of stiffness in the morning. At first my family thought it was growing pains. But the orthopedic doctors thought what I was experiencing had nothing to do with growing pains. They soon suggested that I see a rheumatologist, so we were referred on to a doctor at the Children's Hospital in Denver, Colorado. I had several tests done, and it was then determined that I had a form of juvenile rheumatoid arthritis called ankylosing spondylitis.

When the doctor first told me that I had arthritis, I was shocked. My grandma has arthritis, but I did not know that kids could get arthritis too. I was depressed to hear about my diagnosis and because I no longer had a day without pain. I tried several types of medications with the doctor's help before we found a treatment that worked for me so that I could feel somewhat normal. There are still days that I do not want to get out of bed or even walk, but they are not as frequent now. It makes me mad at times that my body does not always cooperate. I cannot always do the things that my friends do. I used to be able to run, jump, and play sports and not have any pain, but that is not the case anymore. Right now, I'm currently taking several anti-inflammatory and pain medications to help with my symptoms. I also have to take two Enbrel injections a week. I do not like taking them sometimes, but I know they are all used to help me. Now that I take them I can do almost everything I like.

Last year, my family and I went to see a pain management team at the Children's Hospital. I had several pain block treatments. It was just like getting an epidural in your back. The doctors and my parents hoped that it would help alleviate some of the discomfort that I felt in my lower body. My pain doctor told me that through several treatments the pain blocks would help to lessen my discomfort and then I wouldn't have to take so much medication.

This was a long process to do, because it had to be done on an outpatient basis. I was put to sleep for them to do the treatments. My parents and I think it was a success. But it was very costly to my family to have the treatments done, and it takes several trips to the hospital to make it worth your while.

Right now, I am currently playing football and baseball. I can't always play a full game, but I am grateful I can at least play sports. I also like to skateboard, and I try to do it every day. Even though I have arthritis, it does not stop me from doing the things that I like, and it should not stop you. If you have arthritis, don't let it get you down. If your body isn't feeling good, a sea salt bath always helps me. If you are just mad about the situation, there are chat rooms with kids who have arthritis; they can help cheer you up, or just talk to a close friend or family member.

The Arthritis Foundation is also a good place to start. The foundation is always raising money to help find a cure and for research. This year, I was asked to be the 2008 Arthritis Walk honoree for the Rocky Mountain Chapter of the Arthritis Foundation. It was a great experience. I got to do many speeches on arthritis and I also helped by donating my time to help bring awareness. My motto is: "Anyone can get arthritis, even kids like me." So don't lose hope if you think there will never be a cure. Maybe you, too, can help make a difference with this disease by bringing awareness and support.[1]

Once you find a treatment plans that works, you may not need to visit your doctor as often. However, from time to time—depending on what medications you are taking—your doctor will request that your blood be tested to determine if the disease is active and whether any of the medications are harming your body.

TREATING JUVENILE ARTHRITIS TODAY

While you might not be thrilled to have a daily medicine regimen to adhere to, you should take some comfort in knowing that treatments for juvenile arthritis have come a long way over the past twenty years in terms of inhibiting the progression of the disease and reducing pain.

Looking back twenty or thirty years for comparison's sake, doctors often instructed young patients with juvenile arthritis (and even many adults with arthritis, for that matter) to take a significant amount of aspirin each day. "In the '70s and '80s, aspirin was the best thing running," Dr. Harry L. Gewanter says.

You are probably wondering how much good taking aspirin actually did in terms of fighting the arthritis—and the answer is: Not much. But at the time, doctors were afraid to be overly aggressive in their approach to treating the disease because they were unsure about how much damage medications approved for adults could cause in children and teens. This is because "children's immune systems are not fully formed" and drugs may react differently in them, explains Helene Belisle, executive director of the Arthritis National Research Foundation (ANRF). Therefore, aspirin and other mild drugs were considered the safest treatment options among what was available then.

After starting a young patient on baby aspirin, doctors gradually prescribed stronger medications. Shaun-Marie Robbins said her rheumatologist at Children's Hospital of Philadelphia did exactly that. "My first treatment was baby aspirin. [I took] Bayer—thirty tablets a day. Then I was put on Naprosyn," she says.

Nowadays, aspirin is rarely prescribed to treat juvenile arthritis. But when it is, doctors usually have patients take large doses about three to four times a day in order to minimize pain and swelling or to control fevers.[2] However, in most cases, doctors are more aggressive in their approach to treating the disease. In 2008 "the immediate goal" of drug therapy today has been to reduce inflammation, pain, and swelling, in addition to improving function.[3] Dr. Stanley B. Cohen, medical director of the Metroplex Clinical Research Center in Dallas,

Texas, and clinical professor of medicine at the University of Texas Southwestern Medical Center at Dallas, says that "clinical trials demonstrated that early aggressive treatment is necessary to prevent joint damage and disability. Studies have demonstrated that patients treated in the first year of disease with biologics such as TNF inhibitors (like Enbrel, Humira, and Remicade) in combination with methotrexate, disease remission is achieved in up to 40 percent of patients."[4] (These drugs, including biologic agents and TNF, will be discussed in more detail later in this chapter.)

"What you do changes over time [depending] on what information you have," Dr. Gewanter says. "What we've learned over time is that by the time you got to the stronger meds, there was a lot of damage [to a patient's joints] already."

Since about the early '90s, rheumatologists have been prescribing stronger medications at the onset of the disease in order to prevent joint and tissue damage, and then they gradually decrease the dosage or number of medications a patient takes over time. "In a sense, the therapeutic pyramid where you start out slowly [and then progress] has been turned upside down. [Today], you really want to turn everything off [in relation to the disease] as fast as you can," Dr. Gewanter says. He also points out that when treating those who have arthritis in many joints, doctors might recommend they have their joints injected with corticosteroids in an operating room in an effort to quickly shut down the disease. Or a patient might be started out on high doses of oral steroids and methotrexate, which is used to relieve inflammation. In addition, doctors might suggest patients begin using a biologic drug within one month of their diagnosis, with the plan being to taper steroid use once the biologic drug kicks in.

Dr. Marisa Klein-Gitelman says she typically prescribes biologic drugs and methotrexate to her patients who have moderate to severe arthritis. Like other doctors, her goal is also to get the disease under control, and then she begins reducing the amount of medication a patient is taking as soon as it is physically possible. "As opposed to fifteen years ago, [there is a] tendency to be more aggressive," she says. "I think people understand that earlier control is very helpful."

BIOGRAPHY OF GALE A. GRANGER, PhD

Figure 4.2.   Dr. Gale "Morrie" Granger, who
worked as a professor of immunology at
the University of California, Irvine, for
thirty-six years. In addition, he has served
on the board of directors of the Arthritis
National Research Foundation since 1990.

Early in his career as a researcher at the University of California, Irvine, Dr. Gale
"Morrie" Granger received funding from the Arthritis National Research Foundation to
study the immunological processes occurring in the tissue destruction observed in
idiopathic arthritis.

This research ultimately led to the discovery that the white blood cells present in
the joints of RA patients induce tissue destruction by releasing molecules termed
cytokines. Simply put, "Dr. Granger is actually the man who discovered the molecule
lymphotoxins (LT), which were later renamed tumor necrosis factor (TNF)," explains
Helene Belisle. "He was funded by this foundation for a number of years in the 1970s.
That's an amazing part of our story because he had a cutting edge idea that the rest of
the science community said was against the grain."

In spite of opposition by the scientific community, ANRF agreed to provide Dr.
Granger with a grant in support of his research. Ultimately, his findings paved the way
for the recent development of biologic agents that block cytokine activity and hold great
promise for therapy for patients with this debilitating disease.

For thirty-six years, Dr. Granger worked as a professor of immunology at the
University of California, Irvine, until his retirement. He was also a consultant to
numerous hospitals, research institutes, and the National Institutes of Health (NIH). In
addition, he has served on the Arthritis National Research Foundation board of directors
since 1990, including as president from 1997 to 1999. In fact, it was his vision and
guidance that led to the establishment of ANRF's Scientific Advisory Board in 1998. The
Scientific Advisory Board is made up of world-renowned doctors and research scientists
who help select new grant recipients each year.

As the director of a multi-disciplinary, multi-institutional research program, Dr. Granger was responsible for supervising basic research in cancer and autoimmune diseases as well as conducting clinical trials in patients. This program was designed to bring basic and clinical scientists together with the objective of understanding how the body's immune system induces tissue destruction as seen in rheumatoid arthritis and how it interacts with cancer cells. The results of these basic studies are then employed to design and test new methods of therapy for these diseases.

Dr. Salvatore Albani, professor of medicine and pediatrics and director of the University of Arizona Arthritis Center, agrees. "The whole field has changed a lot in the last ten to fifteen years," he says. "We are moving from immune suppression to immune tolerance."

According to Dr. Gale Granger, who worked as a professor of immunology at the University of California for more than thirty years, "research over the past fifteen to twenty years has revealed that host white blood cells also have an important role in causing the damage in these tissues—patient white blood cells invade the joint and other tissues and release a host of soluble factors termed 'cytokines.' These cytokines are responsible for the inflammation [pain, swelling, and redness], tissue damage and scarring that can result."

"Researchers have developed new methods to control the release of the cytokines from the white blood cells [or WBC] and to block their activity once released," Dr. Granger adds. "The ability to control the activity of the white blood cell could lead to many new and exciting treatments. In fact, the ability to block cytokine activity has facilitated the development of a totally new therapy, which blocks the activity of a cytokine termed TNF, and has [as a result] helped many RA patients."

In spite of these advances, Dr. Gewanter notes that methods used today still depend in part on the severity of a patient's condition and the type of arthritis he or she has when considering what is appropriate among the new treatments that are available. "There are certain medications that work better for certain subtypes than others," he says.

TYPES OF TREATMENTS

Medications

Various types of medications the Arthritis Foundation has found to be commonly used in treating young people are discussed throughout the following portion of this chapter. Please know that not all of the drugs listed below have been approved for young teens or children. Check with your doctor for updates.

While there may not be a cure for juvenile arthritis just yet, taking all of the medications your doctor prescribes for you can alleviate some or most of the pain you're experiencing and help to slow the progression of the disease. There are many more drug treatment options today as compared to twenty or even ten years ago. So if a particular medication doesn't seem to be working for you, don't be afraid to tell your doctor. There is a good chance he or she will find something else that does the trick.

To give you an idea of the types of medicines used to treat arthritis today, here is an overview of what you might be prescribed and how each medication can help.

Analgesics

Analgesics are given to patients who have ankylosing spondylitis, juvenile idiopathic arthritis, fibromyalgia, lupus, and scleroderma, among other conditions.

Doctors might recommend you take this type of medication after your initial diagnosis, especially if your arthritis is mild to

Most teens with juvenile arthritis need to take medicine daily to keep the disease under control.

moderate in severity. Analgesics are used almost solely to provide pain relief. Drugs like Tylenol Arthritis and Excedrin, which are classified as acetaminophens, fall under this category and are the most commonly used analgesics.[5] Although the pain relief they provide is only temporary, they can be purchased without a prescription.

Other analgesics, like tramadol (Ultram) or tramadol with acetaminophen (Ultracet), require a prescription and are taken when patients are in severe pain.

Nonsteroidal Anti-Inflammatory Drugs

Nonsteroidal anti-inflammatory drugs (NSAIDs) are given to patients who have ankylosing spondylitis, juvenile idiopathic arthritis, lupus, psoriatic arthritis, pericarditis, and scleroderma, among other conditions.

NSAIDs are commonly taken by patients with juvenile arthritis as part of their initial treatment plan. NSAIDS are typically used in an effort to reduce "the production of prostaglandins, which are chemicals in the body that promote inflammation" and can cause pain, fever, and muscle cramps.[6] Therefore, taking NSAIDs can help to reduce stiffness, swelling, and possibly even joint pain.

There are three subcategories of NSAIDs: traditional NSAIDS, COX-2 inhibitors, and salicylates. Some types of NSAIDs, like Advil, can be purchased over the counter, while others require a prescription. Celebrex, ibuprofen, and naproxen (also known as Naprosyn) are some of the more well-known drugs in this classification of medicine. NSAIDs come in liquid and pill form, and may be taken one to three times a day, depending on the particular drug. If you take aspirin, avoid chewing or sucking on the pill, because it can damage the surface of your teeth and irritate your gums. As an alternative, you can crush the pill and put it in yogurt or a similar food if swallowing it proves difficult.[7]

If you are taking NSAIDs, beware that they can cause ulcers, gastrointestinal bleeding, upset stomach, and, in rare cases, stroke or heart attack. COX-2 inhibitors are thought to be easier on the stomach, but can bring on a stroke or heart attack, as well as blood clots and skin problems. They can also raise blood pressure, cause fluid retention, and reduce kidney function, among other side effects. Those taking aspirin may also experience stomach pain or bleeding. They must also watch out for toxic reactions and other side effects, like ringing in the ears, vomiting, black stool, irritability, drowsiness, and rapid or deep breathing.

Corticosteroids

Corticosteroids are given to patients who have ankylosing spondylitis, giant cell arteritis, juvenile idiopathic arthritis, lupus, psoriatic arthritis, scleroderma, and Wegener's granulomatosis, among other conditions.

This type of medication is often prescribed to those with severe arthritis or in cases where a patient has not responded well to other types of medications. Corticosteroids are used to alleviate pain by reducing inflammation and swelling quickly. These drugs are "related to the natural hormone in your body called cortisol" and are usually given in low doses.[8] Synthetic forms of cortisol "can be taken in pill form or injected directly into joints or other tissues." Injections are usually given no more frequently than every three months because they can cause side effects. Pills or liquid forms of the medicine can also cause side effects, like high blood pressure, osteoporosis, cataracts, mood swings, slowed growth, increased appetite, and reduced resistance to infection. Those taking oral corticosteroids also run the risk of developing Cushing's syndrome, which involves weight gain, muscle weakness, moon (round) face, osteoporosis, and thinning skin. Therefore, individuals taking corticosteroids are often required to take calcium and vitamin D supplements to strengthen their bones.[9]

Prednisone is one commonly prescribed corticosteroid that is known to help relieve pain, stiffness, and inflammation soon after patients begin taking it. It is taken orally or by injection. While taking prednisone can be a huge relief for someone with arthritis, the drug does not come without side effects. Like other corticosteroids, it can cause moon face, weight gain, and high blood pressure, as well as acne, blurred vision, stomach ulcers, and dark facial lines. And if patients try to stop taking it abruptly, it can cause pain or the disease may flare up. "The only drug you really can't stop every day if you're on it is prednisone," Dr. Klein-Gitelman cautions. "You can get very sick if you just abruptly stop it."

When you and your doctor decide it's time for you to stop using prednisone, you will likely have to decrease your dose gradually so the disease does not flare up. In addition, tapering doses is necessary because regular use of corticosteroids, like prednisone, suppress the adrenal gland, and stopping the medication abruptly could cause low blood pressure, rapid heart rate, and fatigue.

Disease-Modifying Antirheumatic Drugs

Disease-modifying antirheumatic drugs (DMARDs) are given to patients who have ankylosing spondylitis, juvenile

MONITORING THE EFFECTS OF MEDICATION ON YOUR BODY

Aside from testing your blood to monitor the effects of medication on your body, your doctor might request a urinalysis to ensure that your kidneys are functioning properly. Simply put, you will need to urinate in a special cup so that the urine can be tested. A urinalysis is typically conducted while you are at the lab or in the doctor's office.

idiopathic arthritis, juvenile dermatomyositis, lupus, psoriatic arthritis, scleroderma, and Wegener's granulomatosis, among other conditions.

Although DMARDs can take weeks or months to work, they are used to help slow the progression of the illness and prevent further joint damage. DMARDs are also prescribed to reduce inflammation and lessen pain. Because they take a while to work, DMARDs are also referred to as slow-acting antirheumatic drugs (SAARDs). Recognizing this, doctors prescribe DMARDs in conjunction with NSAIDs, which help control the pain until the DMARDs kick in.

Some of the more recognizable DMARDs include methotrexate (Rheumatrex or Trexall), leflunomide (Arava), and sulfasalazine. Methotrexate, which was originally developed to treat cancer, is the most commonly prescribed DMARD. It can be taken orally or by injection and has been proven to have long-term benefits for those with idiopathic arthritis. Typically, it takes about two months to take effect. Sulfasalazine and leflunomide both come in pill form, although sulfasalazine can be made into a liquid. Both have proven to be effective treatments for those with arthritis. Those who do not respond to methotrexate might be prescribed azathioprine (Imuran). This is an immune system–suppressing medication that comes in pill form and takes about three months to work.

Another option for treatment is hydroxychloroquine sulfate (Plaquenil). Although not a true DMARD, it is often classified under this category and prescribed to children with mild arthritis in order to reduce joint pain and swelling. It comes in pill form, but can be made into a liquid. Side effects can range from diarrhea to rashes to problems with vision.

Since DMARDs suppress the immune system, those taking them must watch for infections and advise their doctor before receiving vaccinations.[10] Side effects depend on the drug, but can range from dizziness to hair loss to abdominal pain or upset. Methotrexate can also cause nausea, diarrhea, rashes, mouth sores, and, in rare cases, liver problems. When taking DMARDs, regular blood tests are required to monitor for toxicity, which means contamination of the blood.

Biologic Agents (or Biologic Response Modifiers)

Biologic agents are given to patients who have ankylosing spondylitis, juvenile idiopathic arthritis, Kawasaki disease, and juvenile psoriatic arthritis, among other conditions.

"A new generation of drugs called biologics has been developed, which is much more efficient than prior medication in controlling . . . symptoms and also to reduce or even prevent joint damage," says Dr. Albani. Biologic agents, or biologic response modifiers (BRMs), are also used to reduce inflammation.

This type of medication is given by injection or intravenously, although pill forms are in development. Basically, when it comes to treating patients, "this sort of approach is often a mixed approach, a combination therapy in which you put together a few different drugs [and] . . . it is rare these new medications are used alone. There are still older medications which are used in combination therapy," Dr. Albani says. As a result, "not as many children are as completely disabled as in the past."

One of the most commonly used biologic agents in individuals with JIA is called Enbrel or etanercept. The drug is often prescribed along with methotrexate. Drugs like Enbrel "block the action of a protein known to contribute to inflammation called tumor necrosis factor or TNF," since people with idiopathic arthritis have too much TNF in their bodies.[11]

Enbrel is usually injected once or twice a week into the legs, abdomen, or back of the upper arms. Those who inject once a week can use the drug manufacturer's "SureClick" autoinjector. By simply clicking a button at the top of the autoinjector, the medicine is released subcutaneously (into the skin) via a thin needle. At a regular time each week, the patient can do this easily in the comfort of his or her home. In fact, a video demonstration is even posted on the company's Web site, www.enbrel.com, to show you how it's done.

While Enbrel can be highly beneficial, like most drugs, it does not come without risks. "Enbrel has several risks and those risks are not as clear in children," Dr. Klein-Gitelman says. Side effects that can result from using Enbrel include

TIPS TO FOLLOW WHEN SELF-INJECTING

◎ Your rheumatologist might give you a demonstration on how to self-inject. However, make sure that you still read the directions carefully. Also, procedures may vary slightly, depending on the type of biologic agent you are using. So if you have any questions specific to the biologic agent you are receiving, call the company directly. Most companies have special telephone numbers for patients to call if they have questions.

◎ Make sure the medication is stored at the proper temperature. This means you will need to refrigerate it, but it is usually okay to take the medicine out of the refrigerator about fifteen to thirty minutes before injecting it so that it is not as cold when you inject it.

◎ Some people find injections to be quite painful, so consider numbing the injection site with ice or lidocaine cream or patches beforehand to make the process a little less painful. Massaging the area before you inject can help ease the pain, too.

◎ Gather everything you need before injecting, including the shot, an alcohol wipe, a bandage, and a tissue.

Have a Band-Aid ready in case you
bleed after injecting medicine.

◎ Wipe the skin with the alcohol wipe before injecting yourself in order to kill bacteria. Make sure not to touch the area with your fingers or anything else after wiping it.

◎ If you find you usually get injection site reactions, ask your doctor about taking allergy medicine, like diphenhydramine (Benadryl), in order to prevent that from happening.

◎ Ice the area afterward if it hurts.

◎ Let your doctor or the drug company know immediately if you experience a serious allergic reaction.

◎ If you are unable to give yourself the injection, make sure a family member or friend has been trained on proper procedure so he or she can help out when needed.

◎ Never reuse or share needles.

irritation at the injection site, headaches, or dizziness. If you experience other symptoms, like tingling, changes in vision, weakness, or bleeding, call your doctor immediately. Allergic reactions are also possible, but unlikely.

Other popularly prescribed biologic agents include the injections known as Humira (adalimumab) and Kineret (anakinra), as well as the intravenous infusions called Remicade (infliximab), Rituxan (rituximab), Orencia (abatacept), and intravenous immunoglobulin (IVIG). Kineret is taken on a daily basis, whereas Humira is injected every other week. Like Enbrel, Humira was recently approved by the Food and Drug Administration (FDA) to treat individuals as young as four years old.

IVIG is given once a month, and it may help patients, including those with Kawasaki disease, anywhere from just a couple weeks to three months. Basically, IVIG "is given as a plasma protein replacement therapy (IgG) for immune deficient patients [who] have decreased or abolished antibody

During visits to your doctor, make sure to let him or her know when your disease is flaring up so he or she can adjust your medication accordingly. "For a long time, my treatment remained the same," says Shaun-Marie Robbins, who went into remission at the age of fifteen. "It wasn't until I was about twenty-one that I came out of remission. I then started back on Naprosyn, Bextra, and prednisone. When that wasn't working, I started Remicade."

At that point, Shaun-Marie began receiving infusions of Remicade about every eight weeks. "I took that, Bextra, methotrexate, prednisone, and folic acid," she says. "I seem to have responded well to that, but soon Bextra [an NSAID] was taken off the market and it was replaced with Celebrex, which I haven't responded well with." As a result, Shaun-Marie's doctor increased her Remicade treatments to every six weeks.

production capabilities." Furthermore, IVIG may also regulate the immune response by reacting with a number of membrane receptors on T cells, B cells, and monocytes. In effect, IVIG has been shown to reduce levels of TNF-alpha and interleukin-10, another anti-inflammatory cytokine. Side effects range from headaches to infections to allergic reactions.[12]

Remicade is prescribed to relieve moderate to severe arthritis pain and stiffness as well as to prevent further joint damage. Those receiving Remicade get an intravenous infusion about every two months after the first three infusions, which are scheduled closer together. Infusions are given in the rheumatologist's office or at a local lab and last about two hours. Remicade is often given in conjunction with methotrexate. Common side effects associated with Remicade include headaches, stomach pain, rashes, and respiratory infections. Signs of a serious infection include fever, fatigue, flu symptoms, and warm, red, or sensitive skin.

Remicade and Humira, like Enbrel, also block TNF. People who have arthritis have TNF-alpha in excess, which "can cause the immune system to attack normal healthy parts of the body."[13] Kineret, however, "blocks a cytokine called interleukin-1 (IL-1)," which is an inflammatory protein. "Abatacept (Orencia) blocks the activation of T cells."[14]

Rituxan is given to adults who have not responded well to other TNF antagonist therapies. It is often prescribed in conjunction with methotrexate. Those with moderate to severe arthritis may experience relief for up to six months after two infusions.

According to literature provided by the manufacturer, Rituxan "works by getting rid of certain B cells in the blood," which are a type of white blood cell. Because of this, it's possible that healthy blood cells could be eliminated, therefore increasing the chance of infection. Other possible side effects include, but are not limited to, hives, dizziness, blurry vision, fatigue, headaches, heart problems, and bowel or stomach problems.[15]

Overall, biologic agents can take anywhere from just a couple of weeks to several months to take effect. Also, if you

begin using a biologic agent, beware that they can lower your
resistance to infections since they affect your immune system.
"It clearly is an immunosuppressive risk, so if you're sick, you
shouldn't take it," Dr. Klein-Gitelman says. That also goes for
drugs like methotrexate and prednisone. If you are weighing the
risks involved with taking biologic agents versus drugs like
methotrexate and other DMARDs, Dr. Cohen says, bear in
mind that it still hasn't been determined which have a greater
risk of infection.[16]

Opioids

If you are in extreme pain or have pericarditis, your
rheumatologist may prescribe opioids to help prevent pain
signals from reaching the brain. Morphine and codeine are both
forms of opioids and may be prescribed for short periods of
time. However, some physicians may allow you to take opioids
for extended periods of time as long as they are able to monitor
your condition regularly.

Muscle Relaxants

Typically prescribed for short-term use, muscle relaxants are
known to reduce the number of "muscle spasms that often
trigger pain signals." Common forms of muscle relaxants
include carisoprodol and cyclobenzaprine.[17]

Anticonvulsants

Typically used to treat seizures, anticonvulsants are also
prescribed to relieve pain in some cases. Commonly prescribed
anticonvulsants include clonazepam, gabapentin, phenytoin,
valproate, and carbamazepine.

Nerve Blocks

If a certain area of your body is in particularly great pain,
your doctor might inject the surrounding nerves with anesthetic

drugs known as nerve blocks. These injections are not long lasting, but can aid in relieving pain in your muscles, ligaments, tendons, and nerves temporarily. One possible side effect to watch for is temporary muscle weakness.

Antidepressants

Aside from being prescribed to treat depression, antidepressants are also occasionally prescribed in smaller doses in an effort to reduce pain. There are different types of antidepressants, and one type, known as tricyclic antidepressants, is often used to treat pain caused by fibromyalgia. Commonly prescribed tricyclic antidepressants include amitriptyline (Elavil and Endep) and nortriptyline. These medications "elevate the levels of certain chemicals in the brain and spinal cord," which helps to reduce pain signals and improve a person's quality of sleep.[18]

Another type of antidepressant, known as selective serotonin reuptake inhibitors (SSRIs), may be used to help people with arthritis who have a lot of pain and are consequently depressed. Commonly prescribed SSRIs include Prozac, Paxil, and Zoloft.

Human Growth Hormone Injections

As discussed earlier, the disease or medications you are taking may stunt your growth or prevent you from maintaining a normal weight. Kristen Delaney's growth was stunted because she took prednisone. "The last four years I've been on prednisone is when I should have been doing my most growing. It does stunt your growth," she says. If this happens, your regular doctor might refer you to an endocrinologist. An endocrinologist is a specialist who treats health problems relating to your glands. To help you grow taller and gain weight, you might need to get daily human growth hormone (HGH) injections. HGH is normally produced by the pituitary gland and helps you grow. While you're on these injections, the endocrinologist will closely monitor your progress to determine how well the medication is working.

WHAT TO DO WHEN YOU FORGET TO TAKE YOUR MEDICINE

According to Dr. Alexander Carney, a rheumatologist from central New Jersey, the majority of medications prescribed to patients with juvenile arthritis are used to provide symptomatic relief. So in most cases, if you miss one dose, "the worst that can happen is you will have a little flare or increase in your pain." However, if you have a heart condition or if you're taking antibiotics, then missing a dose could be a problem. And, as mentioned previously, forgetting to take prednisone could also be problematic, especially if it's a high dosage. If this happens, "as soon as you remember, take it," Dr. Carney says. "That's the one drug you can't abruptly stop."

Keep in mind that this tip doesn't apply to all drugs. Doubling up on doses or taking them too close together could cause complications. So check with your doctor before doing that. Better yet, "when you're going to start a [new] drug, ask the doctor what the side effects would be, and an additional question might be: What should I do if I forget to take the drug?" Dr. Carney says.

Not all doctors agree about whether young people with JA should take HGH. "The most important way to improve growth is to control the disease inflammation with drugs other than corticosteroids. It is not clear that growth hormone will lead to an improved adult height in these settings. There is also some evidence that it may cause the disease to flare," Dr. Cron says. Conversely, those who are overgrowing may need intra-articular steroids, which can stop premature growth.

The treatments discussed here are only an overview of the medications that are typically used to treat arthritis and related conditions. However, there are other treatments available and even more on the way!

FINDING A TREATMENT THAT WORKS FOR YOU

As you've read, not every case of juvenile arthritis is alike. Some teens may have a mild form of the disease, while others find themselves severely affected. And sometimes the disease goes

TIPS TO ADHERE TO WHEN TAKING MEDICATION

- Never take any type of medicine or supplement unless your doctor prescribed it to you or has given you permission to take it.
- Make sure to follow dosage instructions properly so that you do not overdose, which can cause you to become sick and might potentially be fatal.
- Let each doctor and dentist you visit know what medications and supplements you are currently taking. Sometimes one type of medication can conflict with another and cause complications. Your pharmacist should also inform you if he or she notices that certain medications you are taking could interfere with one another. Also, make sure to alert your pharmacist as to what supplements you are taking in case they could cause problems.
- If you are a student, let your school nurse know what medications you are taking in case an emergency should occur.
- If your general physician prescribes antibiotics when you have a cold or similar illness, let your rheumatologist know immediately. Your rheumatologist may choose to temporarily halt some of the immunosuppressive medicine until the illness has subsided.
- If you have any side effects from your medicine, let your doctor and your family know immediately. A list of possible side effects should always come with the medication. Keep a journal to help you keep track of how your medication is affecting you— whether positively or negatively—and let your doctor see it at each visit.
- Remember, in many cases, you should not take medicine on an empty stomach. Your pharmacist should include information on the pill bottle or package that instructs you as to whether you need to eat or drink before taking a specific drug.
- Avoid drinking alcohol if you are taking arthritis medicine.
- Never take medicine that has expired. It could cause you to become ill.
- If you are traveling, make sure you have enough medication packed for the duration of the trip. Also, make sure it is stored at the proper temperature specifications. If you plan to travel by airplane, keep your medication with you. If it needs to be kept cool, store it in a carry-on insulated cooler bag.
- If you take a lot of medicine, consider putting the pills in a pillbox (at home or when traveling) ahead of time to help you keep track of your daily doses.
- If you become pregnant, let your doctor know immediately, since some medications and supplements may not be safe for expectant mothers.
- Keep a list of your medications and dosage amounts with you at all times in case a situation arises that requires immediate medical attention and health-care workers need to know what you are taking.
- Stay informed about your condition and your health care. Don't be shy when it comes to asking your doctor why he or she has prescribed certain medications for you, because you have a right to be proactive when it comes to your health care. Also, doing this will help you to recognize if something will conflict with any of your other medications.
- Never hesitate to get a second opinion on your treatment regimen.

beyond just infiltrating the joints and spreads into other areas of the body, like the organs. So your doctors will create a treatment plan that is tailored specifically for your needs. According to Dr. Klein-Gitelman, doctors formulate a treatment plan based on the type of arthritis, the severity of the illness, whether the patient is having a flare, and the medications he or she has taken in the past.

As mentioned, because every situation is different, it may take a while to find a regimen that works for you. Some patients may respond well to certain medications and not so well to others. And sometimes your body may no longer respond or experience adverse effects after taking a particular drug after a period of time. Whatever the case, don't be afraid to let your doctor know if a medication is not working or if it is bothering you. Doctors are there to help you get well, and any good doctor will work with you to determine the best medications to do just that.

TAKING A BREAK FROM YOUR MEDICATION REGIMEN

There may be times when you decide to forgo taking some or all of your medications, for any of a number of reasons. Some people reduce the number of medications they take when their disease is less active; others stop taking certain medications temporarily in an effort to halt or lessen the chance of experiencing certain side effects.

NOTE OF CAUTION

Not taking medications prescribed by your doctor can aggravate the disease. So before stopping any or all of your medications, discuss the possible ramifications with your rheumatologist so he or she can help decide what is right for you.

In Shaun-Marie's case, when she found out that she was pregnant at age twenty-eight, she decided she didn't want to

PERSONAL STORIES

"I have taken almost every type of medication there is for my type of arthritis," says Kristen Delaney, who has struggled with the disease since her diagnosis. "My pain, the best I was that I can remember, was when I was in seventh grade when I was on Vioxx and Enbrel. Then they took Vioxx [an NSAID] off the market, and everything just went downhill from there."

Like many other juvenile arthritis patients, Kristen also took methotrexate. "I have tried methotrexate in the past and it makes me really sick. I've heard it bothers a lot of kids too," she says. "At first, I tried the [methotrexate] pills and then I went to a shot, but for me the shot was worse."

A few years ago, "I went on an experimental drug study. It was actually for Orencia for kids at the time," Kristen says. At the time she took part in the study, Kristen felt like she was out of options when it came to relieving her pain. So she began making a four-hour trip to Omaha, Nebraska, twice a month to receive the Orencia infusion.

Eventually, Kristen was able to cut back to getting the infusion once a month. "I was actually on it for about two years when I finally decided to stop because the experimental medicine wasn't working for me either," she says. After that, she resumed her Enbrel injections and took several other medications. "I take at least ten pills a day for either anti-inflammatory [reasons] or pain," she says. "I am currently on prednisone now, and I have been on it for years. It masks the pain more; the pain is still there, but it's a lot worse without it."

Like Kristen, Eric Terry also takes prednisone and gets injections of Enbrel. "Enbrel was his wonder drug as we call it. After about the first shot, we saw a big difference once he got on that," his mother, Cynthia, says.

"Enbrel was just life-changing," Eric echoes. However, for a while after his diagnosis, Eric had difficulty coping because his former rheumatologist originally took a cautious approach to treating his condition. "He started off on Motrin—that was like three times a day," Cynthia says.

Dealing with the disease "was a horrible experience," Cynthia adds. "He had a bad bout in his early years."

In fact, Cynthia remembers her son crying in the middle of the night because he was in so much pain. "I spent many nights laying there with him . . . praying with him," she says. "It was tough getting Eric up every morning. When the winter months came, he was so stiff."

Moreover, Eric's pain became so bad that there was a point when he couldn't even stand to be touched. And because of his condition, Eric also needed help with grooming and had to have his brothers give him piggyback rides down the stairs in the morning, Cynthia adds.

Eventually, Eric's doctor put him on Naprosyn because the medicine "stayed in the system longer and he was progressively getting worse too," Cynthia says. To help

---

control the disease, Eric even had his right knee drained and injected with steroids about four times. He had the same procedure done in his left ankle as well.

Today Eric takes Naprosyn three times a day. "Now he is old enough to the point to let us know when he needs it. He might not always need it," Cynthia notes. In addition, Eric takes methotrexate orally.

Because Eric is taking both Enbrel and methotrexate, he needs to visit Dr. Harry Gewanter every other month for a checkup and he has to get his blood tested to make sure the medications aren't causing him any harm. Generally, the number of doctor visits required depends on the medicine a patient is taking and the severity of his or her condition. "We have about thirty-five hundred patient visits a year," Dr. Marisa Klein-Gitelman says, noting that some patients come for a checkup once a month, while others need to come only once a year. Your doctor will let you know how often you need to make an appointment.

---

continue taking her medication since some medicines may harm a developing baby, while other drug companies are not sure how it could affect babies. Shaun-Marie does not have plans to try any alternative methods to manage her disease. "Most women with rheumatoid arthritis tend to feel relief [from pain] when they are pregnant. So I am actually waiting it out to see how I am going to feel in the next coming months. If I need to, I can still take prednisone for flare-ups," she says.

Allyson Shapiro also stopped taking her arthritis medication. In the spring of 2008, "I took myself off Celebrex," she says. The decision was spurred in part by her participation in a detoxifying health retreat the previous summer. "After the detox, I didn't want any more medications," Allyson says. However, she does continue to take daily vitamins, as well as Synthroid for her thyroid condition.

SURGICAL OPTIONS

There are times when treating juvenile arthritis with medicine isn't enough to halt joint damage, pain, or stiffness. As a result, surgery is needed to replace or straighten joints or simply to relieve pain. "It's such an unpredictable disease," says Deborah Yarett Slater, a licensed occupational therapist. "Some people continue to have flare-ups and they go downhill; their joints get very involved and surgical replacements and more aggressive treatment [is needed]."

The good news is that most people with juvenile arthritis will not need joint surgery—at least not early on, anyway. Overall, it really "depends where you are in your growth and development," Dr. Patience White says. "Every patient is unique and you have to take in all these different aspects" before proceeding with surgery.

However, depending on your condition, your rheumatologist may recommend one of the following surgical procedures:

- *Soft tissue release.* This procedure is done in hopes of improving "the position of a joint that has been pulled out of line." To enable the joint to return to a "more normal position," surgeons cut and then repair tight tissues that are causing the contracture.[19]

- *Osteotomy.* In this case, bone—not tissue—is cut and repositioned in people whose joints are out of alignment. The procedure usually involves knees or hips. An osteotomy is also performed on youths who have extremities that are uneven. By cutting the shorter bone, pins can be inserted inside along with a device called an external fixator, which attaches to the pins and slowly pulls the cut bone apart so new growth can occur.

- *Synovectomy.* During this operation, the inflamed synovium—the lining of the joint—is removed in an effort to reduce pain and swelling.

- *Arthroscopy.* By way of placing a special surgical instrument called an arthroscope inside a small opening in the skin, surgeons can view and repair the damage inside of a joint. Arthroscopy is usually done on the shoulders and knees.

- *Joint fusion or arthrodesis.* This surgical procedure involves fusing damaged joints together in order to help reduce chronic pain when splints or medication aren't doing the trick. Essentially, joints are fused into a permanent position, making them more stable and free of pain. Joints commonly fused include wrists, fingers, and ankles.

TURNING A BATTLE WITH JUVENILE ARTHRITIS INTO A CAREER OF ADVOCACY—SETH GINSBERG'S STORY

Figure 4.3.   Seth Ginsberg was diagnosed at age thirteen with juvenile spondyloarthropathy. He is cofounder of TGI Healthworks and the executive director of the Global Healthy Living Foundation.

"When I was diagnosed at thirteen with spondyloarthropathy, I got turned into a little advocacy machine—I had a disease that was as hard to live with as it was to pronounce. I remember the cocktail of pills I was prescribed to swallow and the ordeal they caused. Though it quickly sidelined me from my extracurriculars, it also set me on a trajectory of activism, awareness, and, well, my own self-identity. In retrospect, the day I was diagnosed with arthritis as a young teenager was the day I got put in a box. Five years later—the day I cofounded CreakyJoints—was the day I danced on top of it.

"In 1999, I had a college experience unlike most, especially one sleepless night at 3 a.m. during my first semester up at school. It wasn't caused by too much beer, nor was it from soured pizza. Instead, it was the aches and pains of an isolating disease, which kept me up and kicked me in the butt. To be more precise, it kicked me in the back. I got out of bed, and that was the night that the arthritis world got shaken up a little: CreakyJoints.org was born as an edgy, fun online community for people of all ages with arthritis.

"All these years later, CreakyJoints has grown in size and impact on the arthritis world. We experienced viral marketing before the words were invented (topping twenty thousand members in a few short years with no advertising). We posted blogs before anyone knew what that was (we just called it a 'diary'). Today, being considered a big deal in the arthritis community is about as cool as being the tallest building in Omaha. But hey, everyone has their claim to fame, right? Luckily mine is as a result of taking a lighthearted, practical, and youthful approach to this supposed old lady disease called 'arthritis.'

(continued)

TURNING A BATTLE WITH JUVENILE ARTHRITIS INTO A CAREER OF ADVOCACY—SETH GINSBERG'S STORY (*Continued*)

"Our goal with CreakyJoints is to make a fun, engaging, and unique community for people to visit regularly for news and information, unique content, an advice columnist, and 'new media' downloads like video and audio podcasts. Our subjects cover the very serious 'how to talk to your doctor' to the not-so-serious 'how to build a birdhouse.' Visitors to the site can browse a listing of local clinical trials of new medicines, find out what others are saying about their experiences with various drugs, learn about what goes into these medicines, and hopefully allay fears about taking new medicine.

"But the Internet wasn't enough to keep us happy. We took our programs offline to local communities (numbering over 120 cities in the United States since 1999) for thousands of people to learn how to swim, eat healthier, take their meds the right way, and, most importantly, meet one another and have a good time within a community of people just like them."[20]

Seth Ginsberg is also the cofounder of TGI Healthworks, a grassroots education agency that produces and executes educational programming on various diseases, including arthritis, diabetes, asthma and COPD, ulcerative colitis, Parkinson's disease, cardiovascular disease, hypertension, psoriasis, and cancer. In addition, Ginsberg is the executive director of the Global Healthy Living Foundation, a 501(c)(3) nonprofit, which builds and sustains communities of people with chronic conditions. CreakyJoints is a part of the Global Healthy Living Foundation as its oldest and most mature community.

⊚ *Resection.* This is when surgeons remove all or part of a bone in order to relieve pain and improve function. Most often, resection is performed on feet, wrists, thumbs, or elbows.

⊚ *Joint replacement.* "Joint replacement is the final common pathway that people come to," says Dr. White. Simply put, at this stage of the game, joints are severely damaged and are the cause of extreme pain. With this procedure, surgeons replace an entire damaged joint with an artificial joint. Although the recovery period is often painful and can last four weeks to several months (during which the patient needs intensive physical therapy), replacing a joint can ultimately lead to less pain and enhanced mobility. Joints that are the most commonly replaced include knees, hips, and wrists. However, growth must be complete in order for the surgery to be conducted. The downside to joint replacement is that joints need to be replaced again about every fifteen years or so. This follow-up procedure is called revision joint surgery and is more involved than the original joint replacement surgery.

◎ *Hip resurfacing.* A new procedure called hip resurfacing is similar to joint replacement in that it involves replacing the diseased surface of hip joints with a metal cap. However, unlike an actual hip replacement, "the ball at the top of the thigh bone that fits into the hip socket (which is known as the femoral head) is not removed." Recovery time, which is estimated at about two weeks, is also much shorter than having a joint replaced.[21]

Before undergoing a surgical procedure, find out the risks that are involved and what the recovery process would be like for you. Sometimes patients need to take additional medicine and take part in a rehabilitation program. If the benefits outweigh the risks, see if you can plan the surgery for a time that is convenient for you. Students might find that scheduling surgery during the summer is best, since it won't conflict with their schooling.

FINDING A SURGEON

If surgery is on the horizon, make sure to find a qualified surgeon who has experience operating on patients with juvenile arthritis. You can start by asking your general practitioner or rheumatologist which surgeons he or she would recommend.

Sometimes surgery is needed to repair joints damaged by arthritis.

Family members or friends often know of a reputable surgeon. In addition, check to make sure the surgeon you are considering going to is board certified in surgery. This means he or she has gone through "special training and has passed exams administered by a national board of surgeons." Certifications "should be from a surgical board that is approved by the American Board of Medical Specialties."[22] A surgeon who is a Fellow of the American College of Surgeons (FACS) has received additional training and passed subsequent tests. To verify whether a surgeon is board certified, visit www.abms.org or call (866) 275–2267. Or visit www.facs.org to find a surgeon near you.

When visiting with a surgeon, remember to ask about fees that you will incur if you choose to undergo surgery. Medical bills can be submitted by surgeons, doctors, anesthesiologists, and the hospital or surgical clinic at which you are treated—to name a few. You may also need to make follow-up visits to your surgeon and doctor and receive subsequent care from physical and occupational therapists. If you have health insurance, you should call the company ahead of time to see if you will need to pay any out-of-pocket expenses—and get a response in writing.

ALTERNATIVE TREATMENTS

Here are just a few alternative methods to manage JA. See also chapter 7 for other ways in which to manage your condition, especially any pain you may be experiencing.

Acupuncture

Highly regarded as a safe procedure with few side effects, acupuncture has been touted as an effective alternative treatment when it comes to relieving pain and improving function. Simply put, acupuncture is an ancient Chinese procedure that involves sticking very thin needles into the patient's skin in an effort to stimulate nerves that block pain signals. Often, it also helps with regulating the nervous system and loosening up tight muscles. This treatment method has been found to be effective in people who have rheumatoid arthritis. To find a licensed practitioner near you, visit the National Certification Commission for Acupuncture and Oriental Medicine's Web site, www.nccaom.org.

Biofeedback

Biofeedback treatment involves using electrical equipment that can monitor your blood pressure, heart rate, muscle tension, skin temperature, and brainwaves to enable you to "become more aware of your body's reaction to stress and pain." By looking at the machine's screen or gauge, you can see how your body reacts when it is tense versus when it is relaxed. The purpose of biofeedback is to help individuals change their physiological activity as a way to improve their health and overall function. It also gives people the opportunity to practice relaxation techniques that can be used "to control some of your body's responses to pain" as they occur.[23] Those interested in trying this treatment method can visit a local biofeedback practitioner or inquire about purchasing a biofeedback machine for in-home use. For more information, visit the Association for Applied Psychophysiology and Biofeedback's Web site, www.aapb.org.

Supplements

Glucosamine, Chondroitin, and MSM

Many supplements on the market today contain glucosamine and chondroitin, which are believed to aid in lubricating joints and rebuilding cartilage, although this hasn't been validated by the FDA. One such product, called Flex-a-min, claims that the glucosamine and chondroitin contained in the pills "promote joint comfort and flexibility over time." Flex-a-min also contains MSM, which the manufacturer says helps maintain healthy cartilage, as well as hyaluronic acid to "maintain the fluid between your joints."[24] These claims, the company admits, have not been evaluated by the FDA. Similar products include Joint Juice, CosaminDS, and Move Free. The manufacturer of Move Free claims that it incorporates glucosamine, chondroitin, and joint fluid in its tablets, along with Uniflex, which is an "antioxidant system that protects joints from harmful oxidants that accelerate the breakdown of cartilage and joint tissue."[25] Again, this claim has not been evaluated by the FDA.

Despite claims by these manufacturers, some doctors feel the tablets may not be all that effective, depending on the level of your illness. These products "may help in a small way, but really treating the inflammation makes the biggest difference," Dr. Randy Cron remarks.

Calcium

In order to keep your bones as healthy and strong as possible, your doctor might recommend you take calcium supplements. Unless your diet is calcium-rich (meaning you eat plenty of yogurt, cheese, and green vegetables, along with drinking milk), young people usually need to take about 1,000 mg of calcium supplements daily. Since your body can only absorb 500 mg at once, you need to split the dosage and take tablets twice a day.[26]

There are various types of calcium supplements on the market today. Three of the most widely used include calcium citrate, calcium carbonate, and calcium phosphate. Calcium citrate is the most easily absorbed. However, it's a good idea to buy calcium supplements that contain vitamin D as well, since vitamin D helps your body use the calcium more efficiently.

Herbal Remedies

If you visit your local health food store or surf the Internet, you are likely to find a host of herbal supplements or teas that profess to boost your health the natural way. An article on herbal remedies that was published in *Parade* magazine states that "five billion people worldwide rely solely on traditional plant-based treatments to heal what ails them." The following is a list of a few that might help you:

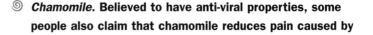 *Chamomile.* Believed to have anti-viral properties, some people also claim that chamomile reduces pain caused by

SHAKLEE CORPORATION

There are many companies out there today that market a variety of supplements online and in stores. While they may claim to have healing effects on arthritis, not all of them actually do. However, one company that has been getting a lot of positive national attention lately—including some airtime on *The Oprah Winfrey Show*—for its commitment to health and the environment is the Shaklee Corporation.

Dr. Forrest C. Shaklee, creator of one of the first multivitamins, founded the Shaklee Corporation in 1956. Since then, the company has remained committed to maintaining sustainable business practices and uses natural ingredients to manufacture its products, which range from household cleaners to nutritional supplements. All its products are touted to be safe for the body and the environment.

"They are the number one nutrition company in the country," says George Piegaro, CEO of Healthier You, Healthier Planet, Inc., a division of Shaklee. "Shaklee leads the industry in analytical methods of testing purity and efficacy. And the company has spent more than $250 million on research and development since its inception."

According to Piegaro, Shaklee manufactures a number of supplements that they believe can benefit individuals who have arthritis. Here is a list of just a few of the products he recommends:

- *Joint Health Complex*. This supplement contains glucosamine and other minerals that are combined to promote collagen synthesis as well as the regeneration of cartilage. It also claims to repair damage to joint surfaces, thereby improving joint function. After using the product for three to four weeks, individuals may notice considerably less pain.
- *GLA Complex*. This supplement, which contains natural anti-inflammatory nutrients, can be taken to reduce arthritis symptoms. Gamma-linolenic acid (or GLA) is an essential fatty acid that comes from plant seed oils; studies have shown that GLA aids in reducing inflammation.
- *Osteomatrix*. According to Shaklee, individuals who are calcium and magnesium deficient feel stiff and have achy muscles and joints. This supplement, which contains calcium, claims to be a natural muscle relaxant. It is also believed to lower blood pressure and increase bone density. Additionally, it may reduce headaches and allow you to sleep better.
- *Alfalfa Complex*. This product contains fifteen minerals and ten vitamins, as well as protein and fiber. It also has enzymes in it that aid in digestion and chlorophyll, which is referred to as a detoxifier. Together, they help reduce pain, swelling, and stiffness in those who have arthritis.
- *OmegaGuard*. Available in softgels, OmegaGuard contains seven natural omega-3 fatty acids, including EPA, DHA, and ALA. This product is suggested for individuals looking to improve joint function, vision, cognitive function, and cardiovascular health.[27]

arthritis. Dr. Isadore Rosenfeld, who wrote the article in *Parade*, also recommends that patients use chamomile to quiet an upset stomach or to help them sleep.

- *Ginger.* If you are taking medication that makes you nauseous (like methotrexate, which can cause nausea), ginger tea or supplements may counteract that feeling.

- *Ginkgo biloba.* People take ginkgo biloba for a variety of reasons, including for anti-inflammatory purposes. It is also believed to be helpful for the vascular system, promoting circulation in the legs, and improving memory—among other benefits.

- *Ginseng.* Possible benefits include boosting energy and improving appetite. Do not take ginseng if you have high blood pressure or heart disease.

- *Hawthorn.* If you have a heart condition, including one of those listed in chapter 3, you might want to look into taking hawthorn, since the NIH claims that it can strengthen the heart.

- *St. John's wort.* This supplement may help those with mild depression, but it can interfere with other medications.

- *Valerian.* Quite possibly the most regularly used sedative in Europe, valerian is taken to promote relaxation and sleep.[28]

At present, clinical trials are being done to determine the actual effectiveness of many herbal supplements. In the meantime, beware that since the FDA does not regulate the companies that manufacture or import herbal supplements, labels may not always be accurate.[29] You need to make sure you purchase products from a reputable source if you decide to incorporate herbal remedies into your treatment regimen. You should also check with your doctor before taking any herbal remedies, because some of them can interact negatively with your prescription medications.

DENTAL CARE

Seeing a dentist regularly is especially important when you have arthritis, since the medications you take may affect your oral health. In addition, oral health can suffer if you have trouble brushing or flossing your teeth due to dexterity limitations or if you simply have difficulty opening your jaw. No matter what the case, you will need to make sure your dentist is always kept up-to-date on your condition and what treatments you are receiving. This is especially important if you are in need of dental work, since you may need to take an antibiotic beforehand.[30]

Your dentist may recommend a variety of products—from special toothbrushes to floss holders to oral rinse—that can be used to keep your teeth and gums healthy. If your dentist doesn't readily offer any suggestions or tips, don't be afraid to ask for ideas, especially if you have limitations.

Since opening your jaw for long periods of time may be difficult (especially for those with TMJ arthritis), you and your dentist might want to try to split up cleaning sessions or dental procedures into a few shorter visits. A physical therapist might recommend jaw exercises that can help to reduce pain and stiffness at future dental visits. Also, if arthritis has prevented your lower jaw from developing properly, creating an overbite, orthodontic measures or surgery may be needed to correct the problem. Your dentist will inform you if this is necessary.

EYE CARE

As discussed earlier, certain forms of juvenile arthritis can cause chronic inflammation of the eye, which is known as uveitis. It especially affects teens and children with pauciarticular JIA.[31] Furthermore, some medications can cause damage to your eyes. For these reasons, you will most likely need to see an ophthalmologist regularly. Your rheumatologist will be able to tell you how often you should schedule eye doctor appointments.

The ophthalmologist will perform a painless examination of your eyes. As part of the process, the doctor will do a slit-lamp exam to look for symptoms of uveitis. If your doctor discovers uveitis, treatment will be prescribed immediately.

NOTES

1. Alex Fernandez, e-mail to the author, June 4, 2008.
2. Arthritis Foundation, "Juvenile Arthritis Treatment Options," www.arthritis.org/disease-center.php?disease_id=38&df=treatments.
3. Arthritis Foundation, *Arthritis in Children* (pamphlet, 2004), 11.
4. Stanley B. Cohen, "Treatment of Arthritis/2008," *LoneStarthritis*, January 2008.
5. Donna Rae Siegfried, "2007 Drug Guide," *Arthritis Today* (January/February 2007): 40.
6. Ibid., 42; Arthritis Foundation, *Managing Your Pain* (pamphlet, 2005), 9.
7. Arthritis Foundation, "Juvenile Arthritis Treatment Options."
8. Arthritis Foundation, *Managing Your Pain*, 10.
9. Arthritis Foundation, *Arthritis in Children*, 14.
10. Siegfried, "2007 Drug Guide," 46.
11. Arthritis Foundation, *Arthritis in Children*, 16.
12. Wikimedia Foundation, Inc., "Intravenous Immunoglobulin," Wikipedia, http://en.wikipedia.org/wiki/Intravenous_immunoglobulin.
13. *Arthritis Today*, Medication Guide—Remicade (ad), Centocor Inc. (March/April 2008): 60.
14. Siegfried, "2007 Drug Guide," 48.
15. *Arthritis Today*, Patient Information Rituxan (ad), Biogen Idec Inc. and Genentech, Inc. (January/February 2007): 18.
16. Cohen, "Treatment of Arthritis/2008."
17. Arthritis Foundation, *Managing Your Pain*, 13.
18. Ibid., 11.
19. Arthritis Foundation, *Arthritis in Children*, 23.
20. Seth Ginsberg, e-mail to the author, May 28, 2008.
21. Kerry Ludlam, "A Hip, New Option," *Arthritis Today* (January/February 2007): 33.
22. Robert S. Dinsmoor, "When You're Considering Surgery," *Arthritis Self-Management* (March/April 2007): 22.
23. Arthritis Foundation, *Managing Your Pain*, 21.
24. *Arthritis Today*, Flex-a-min ad (January/February 2007): 3.
25. *Arthritis Today*, Move Free ad, Schiff (January/February 2007): 82.
26. Kenna Simmons, "Strong Advice," *Arthritis Today* (January/February 2007): 20.

27. Shaklee Corp., "A Natural Approach to Arthritis," Doing Life Intentionally Together, www.healthyfiles.com.

28. Isadore Rosenfeld, "Do Herbal Remedies Work?" *Parade*, March 16, 2008, 18, 21.

29. Ibid., 18.

30. Arthritis Foundation, *Arthritis in Children*, 21.

31. Ibid., 20.

5 Exercising and Maintaining a Proper Diet

EXERCISE

The key to staying as mobile as possible is exercise! Believe it or not, staying active and exercising regularly are as important as taking your medications. This is because physical exercise keeps joints functioning at their optimal level and even helps to strengthen the muscles around them.

To help her strengthen her muscles and joints, Amanda White meets with a personal trainer at her local gym five or six times a week for about an hour each session. "He gives me different exercises to do. Since I can't do different things, like push-ups, he modifies certain exercises so that I can do them," she says.

As part of her exercise routine, Amanda does squats, lunges, and stomach crunches. "Also, because I am a figure skater, I have done things to improve my flexibility, like stretching. I do cardio exercises, too. And I take spin [cycling] classes

"For centuries, people have been talking about how exercise is good. You need to work your muscles all the time. If your muscles are strong, they will support your joints. So by working out and making my muscles stronger, it takes more stress off my joints and that's what makes me feel better."—Amanda, age seventeen

Amanda White lifts weights as part of her weekly exercise routine.

sometimes. Those are really fun. They are a really good workout; they are really good for cardio [health]." Sometimes, Amanda even does exercises using barbells. "I don't lift weights every day—that would be too much," she says. "But I try to lift weights three times a week."

On days when her back or other joints are bothering her more than usual, Amanda likes to swim in the pool at her gym. She also exercises outside of the pool. "I have really closed hips, which makes my back hurt, so I do a lot of hip exercises to stretch them," she says. In addition, Amanda enjoys taking exercise classes offered at her gym. "They have a really cool yoga program." According to information posted on the Web site of the magazine *Yoga Journal*, yoga "is an ancient body of physical, mental, and spiritual practices designed to cultivate inner peace, an open heart, a calm mind, and a strong, relaxed body."[1]

Yoga classes are now offered at about 75 percent of health clubs in the United States.[2] There are several different styles of yoga, which range from low to high intensity. "I ended up going to see this woman, who was an iyengar yoga instructor," says Stefanie Tepley. "[This form of yoga] isn't as stressful as regular yoga on your body and muscles. It is [centered on] long stretches and it helped strengthen my muscles. Of course, I am very stiff in the morning, so [the instructor] taught me how to do stretches in the mornings so I could get out of bed."

As Stefanie notes, traditional yoga may be a bit difficult for people with arthritis and it's recommended that you discuss your limitations with the instructor ahead of time. "My yoga teacher knows I can't do all the exercises, so I sit out sometimes," Amanda says. In spite of the fact that she is unable to do all of the exercises, taking yoga has still helped Amanda to become more flexible and feel better overall.

"It's also really good for your mental health too," Amanda notes. *Yoga Journal* also states that yoga "reduces stress, increases strength and flexibility, improves concentration and alertness, and is non-impactful on the joints." Yoga is even known to improve cardiovascular efficiency and peripheral blood flow. And it can also help decrease systolic blood pressure, strengthen the endocrine system, and keep weight under control.[3]

Whether it's yoga or another recreational activity that piques your interest, Dr. Harry L. Gewanter recommends that teens with juvenile arthritis exercise as much as possible—meaning as much as they can tolerate. "You have [to implement] different goals at different times, and certainly the old philosophy of 'Move it, or lose it' is there," he says.

Amanda recognizes that not everyone with juvenile arthritis will easily adjust to having to add a workout routine into his or her life. "I feel like some people are really afraid of exercise, and some people are afraid of going to the gym," she says. Even if you are embarrassed or scared, Amanda recommends that you should try going to the gym at least once. "Once you go, you won't be afraid of it." But to get a good workout, "you don't even have to go to the gym. There's all kinds of stuff you can do at home."

When at home, Amanda tries to do stretching exercises at least once a day. She also uses a stability exercise ball so that she can practice some of the routines she does at the gym. Stability exercise balls come in different sizes and help users to improve balance, muscle tone, and posture.[4]

Other items that are often used at the gym can also be purchased for use at home, including free weights, a treadmill, or stationary bike. Families on a limited budget may find this

EXERCISES YOU CAN DO WITH A STABILITY BALL

Adapted from Terrie Heinrich Rizzo, "On the Ball," Arthritis Today *(March/April 2008): 49–50.*

Tips for Getting Started

- Choose the right ball size. When sitting upright with your feet flat on the floor, your knees should be level with or slightly lower than your pelvis, with thighs parallel to the floor.
- Position yourself close to a wall or chair for quick balance assistance, if needed.
- Keep your abdominal and buttock muscles tight, and sit tall.
- For increased stability, position feet wider apart and keep arms and legs close.
- Repeat exercises eight to twelve times (one set), and rest for thirty to sixty seconds between sets, unless otherwise noted.

Exercises

1. **Slow Knee March**
   (For core, balance)
   Sit with both hands at sides or on hips. Slowly lift left knee, raising foot two to four inches off floor. Hold for two seconds, then lower and repeat with right knee. As you get comfortable with the movement, lift knees higher and march faster. Do one to three sets.

2. **Hip Rolls**
   (For hips, lower back, balance)
   Sit with feet about hip-width apart and hands on ball at each side for balance, or behind your head for added challenge.
   - *Side-to-Side Hip Rolls.* With knees still, move hips gently from side to side (rolling ball slightly). Pause at the end of each sideways movement for a gentle stretch.
   - *Front-to-Back Hip Rolls.* With both hands on knees, rotate hips to front by tucking buttocks forward under pelvis, then to back by pushing buttocks out behind pelvis. Pause at the end of movements. Don't move knees or chest.

3. **Ball Squats**
   (For legs, buttocks, core)
   Stand with ball propped between lower back and a wall, pressing slightly into the ball. Hands should be at sides or on hips, with feet hip-width apart and slightly in front of you. Bending at knees and hips, slowly move into a semi-sitting position, with knees above ankles. Do not bend knees more than ninety degrees. Hold for three breaths, and push through heels to return to standing position. (Check with your doctor first if you have arthritis in your knees.)

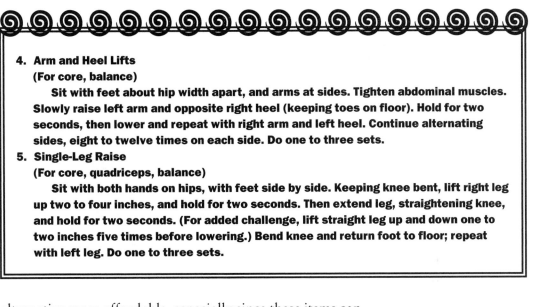

4. **Arm and Heel Lifts**
   (For core, balance)
      Sit with feet about hip width apart, and arms at sides. Tighten abdominal muscles. Slowly raise left arm and opposite right heel (keeping toes on floor). Hold for two seconds, then lower and repeat with right arm and left heel. Continue alternating sides, eight to twelve times on each side. Do one to three sets.

5. **Single-Leg Raise**
   (For core, quadriceps, balance)
      Sit with both hands on hips, with feet side by side. Keeping knee bent, lift right leg up two to four inches, and hold for two seconds. Then extend leg, straightening knee, and hold for two seconds. (For added challenge, lift straight leg up and down one to two inches five times before lowering.) Bend knee and return foot to floor; repeat with left leg. Do one to three sets.

alternative more affordable, especially since these items can often be found on the Internet at reduced cost. However, if you would rather exercise at the gym but don't think you can afford a membership, you should try to work out a deal with management, says Buddy Hayes, a certified therapeutic recreation specialist from Sante Fe, New Mexico. Or you might want to check out the local YMCA, which offers financial aid to members who fit specific criteria.

ARTHRITIS FOUNDATION EXERCISE PROGRAMS

The Arthritis Foundation offers a number of exercise programs as part of its Life Improvement Series. These classes aim to decrease stiffness and reduce pain, thereby increasing mobility. However, according to Peggy Lotkowictz, vice president of mission delivery at the New Jersey Chapter of the Arthritis Foundation, not all of these classes have been approved for teens yet. Fortunately, there is one that has been tested and approved for teens: the foundation's Aquatic Program.

   As part of the Aquatic Program, participants do range-of-motion and other exercises in the water. According to Lotkowictz, "The fact that you're weightless makes it much more easy to move. Because you're weightless, you don't have the force of gravity against your joints, so you can do things in

MS. WHEELCHAIR AMERICA 2008 PROMOTES PHYSICAL FITNESS

Figure 5.1.   Author Kelly Rouba, Ms. Wheelchair New Jersey
2006–08, with Kristen McCosh, Ms. Wheelchair America 2008.
Kristen often mentors and exercises with her friend Lisa Urban,
who has juvenile rheumatoid arthritis.

As part of her platform, Kristen McCosh, Ms. Wheelchair America 2008, has been speaking nationwide about the benefits of proactive physical fitness. Her passion for physical fitness developed after the winter of 2005. Prior to that, she had been feeling the effects of life in a wheelchair. Much of the time, her body was stiff and in pain. She also put on weight from remaining sedentary, and was often tired and had little motivation. Wanting to make a positive change in her life, McCosh made a New Year's resolution to take control of her health.

In January 2006 McCosh joined her local YMCA, which has an extensive adaptive exercise program called the Partnership Program. She soon found a trainer who volunteered to help her get in shape. McCosh then began working out on the YMCA's special equipment three days a week. The other four days of the week, she worked out at home to aerobics videos featuring exercises designed for people who use wheelchairs. She also changed her diet by eating smaller portions, reducing her calorie intake, and cutting out soda with sugar.

If you're looking to get in shape, McCosh suggests you start by investigating what resources are available in your community—whether it be a gym, recreational center, or pool—to help you achieve optimal physical fitness. McCosh also recommends you set short- and long-term goals. Start your exercise program by setting small, realistic goals. McCosh also feels it can be a good idea to bring along a buddy who will help you stick to your agenda. In fact, one of McCosh's best friends, Lisa Urban, has juvenile rheumatoid arthritis and they often work out together. "We like doing yoga and aerobics," McCosh says.

According to McCosh, there are several primary and secondary benefits to exercising. Here are just a few.

Primary Benefits:

- *Endurance exercises.* Increase energy and stamina.
- *Strength exercises.* Increase ability to function independently; reduce weakness.
- *Flexibility exercises.* Decrease stiffness and improve joint and muscle function.

Secondary Benefits:

- *Decreases feelings of isolation and promotes positive-thinking.* Exercise alleviates depression and fosters goal setting.
- *Improves appearance.* Helps with posture, muscle tone, and controlling weight.
- *Improves self-esteem and confidence.* Fosters feelings of accomplishment and can lead to the pursuit of other goals or passions.

water that you can't do on land. Also, if you do the exercises in a warm water pool, it relaxes your joints and tendons . . . and all the connective tissues that surround the joints."

By joining the Aquatic Program, teens have an opportunity to learn new exercises that can increase mobility and quite possibly foster independence and improve self-esteem. Individuals also have the chance to make new friends who share similar experiences living with the chronic illness. The Arthritis Foundation also believes that this type of social interaction can lessen feelings of isolation or even depression.

Typically, the aquatic class is held twice a week. The cost to participate may vary and classes may also be open to adults. "It's really hard to get programs for kids with arthritis, when you think of the number [of children who have arthritis] and where they have to travel [to take the class]," Lotkowictz says. The Aquatic Program is offered at many YMCAs and fitness

Figure 5.2.   Children doing aquatic exercises. Photo courtesy of Jeff Savage, director of programs at the Texas Chapter of the Arthritis Foundation.

centers across the country. For more information, visit your local chapter's Web page at www.arthritis.org and look under "Events and Programs."

Jeff Savage, former director of programs at the Texas Chapter of the Arthritis Foundation, says his chapter also runs the Kids Get Arthritis Too Exercise Program. Presently, the program is offered only in North Texas. According to a program description Savage provided, in order to create interest in the program, staff from the chapter meet with teens and their families during arthritis clinic hours at Texas Scottish Rite Hospital for Children.

Those who agree to participate are evaluated by staff from the chapter, who then formulate individual home exercise programs for participants based on the pain they are experiencing as well as their current activity levels. The routine is explained to the family in detail and participants are asked to keep a log of the exercises they do. Typically, the routine should be performed three times a week for about one hour. Staff from the chapter follow up with participants once a week to make

LET'S MOVE TOGETHER

This excerpt appeared in the Your Stories section on www.letsmovetogether.org, which was created by the Arthritis Foundation. It was written in 2008 by forty-year-old Juliette Rizzo of Bethesda, Maryland. In the past, Juliette assisted with the Surgeon General's Call to Action to Improve the Health and Wellness of Individuals with Disabilities, as well as other disability-related national outreach initiatives of the U.S. Department of Homeland Security and the U.S. Department of Health and Human Services. She also received the Presidential Active Lifestyle Award (PALA) from the President's Council on Physical Fitness and Sport.

The Arthritis Foundation has been moving with me since the doctor told my parents exercise was the key to reducing the joint pain and stiffness associated with my juvenile rheumatoid arthritis onset at age three. From working out with Arthritis Foundation Aquatic Program instructors to chairing an Arthritis Walk in Maryland, and dressing up as Ms. Claus to participate in the Jingle Bell Run, I've learned that exercise can be fun and that it's much more enjoyable with others!

With JRA, scleroderma and fibromyalgia, I must remain vigilant to manage the pain and fatigue, while maintaining my independence and my immune health. Fifty pounds overweight with excruciating hip pain and unable to turn over unassisted in the bed at night, I made a public choice to pursue a healthy lifestyle. Appearing as the first person with arthritis on the Discovery Health Channel's "National Body Challenge" series, I demonstrated that "exercise is for every body," by swimming, strength training, and sailing solo in the Atlantic Ocean. Losing that weight, gaining flexibility and even crossing my legs for the first time in years, a little exercise has certainly taken me a long way![5]

sure they are continuing the program and to see if they are experiencing any difficulties.

Evaluations are also conducted by staff after the teen has been in the program for nine months. This evaluation helps to determine whether the teen is able to do more activity-wise, and whether he or she has less pain, which is often the case.

**Figure 5.3.   A child and instructor at the Tai Chi for Arthritis class.
Photo courtesy of Jeff Savage, former director of Programs at the
Texas Chapter of the Arthritis Foundation. The chapter runs the Kids
Get Arthritis Too Program.**

SPORTS

Because of the pain and fatigue arthritis can cause, it is very
easy to want to remain sedentary. While it's okay to rest your
joints when they are bothering you, getting involved in sports is
one way to keep your joints from losing function. Playing
sports is also a fun way to give your joints and muscles a good
workout.

"Kids [and adults] are encouraged to participate in all sports
that they can," Lotkowictz says. However, before engaging in a
particular sport, it's a good idea to evaluate the type of activity
involved and how it could affect your arthritis. Sports like
football or wrestling might aggravate your condition or cause
serious injuries depending on the severity of your arthritis.
Other activities, like field or ice hockey, jogging, gymnastics, or
even jumping on a trampoline, can also harm the joints and are
not usually encouraged. If you have a mild form of arthritis, it
might be okay to play more rigorous sports, like soccer, but it is

always wise to check with your doctor first. And even with a doctor's permission, it is important to wear protective gear as a precautionary measure.

It is always a good idea to do some warm-up exercises before entering the game. Depending on the type of sport, certain warm-up exercises are done to stretch the muscles that will be used the most during play. "Because there are so many sports, each one will have a set pattern of stretching and warming up. The best idea is to check with the coach or a staff member that is teaching the class. They will have a list of them and, while there, you will most likely do [the warm-up exercises] before each class or training session," says Hayes. "If you are able to join a gym or health club, you can have a session with a personal trainer and they can give you a detailed warm-up and cool-down routine that is tailor-made for you."

Hayes, who has multiple sclerosis and uses a wheelchair, has been an athlete for many years. Based on her experiences, she also recommends doing warm-up exercises before playing sports by yourself or with friends. "For example, if you are

EXCERPT FROM "SURVIVING AND THRIVING WITH JUVENILE ARTHRITIS," BY KARA KUNKEL OF OREGON, MISSOURI

Excerpted from Teen Voices 8, no. 1 (Spring 1999).

Kara Kunkel (now Griffin), then eighteen years old, wrote: "I have always wanted to be just like everyone else, but because of my arthritis my mom and my doctors encouraged me not to participate in sports. Most of the time it was fine with me, but I had to go out for cheerleading because it was always my dream. Luckily, I made cheerleader six years in a row; throughout these years I definitely learned a lot about my disease and how it affects me. I tried never to show any pain while I was cheering, but I must admit I have aches and pains all the time. I never complained because I knew it would not do much good even if I did. Many times I had to limit myself to just certain stunts and jumps."

going to play basketball, you would want to do stretches of the upper body—meaning trunk area, arms, head, and neck. Don't rush the warm-up, as it gives your muscles time to get ready to engage in activity. Most injuries occur because of an inadequate warm-up or cool-down."

Cool-down exercises, which may be similar to warm-up exercises, are performed after engaging in the sport or activity in order to calm the muscles. "This will allow your core body temperature to come back down to what is normal for you. And remember to stay hydrated during your training. If at any time you feel sick to your stomach, stop and rest. This is a good indication you are not hydrated enough," Hayes advises.

However, doing warm-ups, cool-downs, or taking precautionary measures to avoid injuries may not be enough, and playing a particular sport may no longer be possible once the disease has progressed to a certain point.

When Kristen Delaney was in eighth grade, she had to give up playing volleyball because of the pain the activity caused her to feel. Before she made the decision to stop playing volleyball, she tried to cope as best she could. "It was more of a willpower thing than a physical thing. I would take Icy Hot and smother my knees and hands with it until it went numb. I pretty much went through a whole jar of it in three days because I am a competitive person," she says. "[But] I came to realize after seventh grade that I couldn't do it anymore because no matter how hard I've tried, I couldn't play how I wanted to anymore."

It was after her freshman year when she also stopped playing on the high school softball team because she used up so much energy while running the bases that it caused her to collapse. "I was in so much pain and my body didn't want to do that anymore," Kristen says.

In Kristen's case, the disease had progressed so much that it was no longer possible for her to participate in demanding sports or activities. For this reason, it is always best to consult your doctor before engaging in physical or strenuous activities like sports. What types of activities teens should do "varies depending on where the arthritis is," Lotkowictz says. "It really is on an individual basis, which is why [they should ask their doctor before participating]."

"Before any exercise or workout sessions begin, the person [with arthritis] should be cleared by a medical doctor," Hayes echoes. "Any information about the sport should be taken to the doctor appointment so the doctor knows what the person will be doing. It is not safe to misinform the doctor because you think they will not approve you to engage in the sport or activity and it may very well cause physical harm."

According to the Arthritis Foundation, certain sports, like swimming or bicycling, "exercise the joints and muscles without putting weight-bearing stress on the joints" and are usually doctor-approved.[6] Jacqueline Kuhns, a physical therapist at St. Lawrence Rehabilitation Center in Lawrenceville, New Jersey, also recommends swimming as a form of exercise. "Doing range-of-motion [exercises] in the water is good. And so is resisted walking, which is just walking back and forth in the water," she says. By swimming regularly, you will find that it improves muscle tone, as well as the movement of larger joints, more than most other activities.

Dancing can also benefit your joints, as well as the rest of your body. "I approach dance from a professional artistic standpoint, but the healing benefits of dance are very apparent," says Alana Wallace, a dance instructor from Chicago, Illinois. "Dance is a great way to exercise, alleviate stress, promote flexibility, burn calories, cultivate social and cultural interactions, and so on. Thus, all these things promote wellness and well-being. As a post-polio survivor for more than fifty years, I feel dance has helped me to ward off secondary health problems because when I am doing something physical that I love, I feel healthy."

If dancing, swimming, or bicycling does not appeal to you, there are plenty of other sports or recreational activities to choose from that can help you stay in shape. But remember, no matter what the sport or activity, it is always a good idea to pace yourself. You can tell if you've pushed your body too hard if you find yourself in pain one or two hours after a particular activity, and especially if you are still in pain the next day. If

Bicycling is a good form of exercise that won't put too much stress on your joints.

that is the case, you will have to cut back on how long you participate in the activity or decide whether it's something you should continue doing. You may also want to consider cutting back on the time you spend engaged in a recreational activity on days that are already stressful or busy.

ADAPTIVE SPORTS

Some teens with juvenile arthritis may use crutches, a walker, or even a wheelchair to help them get around. If this is the case, joining a regular sports team may not be an option. However, there are a number of leagues and programs in existence today that accommodate people with special needs.

One such group is called the Miracle League. Established in 1998, this nonprofit organization has baseball leagues in forty-four states as well as several in Puerto Rico that accommodate players of all ages who have physical or mental challenges. Games are played on a special field that is flat and made of cushioned, synthetic turf so that youth can move around safely and easily, according to Diane Alford, executive director of the Miracle League Association. The dugouts are also wheelchair accessible. A typical season lasts eight weeks and players are assigned to a buddy who helps them as needed.

It is also possible for teens with physical disabilities, including those who use wheelchairs, to dance. Wallace, who has post-polio syndrome and uses a wheelchair, oversees

Dance>Detour, a fully integrative dance company based in Chicago. A number of similar dance companies or dance troupes exist worldwide.

"As a professional actor and vocalist artist, the inclusion of dance to my career was initially a hard sell to me," says Wallace. "I did not think artists with disabilities could legitimately compete, nor be taken seriously in the arena of dance. But in 1995, I was wowed when I witnessed my first physically integrated dance performance by the Cleveland Ballet Dancing Wheels. What thrilled me most about the company was the fact that their dancers who used wheelchairs were equal participants in the dance. I always thought that people who danced in wheelchairs could only flap their arms and that the non-disabled dancers manipulated their wheelchairs and dominated the movement. Boy, was I wrong! This became a new genre for me to explore, and I was inspired to form my own company, Dance>Detour."

Although Wallace has been a dance instructor for many years, she still finds it hard to describe her method of teaching. "There are no rules. The dance movements we, meaning people with disabilities, create are so individualized. It is a combination of imagination, exploration and pushing our range of abilities beyond what we thought possible," Wallace says. "Dance has changed my life. I now embrace my disability and my body in a way that I never have before."

The Miracle League and Dance>Detour are just two recreational organizations that were created to include people with disabilities. According to Hayes, there are many more out there, including Sailability, Disabled Archery USA, the Handicapped Scuba Association, Disabled Sports USA, the North American Riding for the Handicapped Association, and the National Sports Center for the Disabled. There are also a number of adaptive sports centers located around the country.

At the Adaptive Sports Center (ASC) of Crested Butte, Colorado, teens and their families can enjoy skiing, snowboarding, downhill mountain biking, handcycling, rock climbing, hiking, pontoon boating, sea kayaking, and even whitewater rafting, among other activities—depending on the time of year, of course. According to Matt Kuehlhorn, ASC's summer program director, the center uses adaptive equipment, ranging from special skis to modified paddles, so that people with all types of disabilities can enjoy the recreational activities the organization offers.

ASC is open year-round and individuals usually pay a daily fee to participate. "They can do a lot of different activities. Typically, we'll do one or two [activities] a day," Kuehlhorn says. "A lot of kids really do enjoying whitewater rafting and getting up on the ropes course."

If this sounds too difficult for someone with arthritis, there's no need to worry. "We can accommodate anybody," Kuehlhorn says. "A lady, who is actually one of our [financial] donors, has a form of arthritis . . . and she started with our ski program."

Craig Kennedy, who uses a wheelchair and is president of the Colorado-based company Access Anything, LLC, enjoys skiing each season and encourages other people with physical limitations to give it a try. "For someone with arthritis that can stand but has limited stamina and strength, downhill skiing offers four-track skiing, [which is a] ski with two long crutch-type braces called outriggers that have ski tips on the end. There is also the ski walker that is like a regular walker but has skis on it. For those with more severe cases who cannot stand [up] to ski, monoskis and biskis are 'sit-skis' [that can be used]."

No matter what activity piques your interest, "our doors are open to anybody, and one thing we love to do is work with families. So if one of the kids has arthritis, then we can get the whole family out for some activity," says Kuehlhorn.

The choices of adaptive sports available today are limitless. "You would be hard pressed to find any sport out there these days that is not adapted for people with mobility impairments," Kennedy says.

RECOMMENDED EXERCISE ROUTINES

If you've just been diagnosed with arthritis—or even if you've had it for years—you may not feel up to trying adventurous activities like whitewater rafting or downhill mountain biking just yet. If that's the case, or if you simply aren't a "thrill-seeker," you may want to ask your doctor or physical therapist (see chapter 6) for a list of exercises that you can safely do inside or outside your home.

Athletic trainers at your local gym may also be able to design a workout routine just for you, like Amanda's trainer did for her. However, you want to be sure the trainer is properly certified and knows what exercises are appropriate for someone who has arthritis. According to the Arthritis Foundation, it is a good idea to focus on doing flexibility exercises when first implementing a fitness routine. Flexibility exercises can improve range of motion and increase function overall. After you've become adept at doing these exercises, you can then progress to weight training and endurance exercises, like bicycling.

Dietician Marla Brodsky admits that exercising is usually the last thing that people with arthritis want to do. But she says there have been studies that show strength training and other exercises can decrease pain because they help develop the muscles so that they are better able to support the joints in your body. And this is something she can attest to. A personal trainer from Chicago, Brodsky was diagnosed with multiple sclerosis in 1994. Since then, she has learned to manage her condition through diet and exercise. To date, "I have virtually no symptoms," Brodsky says.

Based on her experiences, Brodsky also recommends including swimming and strength training as part of your exercise routine. "A few times a week, do strength training," she says. Brodsky also notes that when you begin lifting weights, it's best to start with lighter weights of about one or two pounds and then gradually add more weight as time passes. If you have trouble lifting weights due to limited dexterity or general weakness, try using wrist weights, which can be strapped around your wrist with Velcro.

As an alternative to lifting weights, resistance bands can also be used to strengthen the upper and lower parts of the body. Resistance bands, also known as Thera-Bands or exercise tubes, come in various colors depending on their level of resistance.

Unlike weights, they can easily be taken with you if you are traveling away from home and want to keep up with your fitness routine.

When it comes to doing range-of-motion and stretching exercises, they should be part of your daily routine because they increase your mobility, Brodsky says. In addition, she recommends doing endurance exercises such as riding a stationary bicycle, walking, or swimming about twenty to thirty minutes three times a week. "[Exercising] helps to control weight. It makes you feel better, so it actually decreases depression. It helps your heart, and it gives you more energy. It can even help lessen morning stiffness and pain."

Those teens who have juvenile arthritis and are still in school are encouraged to take physical education. However, adaptations to the school's regular gym program may be needed. (See chapter 8 for more information.)

THE BENEFITS OF EXERCISE

"I think [exercise] is an essential part of the treatment plan," says Dr. Marisa Klein-Gitelman. As discussed earlier, exercising makes your muscles stronger. If you do not use a joint that is sore, the muscles around it will weaken or deteriorate, causing even more pain. So by exercising, you are helping to reduce the amount of pain the disease inflicts and you are preventing damage to joints at the same time.[7]

Also, the more you exercise, the more you will build up your endurance. According to the Arthritis Society of Canada, "as the general [physical] condition improves, more active exercises will gradually strengthen muscles. Strong muscles stabilize and protect the joints."[8] There are other benefits to exercising, too. The Arthritis Foundation claims exercise "also helps promote overall health and fitness by giving you more energy, helping you sleep better, controlling your weight, decreasing depression, and giving you more self-esteem. Furthermore, exercise can help [ward] off other health problems such as osteoporosis and heart disease."[9]

RESISTANCE BAND EXERCISES

Resistance Band Squats

1. Start by stepping on the resistance band with both feet shoulder-width apart.
2. Hold the resistance band at shoulder level with both hands. Start into a full squat while holding the band at shoulder height.
3. Return to the starting position and repeat.

Alternate Lying Chest Presses

1. Lie on your back and place the resistance band under your back and hold the ends with both hands.
2. Start by pressing one arm up toward the ceiling and then return to the starting position. Repeat with the other arm.

Triceps Extension with Resistance Band

1. Start by holding the tubing in one hand and placing that hand behind your back.
2. Now grab the other end of the band with the arm that is over your head.
3. Extend the top elbow until your arm is fully extended.
4. Return to the starting position and repeat for the prescribed repetitions.

Lateral Rows with Resistance Band

1. Step onto resistance band with feet hip-width apart and knees slightly bent.
2. Start position: Grasp ends with a neutral grip (palms facing each other). Arms should hang down to sides with elbows slightly bent.
3. Raise band to side of body at shoulder height keeping elbows only slightly bent.
4. Return to start position.

Biceps Curls with Resistance Band

1. Stand with feet shoulder width apart, knees slightly bent, and at a staggered stance.
2. Step onto middle of tubing with back foot or both feet.
3. Start position: Grasp ends with underhand grip (palms facing forward) with arms hanging down at sides. Elbows should be close to sides.
4. Flex at the elbows and curl band up to approximately shoulder level. Keep elbows close to sides throughout movement.
5. Return to start position.
6. Remember to keep back and head straight in a neutral position throughout movement. Shoulders should be stabilized by squeezing shoulder blades together slightly—only the elbow joint should be moving.[10]

EXERCISE COUNTDOWN

Taken from Michele Taylor, "Kid Power," Arthritis Today (July/August 1998).

Before you start exercising, here are 10 things to remember:

1. Your exercise program should include a warm-up and cool-down.
2. Don't do your exercises on a bed or soft surface.
3. Do each exercise slowly and smoothly.
4. Repeat each exercise 3 or 4 times and move your body a little farther each time.
5. STOP if you feel pain 2 hours after exercising. If you have a flare, take it easy for a day or two. When you start back, reduce the number of exercises and see if that helps.
6. Try your moves to music or grab your parents or some friends to join you.
7. Reward yourself after you reach your exercise goal for the day.
8. Make sure you ask your doctor and parents if the exercises you're doing are right for you.
9. Keep an exercise diary to see how many of each exercise you do every day so, at the end of the month, you'll see how far you've come.
10. ALWAYS focus on what you can do, NOT on what you can't do.

Target: Shoulder

Shoulder exercise

1. Lie on the floor with both arms at your sides.
2. Raise one arm over your head, keeping your elbow straight, until the back of your hand reaches the floor.
3. Return your arm slowly to your side. Do this a few times.
4. Repeat with the other arm.

Target: Neck

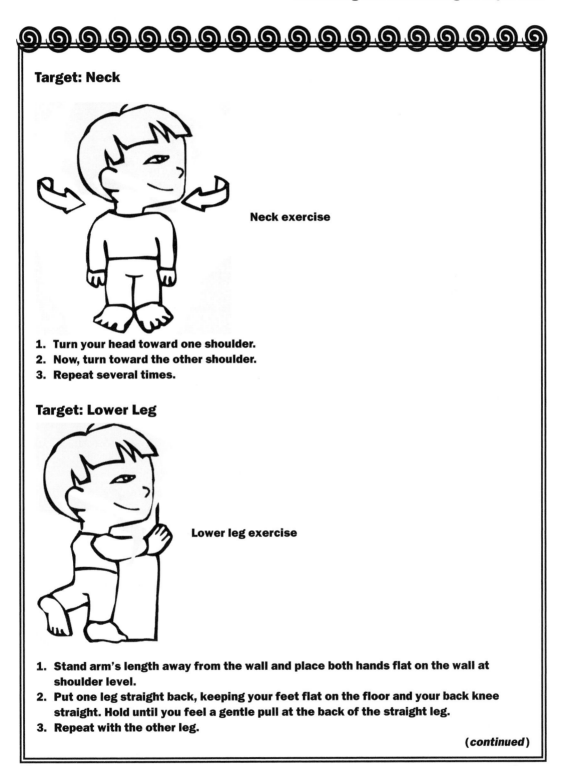

Neck exercise

1. Turn your head toward one shoulder.
2. Now, turn toward the other shoulder.
3. Repeat several times.

Target: Lower Leg

Lower leg exercise

1. Stand arm's length away from the wall and place both hands flat on the wall at shoulder level.
2. Put one leg straight back, keeping your feet flat on the floor and your back knee straight. Hold until you feel a gentle pull at the back of the straight leg.
3. Repeat with the other leg.

(*continued*)

EXERCISE COUNTDOWN (*Continued*)

Target: Neck and Chest

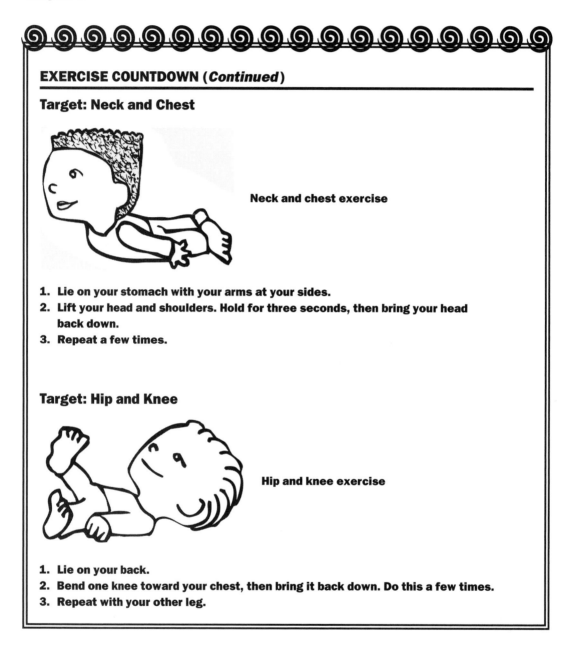

Neck and chest exercise

1. Lie on your stomach with your arms at your sides.
2. Lift your head and shoulders. Hold for three seconds, then bring your head back down.
3. Repeat a few times.

Target: Hip and Knee

Hip and knee exercise

1. Lie on your back.
2. Bend one knee toward your chest, then bring it back down. Do this a few times.
3. Repeat with your other leg.

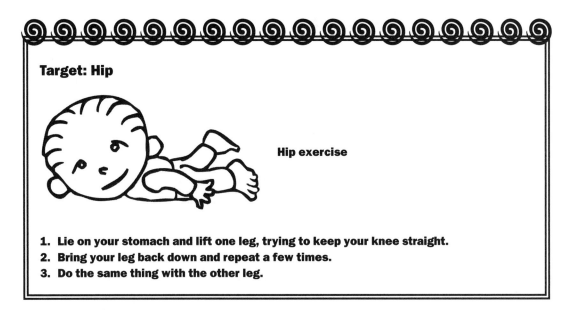

Target: Hip

Hip exercise

1. **Lie on your stomach and lift one leg, trying to keep your knee straight.**
2. **Bring your leg back down and repeat a few times.**
3. **Do the same thing with the other leg.**

The Arthritis Society also recommends that teens implement a fitness routine into their daily schedules, under parental supervision, if necessary. It may even be beneficial to get family and friends involved in the routine to either help with exercises or to make the process more enjoyable. Playing upbeat music may also make you feel more invigorated and ready to work out.

When working out, remember to set limits so you don't exacerbate your condition. Also, at times when the disease has flared up, you may need to alter your routine by reducing the number of exercises you do or only doing those that are the least stressful on your joints. For example, during a flare-up, riding a bicycle may be easier on your body than walking, and it is still a great way to strengthen your hips, knees, and ankles.

If you've just implemented a fitness routine into your schedule, start out slowly and gradually increase your workout. Also, keep in mind that it may take time to experience all the benefits that exercise can bring. Most of all, it will keep you in optimal shape rather than letting the disease take complete control. As we have discussed, exercising might also be a bit painful in the beginning since you are working your muscles more and possibly in different ways—but stick with it, and the results will be worth it!

MAINTAINING A PROPER DIET

Along with exercise comes nutrition, and that means eating foods that are good for your body. Eating right will help you to stay in shape and keep your body in good health. "I want [patients with juvenile arthritis] to take in a good diet and make sure they [follow] healthy living styles," Dr. Patience White says.

So what exactly constitutes a good diet? "I think it should be a calcium- and vitamin D–sufficient diet. A lot of times, children don't eat good quality fruits and vegetables," says Dr. Klein-Gitelman. Teens who have juvenile arthritis need additional calcium and vitamin D to help strengthen their bones, and that's why following a proper diet is especially important.[11]

To achieve this, teens with juvenile arthritis should eat three balanced meals a day. This means having breakfast, lunch, and dinner. Breakfast is the most important meal of the day because it helps energize your body for the day ahead. And, just as importantly, it also helps to coat your stomach so the medication you take does not cause pain, nausea, or vomiting. An example of a healthy, ample breakfast includes nutritious

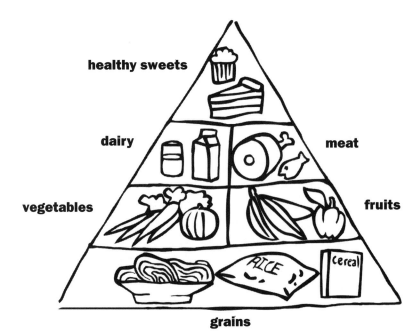

It's important to eat a balanced diet.

I CAN WITH RA . . . IN THE KITCHEN

Food Network star chef Sandra Lee has come together with the Arthritis Foundation and Bristol-Myers Squibb (maker of Orencia) to create a new Web site, www.IcanWithRA.com. The site offers information on arthritis as well as tips for making cooking and grocery shopping faster and easier on your body. The site even features a few recipes that are simple to make. Some of the tips Sandra mentions throughout the site are things she learned from her grandmother Lorraine, who had painful rheumatoid arthritis.

cereal (not the sugary kind) with milk, a piece of toast, and a glass of orange juice.

When preparing your meals, it is important to follow the USDA guidelines and eat something from each of the food groups—dairy, meat and protein, grains, fats and oils, fruits, and vegetables—every day. If you neglect one of these food groups, your body will not get all the nutrients it needs in order to have a balanced diet.

Eating food from each of the six food groups is a great start on the road to eating healthy, but that's just the beginning. You can learn how to make improvements to your diet in a variety of other ways by meeting with a registered dietician. "There's a lot you can do with [your] diet. There's a lot of research on it and [eating right] really can help people," says Brodsky, who also owns Luscious Life Nutrition. Brodsky started the company in 2003 in an effort to provide exercise training and nutritional information to people with inflammatory disorders.

Over the past five years, Brodsky has served as a consultant to the Arthritis Foundation's Greater Illinois Chapter and often gives lectures on the subject of nutrition as well as how particular foods are believed to increase inflammation. According to Brodsky, it is possible to create a diet that will reduce the amount of inflammation caused by juvenile arthritis. "Basically an anti-inflammatory diet, it is pretty much a 'whole foods' kind of diet. There are certain foods that are shown to increase inflammation and others that are shown to decrease inflammation by lowering some of the anti-inflammatory hormones that occur."

"Food is more than just something you eat," Brodsky adds. "It's really biochemistry. It can change your cells significantly so you have less inflammation. Most people are in this chronic inflammatory state. Much of that chronic inflammation may be due to a poor diet. Food has a huge impact on decreasing inflammation. It's something you should put a lot of work and emphasis on rather than just relying solely on drugs [to bring the disease under control]."

To follow an anti-inflammatory diet, you must adhere to several principles. First, you need to identify whether you have any food sensitivities or allergies, since they can trigger inflammatory reactions. "Many people with rheumatoid arthritis are found to have food sensitivities, the main ones being wheat and dairy. Some people also have a sensitivity to corn," Brodsky says.

Omega-6 fatty acids, which are in corn oil, soybeans, cottonseed, safflower, and sunflower oil, are often found in the fats that you get from fried food and later turn into inflammatory hormones after they are metabolized, Brodsky says. "You need some of those when you have a cut. But in the Americanized diet, we have too many of those in our diets. So cut down on lots of those kinds of fats in fried foods and try to shift toward getting a lot of omega-3 fatty acids, which are anti-inflammatory."

To clarify this further, "omega-3 and omega-6 fatty acids play a crucial role in brain function as well as normal growth and development." And research indicates that "a healthy diet should consist of roughly one omega-3 fatty acid to four omega-6 fatty acids. A typical American diet, however, tends to contain eleven to thirty times more omega-6 than omega-3 fatty acids."[12]

So consuming more omega-3 fatty acids can help to reduce inflammation, and incorporating them into your diet is probably easier than you think. These fatty acids come from fish (like salmon, mackerel, tuna, and trout), flaxseed, and pumpkin seeds, among other foods. "If you don't eat a lot of fish, I do recommend taking a supplement of fish oil," Brodsky says. She suggests taking 1,000 to 2,000 mg containing a combination of EPA and DHA, which are essential fatty acids found in fish oil. Of course, be sure to check with your doctor first.

"Leafy greens, like collard greens and chard, [also] can have some omega-3s," she says, adding that however you decide to consume them, "those [fatty acids] are really, really important to get [into your system]."

Another principle of the anti-inflammatory diet is to "eat what is known as low glycemic foods, foods that haven't been stripped of their natural fiber and nutrients through processing, such as white flours, baked goods, and processed grains," Brodsky says. "You want more whole grains, gummy fibers like legumes, and less sugars—things that are absorbed into the bloodstream slowly and don't raise your blood sugar quickly, because elevating your blood sugar can have inflammatory effects."

The next principle is to increase your intake of brightly colored vegetables or fruits because these pigments protect against free radicals that damage cartilage, Brodsky says. "Ones that have vitamin C, like citrus, [are recommended because] vitamin C builds up cartilage." Included in this list are strawberries and kiwi. Pineapples also contain a chemical called bromelain that is known to help arthritis. Vegetables or fruits that are blue, dark green, orange, red, or white in color contain phytochemicals that are also good for your diet. "[They] prevent the free radicals that damage cartilage," Brodsky says.

Brodsky says you should also eat vegetables or fruits that are high in vitamin E (like nuts and seeds) or beta carotene, like spinach, sweet potatoes, and kale. "All plant foods, including spices, are really powerful. So, the goal is to have at least five servings a day of different color rainbow fruits and vegetables. I usually tell my clients to eat a rainbow every day," she notes.

Brodsky also has another tip: "Whenever possible, spice up your food with spices because they are even more potent than fruits and vegetables." For instance, ginger and turmeric can actually mimic the effects of some arthritis pain relievers, like Celebrex and Advil. Brodsky suggests taking turmeric supplements in the amount of 300 mg three times a day, along with a teaspoon of fresh, dried, or supplemental ginger. Or you can add ginger to your diet by eating candied ginger, putting it into Asian or Indian cooking, or slicing some ginger and putting it into the bottom of a cup of tea. "Turmeric and ginger are known to be powerful anti-inflammatory spices. Also, rosemary contains COX-2 inhibiting chemicals similar to pain relieving drugs, and hot chili peppers contain spicy capsaicin, which blocks chemicals from going to the brain (known as substance P), which signals pain. These are all COX-2 inhibitors, but you don't have to have the side effects of drugs— you can actually do it with food." If all else fails, "eat Indian food. Indian food has curry powder and ginger. So as much as possible, make things that have [curry powder in it]. People in India have less arthritis symptoms."

There are also some foods that should be avoided. According to Brodsky, trans fats, which are a type of partially hydrogenated fat often found in snacks or fast food, as well as saturated fat from red meat, are not healthy because trans fats are man-made fats that may trigger an immune response. Saturated fats are converted into inflammatory chemicals. Therefore, you want to limit your intake of junk food and fast food. "And if you're cooking, use extra virgin olive oil or canola oil instead because those fats contain mono-unsaturated fat, which, according to studies on the Mediterranean diet, lowers inflammation as well the green pigments (polyphenols) in olive oil, which are antioxidants," Brodsky adds.

Some juvenile arthritis sufferers have also experimented with particular diets that claim to boost your health. In

DO SPECIAL DIETS WORK?

There are many books and Web sites out there on diets that claim to benefit arthritis sufferers. But do they work?

- **Dr. White:** "The answer is, we don't know if they are helpful at all. There are many, many diets out there. There are many, many supplements out there. But we haven't shown that any of them make a course (change) in JRA at this point." The best thing to do, Dr. White says, is to discuss those of particular interest with your rheumatologist since certain diets can counteract with your medication.
- **Dr. Klein-Gitelman:** "Patients who are taking steroids should be on diets that are low salt and low fat to avoid negative effects that can be caused by the medication."
- **Brodsky:** "I think diet can work with medicine. I believe in integrating the best of all worlds. I think if there are some good disease-modifying medications that are out there for these types of autoimmune diseases, we should take advantage of that. I don't think doing just all diet [modification] can eliminate all of the disease. But I think [a proper] diet can help reduce the number of medications you're taking."

Amanda's case, she followed a diet that restricted her intake of gluten. Gluten is "the protein part of wheat, rye, barley, and related grains."[13]

Amanda says, "Gluten is basically in all bread products. So I reduced my diet of wheat because I [believe] in some forms of arthritis, including uveitis, gluten has been linked to a cause of it." Dr. Ilona S. Szer adds, "It turns out, a lot of people with juvenile dermatomyositis have antibodies to gluten."

According to Brodsky, "Gluten, along with other proteins found in foods, such as dairy (casein) may be absorbed into the bloodstream undigested. This causes the immune system to recognize it as a foreign body and can produce antibodies to it. So different foods may cause food sensitivity—not a true allergy. There has been little research in this area, but more people with autoimmune disorders are finding a link."

EFFECTS OF JUVENILE ARTHRITIS ON WEIGHT

JA and Weight Loss

Aside from causing joint pain or inflammation, juvenile arthritis can also curb your appetite. According to Brodsky, "When you have a lot of inflammation, it turns off the appetite center in your brain." The stiffness in your joints can even make it physically difficult to eat. You also may not have much of an appetite on days when you have a general feeling of malaise or are simply too tired to eat. And those individuals who have TMJ arthritis may find that they experience a lot of pain in their jaw while they are chewing. On top of all that, some medications can also cause you to lose weight.

Having a chronic illness "places increased demands on a child's body and creates a need for additional calorie intake."[14] As a result of not eating ample amounts of food, teens will often lose weight, and their bodies may not grow at a normal rate. They may also feel tired more often. Therefore, it's important to maintain a proper diet by eating well-balanced meals several times a day. The Arthritis Foundation recommends having breakfast, lunch, and dinner at the same time each day. The foundation also suggests having a couple of healthy snacks in between meals.

If you don't feel up to eating, it's important to do so anyway so that your body gets the nourishment it needs. In fact, you may be able to limit your intake of food by "increasing the nutrient content of each bite of food or drink."[15] Along those lines, "eat small amounts of food, but [eat] frequently and make them concentrated in calories. Try to consume things like trail mix or fruits and nuts, which have a lot of calories," Brodsky says. She also recommends eating cheese and drinking smoothies because they contain protein and lots of calories.

The Arthritis Foundation adds to that list gravy, margarine, and dips, along with whole milk.[16] If you are not allergic to milk, "the proteins in cow's milk sometimes can simulate your immune system," Brodsky notes. Also, milk contains vitamin D, as do wild mushrooms and oily fish, which your body needs. By following this advice, you should be able maintain a normal weight. However, if you continue to lose weight, you must inform your doctor.

When patients continue to lose weight, their doctors will meet with them to figure out why it is happening. Generally speaking, there could be several reasons why patients lose weight. In some cases, the arthritis pain in the jaw could cause a teen to chew more slowly, and, consequently, when everyone else is done eating, the teen may not want to finish the meal alone, leaving it uneaten. At school, the teen may not get to finish lunch because part of that period is spent getting medication from the nurse.

Sometimes, however, the problem may not be as evident on the surface. According to Dr. Szer, when teens have an illness like arthritis, it may seem like very little in their life is under their control. Instead of expressing their emotions, teens look for something they can control. "The biggest part you can control, is you don't eat," Dr. Szer says. But not eating will only make the condition worse—something young people don't anticipate.

Another reason for weight loss can be because teens "who are inflamed may have gut inflammation as well, so they may not absorb [food] as well as other people," Dr. Szer says. Therefore, when these individuals eat, a portion of the food nutrients goes to feed the inflammation.

Since there could be a variety of reasons for losing weight, it is important that individuals with this problem see a doctor quickly so that the situation can be addressed before it gets worse. Remember, when you have a chronic illness like juvenile arthritis, losing too much weight can put a strain on your health more than it would someone else, since your immune system is already weakened.

JA and Weight Gain

Not all teens with juvenile arthritis will lose weight. In fact, some teens with arthritis gain too much weight. There are a few reasons this could happen. One is that certain medications can cause you to put on extra pounds. Prednisone is one example, since it raises your blood sugar. "I gained weight from the

BOOSTING YOUR WEIGHT

If you find that keeping your weight up seems to be an issue, here are a few tips recommended by Dr. Ilona Szer:

- Make eating a family affair. "Parents should make time for eating."
- Try eating smaller meals, but more of them. "Children with arthritis may benefit from eating smaller meals because they think that eating is a chore."
- Eat more. Feeding an illness requires more nourishment to keep your body healthy.
- Drink a shake. "At the end of the day, I often recommend a really good milk shake." When making the milk shake, put in half-and-half (or even double-strength milk) and protein powder. Drinking the milk shake at night is recommended because your body won't burn off the calories as easily while sleeping.
- Eat protein bars and drink Boost or Ensure, which contain various nutritional supplements.

prednisone. You can see the moon face [I have because of it] and the weight fluctuation is just crazy," Kristen says.

Furthermore, it is easy to gain weight when your arthritis is preventing you from being as active or mobile as you once were or like someone your age typically would be. It's important to monitor your weight, since gaining even a few extra pounds can put more stress on the joints in the lower half of your body.

To help keep your weight down, it is imperative not only to eat a balanced diet, but also to exercise regularly. According to Brodsky, "Every extra pound of weight that you carry is [like] three additional pounds on your joints. Exercise is key. I know a lot of people who have arthritis don't feel like exercising because it hurts, but it's kind of important to push through some of that when you are not in an active flare-up and try incorporating it slowly. Muscle tissue is active; it burns calories."

Allyson Shapiro says she works out several times a week in order to stay in shape. A couple of years ago she even went to a fitness camp, and last year she took part in the Martha's Vineyard Holistic Health Retreat, which is designed to help individuals cleanse themselves both physically and emotionally. "My mom was really good friends with the writer of *21 Pounds in 21 Days (The Martha's Vineyard Diet Detox)* and I thought that it would help me a lot," Allyson says, noting that she wanted to lose weight to make movement easier on her joints.

According to the retreat's Web site, naturopathic doctors, emotional healers, trainers, and other health practitioners supervise participants during the entire detoxification process, which rids the body of physical and emotional toxins that prevent the "immune system from effectively producing the millions of healthy cells needed for day-in/day-out strength and vitality."[17]

During her eight-day stay at the retreat, Allyson also worked out regularly on several exercise machines and did not consume any solid foods. "There was no chewing. It was all liquid [consumption] so you could get your toxins out. I lost ten pounds," she says. "I gained it back quickly afterward, but I felt better."

Staff also talked to Allyson about which foods could harm or benefit her body. Today she eats more natural and organic foods. She also makes sure to avoid those foods that could cause her arthritis to flare. "They told me tomatoes can cause inflammation . . . and potatoes too," she says. "I looked at a lot of things differently [after being in the program]."

Although she was lonely at times during the retreat, the quiet atmosphere was beneficial because "there was a lot of free time to clear your mind," she says. And after returning home from the trip, Allyson noticed her health had improved not just physically, but mentally.

Like Allyson, you might consider trying a special diet or exercise program to help you lose weight or better manage your health. There are countless diets and retreats to choose from, but remember to always consult your physician for advice before you try something new.

Supplements

Even while following a diet regime, it's still possible your body may need a boost when it comes to certain vitamins or

WEB SITES WORTH CHECKING OUT

- *The National Center on Physical Activity and Disability.* Visit www.ncpad.org or call (800) 900–8086 for a vast array of information, tips, and guidelines relating to physical activity, including exercise.
- *Luscious Life Nutrition, Inc.* Web site: www.Lusciouslifenutrition.com; e-mail: mbrodsky@ameritech.net; phone: (773) 330–8275.
- *Access Anything, LLC.* For guidebooks and travel tips relating to the accessibility of vacation destinations, visit www.accessanything.net.
- *YMCA.* A number of YMCAs around the country offer the Arthritis Foundation YMCA Aquatic Program. To find out if the program is offered near you, visit www.ymca.net.
- *Sailability.* Sailability is a nonprofit organization focused on providing people with all types of disabilities an opportunity to sail—no matter what their financial situation. To learn more, visit www.sailability.org.
- *Disabled Archery USA.* The sport of archery can easily be adapted to your abilities. To join a disabled archery team near you, visit www.da-usa.org.
- *Handicapped Scuba Association (HSA).* Dedicated to improving the physical and social well-being of people with disabilities, HSA offers training, certification, and diving adventure programs worldwide. Visit www.hsascuba.com for more information.
- *Disabled Sports USA.* This nonprofit organization offers a variety of sports rehabilitation programs, from skiing to water sports, to individuals living with disabilities nationwide. To learn more, visit www.dsusa.org.
- *North American Riding for the Handicapped Association (NARHA).* At more than eight hundred centers in the United States and Canada, individuals with disabilities can participate in NARHA's Equine Assisted Activity and Therapy (EAAT) programs, which include activities like therapeutic riding. Visit www.narha.org to learn more.
- *National Sports Center for the Disabled (NSCD).* From kayaking to snowboarding, this agency offers adaptive recreation programs in more than twenty sports. NSCD also hosts AbilityCAMPS nationwide for disabled youth ages six to eighteen who are interested in sports. For more information, visit www.nscd.org.
- *Adaptive Sports Center (ASC) of Crested Butte, Colorado.* A nonprofit organization, ASC provides year-round recreational activities, from handcycling to whitewater rafting, for people with disabilities and their families. Visit www.adaptivesports.org for more information.

minerals. Because of this, the Arthritis Foundation recommends taking a multivitamin with breakfast.[18] Brodsky also suggests taking supplements of fish oil, as discussed previously, and vitamin D3. Most of your vitamin D intake comes from the sun, and information about its benefits is still surfacing. "It helps keep your bones strong and it helps you to absorb calcium," Brodsky says, adding that it can also help reduce muscle pain and prevent certain autoimmune diseases. Depending on your condition, it may be beneficial to take 1,000 to 2,000 international units (IU) of vitamin D3—but check with your doctor first.

The National Institutes of Health estimates that more than half of Americans take dietary supplements, so talk to your doctor about which ones are right for you.[19]

NOTES

1. *Yoga Journal*, www.yogajournal.com.
2. Ibid.
3. Ibid.
4. Ibid.
5. Terrie Heinrich Rizzo, "On the Ball," *Arthritis Today* (March/April 2008): 49–50.
6. Arthritis Foundation, *Arthritis in Children* (pamphlet, 2004), 18.
7. Arthritis Society of Canada, "Juvenile Arthritis," www .arthritis.ca/types%20of%20arthritis/childhood/default.asp?s=1.
8. Ibid.
9. Arthritis Foundation, "Introduction to Exercise," www.arthritis.org/exercise-intro.php.
10. Exercise descriptions courtesy of Ryan Lee, www.ryanlee.com.
11. Arthritis Foundation, *Arthritis in Children*, 22.
12. University of Maryland Medical Center, "Omega-6 Fatty Acids," www.umm.edu/altmed/articles/omega-6–000317.htm.
13. Chek Med Systems, Inc., and Jackson Siegelbaum Gastroenterology, "Gluten-Free Diet," www.gicare.com/pated/ edtgs06.htm.
14. Arthritis Foundation, *Arthritis in Children*, 22.
15. Ibid.
16. Ibid.

17. Martha's Vineyard Holistic Retreat, "Detox Spa Retreat," www.mvholisticretreat.com/ofsspadetox.

18. Arthritis Foundation, "Diet & Nutrition," www.arthritis.org/juvenile-arthritis-nutritiondiet.php.

19. Isadore Rosenfeld, "Do Herbal Remedies Work?" *Parade*, March 16, 2008, 18, 21.

6 Physical Therapy and Occupational Therapy

PHYSICAL THERAPY

Depending on the form or severity of your arthritis, you may be required to see a physical therapist. Last year, Eric Terry's "whole summer was spent twice a week going to physical therapy," his mother, Cynthia, says. "He did physical therapy two others times in the past, but this time [he went] because he was limping so bad . . . and he didn't have full range of motion in his legs."

Physical therapist Jacqueline Kuhns says physical therapy is usually required when a patient's condition declines and he or she is having difficulty completing everyday tasks. She explains that "with juvenile arthritis, especially rheumatoid arthritis, the patient's mobility becomes restricted pretty quickly and physical therapy helps to keep the joints and muscles within a functional range. Physical therapy is about keeping you functioning— meaning doing activities of daily living, keeping you walking for as long as you can, and just keeping the joints within the greatest range of motion they can be. It's all about function."

In addition, physical therapists help patients protect their joints by building up their muscles. "So the stronger the muscles are around the joint, the better it is for the joint," says Sandra McGee, a physical therapist/pediatric certified specialist from Children's Hospital of Philadelphia.

Since Eric went to physical therapy, "we've seen a tremendous difference, and he enjoyed it" Cynthia says. Although Eric is no longer seeing a physical therapist, Cynthia said his doctor will arrange for him to work with one again if his condition declines any further.

To receive physical therapy, you will need a prescription from your physician stating your specific needs. Depending upon your health insurance plan, you may be sent to a local hospital or clinic for physical therapy services. Some practices have a home-care program, which enables physical therapists to come to your home or school in order to provide treatment. However, where you are treated may depend on your health insurance. There may be some flexibility if you happen to prefer one particular provider over another, although you might have to pay the difference in cost in some cases.

Some teens may need to work with a physical therapist only a few times, while others may need to go for much longer periods of time, sometimes months or years, depending on the severity of their condition and whether joint damage continues to progress. There are also times when a teen may need to go into the hospital to receive more intensive physical therapy several times throughout the day. Exactly how much physical therapy a teen needs is usually determined after the physical therapist assesses the patient's condition.

When you first meet with a physical therapist, an evaluation is conducted to see how you move your body. You will probably be asked to walk, run, climb steps, and perform other activities so the physical therapist can see how your movements compare to other teens your age. Furthermore, your posture will be evaluated to ensure that you are standing up straight and that the disease has not affected your spine.

To aid them in determining how well your joints bend, physical therapists use a tool called a goniometer. The distance

A goniometer measures how well your joints bend.

EXERCISING THE VIRTUAL WAY

A personal message from the author, Kelly Rouba, who was diagnosed with juvenile rheumatoid arthritis in 1982 at the age of two.

I remember when my brother Kevin stood in line for about a half hour so he could be one of the first people to get Nintendo's latest video game system called Wii in 2006. At the time, I didn't really understand what all the hype was about until he brought the system to my home so I could try it out. After he popped in the first sports game CD, I found myself immediately engrossed in virtual games of baseball, boxing, and golf, among others. Because of the severe physical limitations arthritis imposed on my body, I had never been able to play these sports before. Instead, I always sat on the sidelines watching my brother play baseball and soccer as he grew up. Now, for the first time, we could play together—even if it was virtually—and I even broke a sweat!

"Keep Up with the Wii"
by Sean R., a fifteen-year-old from Bondville, Vermont,
CreakyJoints member and JRA patient since age nine

Keep up! They yell all the time.
They don't know what it's like.
They keep the pressure high, they keep the yelling loud.
They don't know what it's like.

The walk down hill is much easier.
The stairs up are a bother.
Lifting the equipment bag makes me feel weak.
I try to tell them why it hurts and they don't care.

Why can't everything work out OK?
I just want to play the Wii.
My hands hurt.
I just want to play the Wii.

your joints can move is referred to as their range of motion. Physical therapists will also test your strength by pushing on your muscles in different areas to determine your level of resistance. This helps the therapist "to assess your muscle function, and how much force or power your muscles can generate through the range of motion," explains Melissa Lee, a physical therapist at Hamilton Physical Therapy Services (HPTS), which has several offices in New Jersey.

Therapists may also measure the length of your limbs, since arthritis has been known to cause them to grow unevenly in some individuals. In addition, therapists will look for joint contractures, which are commonly found in patients with juvenile idiopathic arthritis. Simply put, a contracture means that a joint is stuck in its current position as a result of not moving it due to pain or stiffness. "People with JIA are likely to get contractures in the wrists, elbows, hips, knees—basically, any of the major joints. This means that certain muscles become shorter and tighter and they pull on the joints differently and then you get a joint contracture," according to Kuhns. Once an evaluation is completed, the physical therapist will determine your needs and create a fitness program that is right for you.

PHYSICAL THERAPY ROUTINES

According to McGee, most of her patients with juvenile arthritis are newly diagnosed. Typically, these patients come in for physical therapy for about an hour once a week for four to six weeks. If they find they are going through a flare or their arthritis is more active, they usually come back for a few visits until the disease is under control.

At age three, Kristen Delaney first went to see a physical therapist because she was limping. The limp "is still kind of there, but it was really bad when I was little." Kristen continues to see a physical therapist every so often so she can learn new exercises to help her body stay in shape. "I think physical therapists and occupational therapists have learned a lot about stretches you can do to help prevent the possible deformities of the disease. My fingers aren't straight because of the arthritis in my hands, but because I've been good about doing exercises and doing what my physical therapist has told me to do over the years, I am not as deformed as I could be and I am actually pretty functional."

Stretching is just one way of helping teens with arthritis to maintain their mobility and ability to function. Physical and occupational therapists (OTs will be discussed later in this chapter) also help patients do other exercises besides stretches that are intended to alleviate pain and prevent further deformity and disability. Moreover, physical therapists are able to accomplish something that medications can't always do, and that's restoring the loss of joint function.

During a typical visit, the physical therapist will concentrate on loosening up those joints that are affected by arthritis as well as any others that have become stiff due to overcompensation. As part of a normal routine, patients are required to do range-of-motion exercises to help their joints stay flexible. Range-of-motion exercises can also help reduce stiffness and loosen up contractures in teens.

There are some types-of-range of motion exercises you can do without assistance from a therapist. These are known as active range-of-motion exercises. "Active range of motion is when you actively do the exercise yourself, using your muscles to move through range of motion," says Allison Davis, a physical therapist assistant at HPTS. When doing active range-of-motion exercises, try to move your joints as far as possible so that you can feel the muscle stretching.

Some examples of active range-of-motion exercises include moving your head and feet up and down or from side to side. Another great exercise is raising your arms up above your head or out to the side. Or bend your arms so that your hand touches your shoulder and then straighten your arm out. You can also try facing the wall with one leg bent and one leg remaining straight. Then lean toward the wall so you feel a stretch in the back of the leg that is kept straight. It may also help to lie on your back and pull one knee to your chest while keeping the other leg straight.[1] You can alternate legs, and then try pulling both knees to your chest. Then practice touching your toes or moving your leg out to the side as far as possible.

While these are all things that you can do on your own, a physical therapist may assist you with these exercises so that you get the best stretch possible during your visit. "This is known as active assistive range of motion, which is when we move a body part through range of motion and you help move it too," Davis says.

There are also times when a physical therapist will move your joints for you entirely. This is referred to as passive range of motion. "True passive range of motion is when someone or something does the motion for you. For example, we may use pulleys to exercise your shoulder. Or we will move your knee or arm for you without you contracting a muscle," Davis says. Unless your joint is swollen, a physical therapist will try to move the joints and muscles as far as they should go—which can be painful sometimes. If you experience a lot of pain, let the therapist know as it occurs. Also, at times when the joint is swollen, a physical therapist will still continue to exercise it, but in a less aggressive manner.[2]

Physical therapists also rely on strengthening exercises to build up muscle and endurance. Strengthening exercises typically involve weights and can also include:

- Aerobic activities, like cardio-bicycling
- Nonimpact or low-impact aquatic exercises, like walking or swimming
- Postural exercises, including seated rows and lateral pull downs
- Upper and lower extremity strengthening—beginning with isometric exercises and gradually progressing to resistive exercises

The Arthritis Foundation also recommends performing isometric exercises in addition to isotonic exercises. Isometric means that "you tighten your muscles but do not move your joints." These exercises can help you build muscle even when it's too tough to move painful joints. An example would be tightening the large muscles at the front of your thighs. Conversely, isotonic exercises do require you to move your joints in order to strengthen your muscles. One example of an isotonic exercise would be to extend your leg out straight while seated and hold it in place for several seconds.

For those teens who have arthritis in their knees, McGee uses several exercises. One such exercise is to have the teen sit in a chair or on the edge of a bed so that his or her knee is dangling. Then McGee helps to stretch it out straight. At times, she will even put a weight on a patient's ankles for added resistance. In addition, she will often have individuals lie on their back and raise their leg up while keeping it straight. This exercise is called a straight leg raise.

"As they get stronger, we'll do things like stepping up onto a step," McGee says. At first, patients are asked to do this five times. Once they are ready, McGee has them progress to ten repetitions, and then two sets of ten. Next, she usually increases the height of the step or adds weights to a patient's ankles. Stability balls can also help increase flexibility in the knees and hips, but because stability balls can be difficult to use, she usually recommends that teens use them under the supervision of a physical therapist.

McGee also has plenty of exercises for those who have arthritis in their arms and hands. "Most of the time when I see kids with arm involvement, it's in their wrists," she says. To strengthen their arms, McGee sometimes has children do exercises with Thera-Bands and then she has patients play with Play-Doh to loosen up their wrists. "Squeezing things and releasing, like [with] Play-Doh, is a good one. They can [even] do that at home [to] work the wrist and the fingers." You can also try making a fist and then straightening your fingers or lifting your wrists up or down.[3]

In addition, McGee has patients practice turning their palms up and then turning their palms down. And "we put their hands in the prayer position and then kind of push [their] elbows out to the side so that the wrists bend," she says.

Kuhns does many of the same exercises with her patients, as well as a few more. In one case, Kuhns treated a school-age girl with juvenile idiopathic arthritis. "She had some pain, but she had full range of motion in her joints and she walked independently [without assistive devices]. Her biggest complaint was joint stiffness in the mornings," Kuhns says.

When Kuhns visited the girl at her school, she began each session with range-of-motion exercises, like arm, shoulder, and ankle circles. "We would always do active range-of-motion exercises because she has full range of motion in all joints and I wanted to keep her joints loose," Kuhns says. "Then, we worked on cardiovascular fitness and endurance training by doing exercises like jumping on a trampoline. That is a workout!"

The two also played kickball, which requires players to use multiple joints. It also helps with balance since the person has to rest on one foot in order to kick the ball. And they focused on abdominal strengthening by doing sit ups and tossing a ball while lying down. "Overall, we worked with the neck all the way down to the ankles," Kuhns says, adding that they even played music to make it more enjoyable.

Kuhns also recommends that teens with juvenile arthritis lie on their stomach about fifteen to twenty minutes each day if their hips are getting tight. "That stretches out the hip flexors—the muscles that bend the hips. They tend to get tight and shorten, so if you lie on your stomach, that helps stretch them out. This exercise, for [young people] especially, makes the hip flexors more functional," Kuhns says. McGee notes that gravity also helps the knees to straighten out while the teen is lying down. During that time, teens can watch television or listen to music in order to make the exercise more bearable. Kuhns says it's a good idea to set a timer if you plan to lie on your stomach so you know when it is time to get up.

Another thing Kuhns works on with patients is having them sit or stand up straight. Most teens tend to slouch, or become rounded, which means their head and shoulders slump forward. During their visits, "we work on proper posture, so they don't get rounded, because that's the tendency with the disease," Kuhns says. Slouching can cause added pain because it puts more stress on other joints and can even make you feel tired.

According to the Arthritis Foundation's brochure *Managing Your Activities*, to achieve proper posture while standing, keep your shoulders back and tuck your chin in. Stand as straight as possible without locking your knees and keep your feet planted slightly apart. Tighten your stomach muscles and tuck your buttocks in at the same time. When you are sitting, make sure your feet touch the ground and that your knees are bent at a 90-degree angle. Also, make sure that your spine is supported. You may even try putting a pillow behind your lower back. Again, keep your shoulders back and your chin tucked in. Maintaining proper posture helps reduce stress on your neck, back, knees, and hips. And "the less slouched over you are, it helps you do more. It all goes back to daily living," Kuhns says.

More Than Just Exercise

Sometimes your physical therapist may use other measures or devices to help your joints feel better. If you are stiff, your physical therapist may apply hot packs or ice packs to your joints before you exercise. This can also be done at home. "[We use] heat probably more than ice," McGee said. "The joints tend to chill down too quickly and kind of like gel [with] ice, so we usually recommend heat instead." However, Kuhns notes that it's best to avoid heat at times when your joints are inflamed or swollen because heat tends to make the body swell.

Some physical therapy offices also have a big metal whirlpool bathtub that patients can go into in order to loosen up before exercising. It can also be used just to soak the arms or legs in warm swirling water. Furthermore, exercises can be done both inside and outside of the whirlpool bathtub. "At our facility, we have a pool. We do use the pool a lot [for therapy],￼" McGee says, noting that some of the exercises they do in the pool can be done at home in the bathtub. Kuhns says that aquatics therapy makes it easier for a person with arthritis to move and is often less painful. "It takes away the pressure of gravity, and it kind of 'un-weights' the joints. It's like a gravity-free environment—it's like being in outer space," she says.

When it comes to working with a patient's fingers and wrists, physical therapists also have another treatment option they can try called paraffin wax. When doing this, patients dip their hands into a small tub containing the warm wax several times. Then the therapist puts a plastic bag around their hands. Once the wax has cooled, it can be peeled off. This same treatment can also be done on the feet. Basically, paraffin wax treatments are utilized because they are known to help sore muscles. "The wax is beneficial because it will evenly distribute the warm temperature throughout the hand or foot. It also provides moisture to the skin," Davis says. Paraffin wax systems can even be purchased for home use so patients can continue treatments whenever needed.

Sometimes physical therapists resort to a variety of other treatments that are not as commonly used today in an effort to help relieve pain and promote function. One such treatment is called transcutaneous electrical nerve stimulation (TENS). This device has electrodes that are taped to the area of the body where there is pain. The electrodes have wires that are attached to a battery-operated stimulator so they can send mild electrical pulses to the nerves. Depending on the type of TENS device used, it either causes the patient's body to release endorphins (chemicals that help lessen pain) or it blocks the pain by stimulating large nerves.[4] TENS does not hurt; it merely tingles. Although TENS is not used as often these days, "if there's a lot of pain involved, it's still something we might use," McGee says.

Physical therapists might also elect to perform an ultrasound of joints and muscles that are particularly painful. When conducting an ultrasound, a physical therapist will put lotion on the inflamed area and then rub the ultrasound machine head, called a transducer, over the muscles and tissues in that area. The machine omits high-energy sound waves and its "effects can either be thermal, meaning it has the ability to increase the temperature of the tissue, or non-thermal and thereby facilitates the healing of tissues and helps manage inflammation. It can also be used to apply certain medications transdermally, or through the skin," says Lee.

While they can be beneficial to a patient, ultrasounds are usually performed only on adults. According to McGee, ultrasounds are rarely done on youths because "there are precautions to doing it over the growth plate because kids are [still] growing."

While visiting a physical therapy clinic, you may also be introduced to a number of exercise machines that can help with range of motion, strengthening, and endurance. These include treadmills, stationary bicycles, and universal equipment like the Total Gym. Allyson Shapiro receives physical therapy twice a week; while there, she uses several machines and even lifts weights to help stay in shape.

Continuing Physical Therapy at Home

Although you may not own fancy exercise equipment, it is still possible to do many of the exercises your physical therapist has taught you at home. In fact, physical therapists often encourage teens to practice the workout routines they learned so that their juvenile arthritis does not consume their joints completely.

"If a child had some range-of-motion decline, then we usually recommend they do the range-of-motion exercises every day. If it's a strengthening issue, then [they should do them] three to four times a week," McGee says.

Some exercises that require assistance from a physical therapist, like range of motion of the joints and stretching of specific muscle groups, can also be taught to family members so that they can move your joints for you. By having a family member assist with certain exercises, it can help stretch your joints beyond what you are capable of doing by yourself. Also, in terms of doing everyday activities, "physical therapy is [designed] to teach families how you want people [with juvenile arthritis] to move and what kinds of moves you want to encourage," Dr. Harry Gewanter notes.

Although it may not seem like fun having to exercise several times a week, strengthening joints and muscles requires continuous effort. "Even though it hurts to try to do the stretches, I still try to do them periodically throughout the day because I don't want to lose the motion in my [body]," Kristen says.

Stefanie Tepley takes part in what is called a month-to-month program, through which she is expected to follow a physical and occupational therapy routine at home. "Basically, the month-to-month means I have a home [exercise] program that I have to follow and do every day. And if I have any trouble, I can call the physical therapist, but otherwise I just see them once a month and we assess what's going on." When Stefanie meets with her physical therapist, her program is updated based on her current needs. "If something's not working for me or she wants to mix it up a bit" or if certain joints are bothersome, changes to my program are made, Stefanie says.

Before implementing a home exercise routine, always remember to consult your physical therapist and physician. They will be able to tell you what exercises are right for you and what will provide the most benefit to your body.

"I think [exercising] is an essential part of the treatment plan [for JA]," says Dr. Marisa Klein-Gitelman. "We often work with physical therapists and occupational therapists to give them certain exercises [for our patients]." Therapy helps keep muscles and bones strong so they remain limber and have a good range of motion, she adds. "Getting people up and in motion . . . is important to bone and joint health."

EXERCISING CAUTION

While exercising is crucial to improving your condition and keeping your body in shape, it is extremely important not to overexert yourself. "Exercises should be done in moderation, which also depends on the kind of exercise," Kuhns says. Most exercises can be done on a daily basis, but should usually be kept to a half hour. Kuhns recommends swimming, yoga, and bicycling since they are not as high impact as some other activities.

"We like to have the kids stay as active as they can without overdoing it," McGee says. "So walking is something we always encourage." Those who have trouble walking may want to try bicycling instead. In addition, "elliptical machines are really good because they work the arms and legs and don't put pressure on the joints. They are not as hard on the body as treadmills," according to Kuhns.

Conversely, running and jogging are both considered to be high-impact activities and can cause joint damage to the lower part of your body. "You're weight bearing a lot through the joints and they may get sore. I would say the aquatic therapy is the preferred method because doing those exercises in the water takes pressure off joints and won't make you feel as sore later," Kuhns says.

Kuhns recommends that teens try to rotate the joints they exercise. "Don't work the same muscle groups two days in a row." Additionally, it's a good idea to make return visits to your physical therapist if you are not seeing him or her on a regular basis, just as Kristen does. This way, exercise routines can be modified based on your current condition and will still help you to get the most out of your workout.

OCCUPATIONAL THERAPY

An occupational therapist (OT) is trained to help people with all types of physical impairments better manage everyday tasks they would normally encounter at home, at school, at work, and even during times of leisure.

While physical therapy is also known to help those who have juvenile arthritis keep up with daily living, there are certain activities, like dressing or showering, "that sometimes fall under the category of occupational therapy," Kuhns says.

Just like with physical therapy, occupational therapists also see patients at hospitals, clinics, homes, and schools. If you meet with an OT at a clinic or hospital, you may notice that he or she works in a setting that resembles the inside of your home. In fact, there might be computers, stoves, ovens, washers, dryers, and a variety of other appliances and electronic devices on-site. Because of the pain or joint damage caused by your arthritis, it can be difficult to carry out all kinds of everyday tasks, from grooming to typing. By working with an occupational therapist in an environment that resembles a typical home, you will learn various ways to adapt your lifestyle so that your physical limitations become less of a hindrance. Furthermore, you will likely be introduced to assistive devices that make certain tasks easier. An occupational therapist can also show you ways to manage pain, conserve energy, and reduce stress on your joints as you go about your normal activities.

At the first meeting with an OT, the patient's physical condition is evaluated by the occupational therapist. "A basic evaluation would include, in general, [assessing] range of motion, muscle testing, and muscle strength," says Deborah Yarett Slater, who is both practice associate and staff liaison to the Ethics Commission at the American Occupational Therapy Association (AOTA). Slater is also a fellow of the AOTA, a designation that is bestowed upon those who have provided exemplary research and leadership in the profession. "If you have a big flare-up, it would be contraindicative [for occupational therapists] to do resistive stuff. We might test sensation. It's not often a problem in RA patients, but sensation is important because if you can't feel anything, you can't hold anything."

Using a goniometer, the OT will measure the range of motion in your fingers, wrists, elbows, and shoulders. Patients may also be required to squeeze a dynamometer, which measures the strength in their hands, or a pinchmeter, which assesses how well they can pinch. Pinching, grasping, and performing routine upper body motions can be difficult for people with arthritis.

"I have a lot of experience with adults with rheumatoid arthritis," Slater says. "The small joints are the ones that are usually compromised. If you have involvement in the small joints of the hands, then a lot of the fine-motor [activities] would be tough if you're having a flare-up—[like] writing, keyboarding, and fastening clothes."

During the evaluation process, occupational therapists often ask their patients a series of questions in order to find out what they can and can't do, what they need or want to do, and what activities or tasks are most important to them. "The basis of occupational therapy is around occupational performance," Slater says. "The other thing I would spend a lot of time on is [asking about their] self-care, or what we call activities of daily living—bathing, dressing, feeding, mobility."

Overall, the goal is to find out where the occupational performance problems lie. Slater says that OTs are likely to ask a new patient the following questions:

- Can you get up?
- How far can you walk?
- Do you need any gait (walking) aids to walk?
- Have you had any surgeries or joint replacements?
- Can you get on and off the toilet and in and out of the shower?
- Is dressing difficult? If so, in what way? And does the difficulty involve fastenings?
- When you have a flare-up, what is your status then versus how you function normally?
- On a scale of 1 to 10, what is your current level of pain?
- Do you have more pain at night or during the day?
- Are there any points during the day when the pain is worse?
- Are there any types of activities that increase your pain level?
- What do you do to feel better?
- Does heat help you?
- What types of adaptive equipment do you need or presently use? ("A lot of time [this includes] adaptive feeding utensils, adaptive fastening [tools], and splints, too, if you're dealing with hands especially," Slater says.)

When patients are of school age, occupational therapists often ask them to describe their daily routine. OTs also pose questions related to activities that take place at school. Typical questions include:

- What problems do you experience while at school?
- Can you hold a pencil?
- Can you type on the computer?
- Can you reach the items you need?
- Can you carry your books?
- Do you do any leisure activities or have any hobbies? If so, are they difficult for you to do?

Exercise Routines

After the initial evaluation is complete, the occupational therapist will create an exercise plan designed to increase the patient's strength and flexibility. These exercises can also help patients to loosen up their joints at the start of their day. Exercises routines will also vary depending on the person's age and condition. "When you're dealing with kids, you try to make it more fun. It's different than with adults; adults may be more tolerant of straight exercises," Slater says.

During a typical visit, patients may do some light range-of-motion exercises, including flexing and extending joints. They may practice squeezing stress balls and do a few exercises with a Thera-Band. Both of these are activities that can also be done at home. "One of the things I tend not to do with arthritics is resistive exercises," Slater notes.

When working with teens who have arthritis, "the main thing is to keep joint mobility [by engaging in] anything that promotes range of motion," she adds. "[Occupational therapists] can also do some light strengthening, but certainly not when patients are having a flare-up. And I would never do aggressive strengthening."

Overall, the objective when creating an exercise routine for patients is "just to keep them moving because that's really what it's all about with arthritis—not to lose joint motion and not to destroy the joint more," Slater explains.

Assistive Devices and Conserving Energy

Depending on a patient's physical condition, an occupational therapist may recommend a number of assistive devices that can help make everyday tasks easier. It is also possible that an OT will modify a particular tool or device to make it simpler to use. Although young people are sometimes too embarrassed or can't be bothered using assistive devices, it is to their benefit to do so.

In some cases, occupational therapists find that teens with juvenile arthritis have trouble writing or cutting food. Therefore, they may put special rubber grips on pens, pencils, or silverware that make the handles bigger and easier to grip. Also, many people with arthritis have trouble turning keys, due to limited dexterity or a weak grip. If this is the case, they can use a key turner, which is a slightly curved plastic handle that attaches to your keys in order to provide extra leverage when opening locks. According to Slater, "there's things you can put on door knobs to make them easier to turn."

Patients with juvenile arthritis may also have difficulty with buttons, zippers, and snaps. OTs might suggest certain types of clothing that are easier to fasten. Or they can provide patients with special items, like button hooks (also known as button aids) or zipper pulls. Sometimes, OTs may replace buttons with Velcro in an effort to make dressing easier so that the person is not limited to wearing pants with elastic waistbands or shirts without buttons. "Velcro is good as a fastener—if it's not too tough to pull apart—if people are really having trouble with small snaps and that kind of stuff," says Slater. An OT might also recommend slip-on shoes for patients who have problems reaching over to tie their shoes.

Stefanie says, "There's a lot of tools that I've gotten over the years, like button hooks because I can't do buttons because of my fingers. . . . [I've also gotten] thicker brushes so that I can brush my hair easier and rocker knives to cut things when people aren't home to help me. There are so many tools out there."

Ag Apparel is an adaptive clothing company that was recently recognized by *O, The Oprah Magazine* for offering fashionable, yet accessible, clothing. Founder Jordan Silver's mother has rheumatoid arthritis. Silver has her mother test each piece of clothing for ease of use before she markets it. You can find Ag Apparel on the Web at www.agapparel.com.

Sometimes an occupational therapist will visit a patient's home, school, or place of employment to determine how he or she can modify or rearrange items to make certain tasks quicker and easier. "A lot of OTs do that and they do it through home-care [programs]," Slater says. "If someone's in an outpatient clinic, you can usually do one home visit."

Visiting the home, workplace, or classroom of a particular patient can provide occupational therapists with a lot of insight

ACCESSIBLE CLOTHING OPTIONS

The following information, compiled by author Kelly Rouba, appeared on Arthritis Today*'s Web site at www.arthritis.org/dress-for-success.php.*

Looking stylish is often easier said than done, especially when arthritis affects your ability to put on tops or pants that have troublesome snaps and buttons or simply fasten in hard-to-reach places. Check out these sites for accessible clothing for women, men, and children.

- **WheelieChix Chic: Offers designer fashions for women with physical limitations who use wheelchairs. Owner Louisa Summerfield was diagnosed with juvenile rheumatoid arthritis at the age of nine. Because she knows firsthand how difficult dressing can be, her line includes tops and pants that are made with disguised magnetic fastenings, and garments are relaxed in the waist. Visit www.wheeliechix-chic.com.**
- **Buck & Buck: This company has a special section of clothing designed especially for people with arthritis. Outfits are made with Velcro, zippers, and elastic waistbands to make dressing easier. Grab loops can be put on pants, if requested. Call (800) 458–0600 or visit www.buckandbuck.com.**
- **Easy Does It: Clothing is made with independent living in mind, especially for those with arthritis. Garments have "decorative buttons, snaps, hooks or zippers that conceal Velcro fasteners" that are secure and easy to use. Visit www.myeasydoesit.com.**
- **Dignity by Design: Designer clothing for people with physical challenges and dexterity limitations. Call (612) 325–4889 or visit www.dignitybydesign.com.**
- **Silvert's: Comfortable and fashionable outfits are designed for people with arthritis or other physical disabilities. Call (800) 387–7088 or visit www.silverts.com.**
- **Clothing Solutions: Company features adaptive clothing designs, some of which have zipper front openings to make them easier to put on. Other designs are made specifically for wheelchair users. Adaptations to clothes are disguised so the person wearing it can maintain their dignity. Call (800) 336–2660 or visit www.clothingsolutions.com.**
- **Adaptations by Adrian: Company offers adaptive clothing that is fashionable and easy to put on. 877/6-ADRIAN; www.adaptationsbyadrian.com.**

related to the person's condition. "Once we walk through a day with someone and find out what causes the problem and where the fatigue [comes in], then we can make individualized suggestions about how they may be able to consolidate activities, do things in an easier way, or rearrange their bedroom so that things are more easily reachable," Slater says.

Rearranging also applies to other areas of the house besides the bedroom. Occupational therapists can make suggestions on how to improve accessibility in almost any room in your house. "If I were looking at a kitchen, I would look at keeping the more frequently used items right there on the counter in front of you," Slater says. She also recommends that individuals use a cart with wheels to transport items around the kitchen while they are cooking in order to save them from making extra trips back and forth when their arms are full. And items like one-handed cutting boards and utensils with larger handles can be helpful, she says, adding that using oven mitts on both hands can also prevent strain when lifting hot and heavy pots.

TIPS FOR SAVING ENERGY AT SCHOOL

Licensed occupational therapist Deborah Yarett Slater also has a few tips for students to try at school:

- Use book bags on wheels instead of carrying them.
- Get your classes scheduled close together so you don't have to walk far.
- Plan your day so you have rest periods. Or ask for a study break partway through the day so you can sit or lie down.
- Use a scooter for long distances if you have trouble walking.
- Get a locker that's in a central location, so you can put away heavy textbooks once class is over instead of carrying them around for hours.
- Limit after-school activities so you do not get overwhelmed or fatigued.

"I think legally and in every other way [schools] have to make the accommodations that they need to—that are reasonable to do [for students with special needs]," Slater says.

Making your home, office, or classroom more accessible can help you to maintain independence so that you do not need to ask for help from others as often. You may also notice that rearranging your space allows you to conserve energy as well as reduce joint strain or pain. "Arranging your physical surroundings so that things are easy for you and minimize how much work you have to do" is an important part of pain management and something occupational therapists highly encourage, Slater says.

For a more extensive look at the various types of assistive devices available, see appendix A.

Joint Protection

Watching teens in action at home, work, or even at school enables occupational therapists to see whether they are causing harm to their joints. If that is the case, an OT will recommend

TIPS TO PROTECT YOUR JOINTS

There are many ways of protecting your joints. Here are a few that you should always keep in mind:

1. Be careful when moving inflamed joints, since movement can cause more pain. However, make sure you continue to do your exercises—although you may want to tone down the routine a bit.
2. Try to keep your joints straight while engaged in activity if they are developing contractures.
3. Change positions often and stretch every twenty to thirty minutes, if possible, so your body doesn't become stiff. If you are engaged in activity, you might want to take a break so that you don't tire your muscles.
4. Use larger joints when doing more difficult tasks, like carrying objects. If you carry a book bag, place it around both shoulders instead of holding it in your hand.
5. Stop what you are doing if your joints are hurting, your muscles feel weak, or you are feeling tired. This means you have overstressed your joints, and if you don't stop, it will only cause more pain.
6. Use your joints in a safe way and maintain good posture.
7. Remember to ask for help when needed.[5]

an alternative way of doing particular tasks that it is easier on the patient's joints. Chances are this "new way" of doing things will be less painful, too.

For example, your therapist might instruct you to carry objects using the palms of your hands instead of your fingers. When lifting objects, keep them close to your body as to not put pressure on your arms or back. Also, when going up stairs, lead with your stronger leg. When going down stairs, lead with your weaker leg.[6]

Splints and Braces

To preserve or restore the function in a patient's wrists and fingers, some occupational or physical therapists with additional training (particularly certified hand therapists) may design splints for him or her to wear. Splints are also known to help prevent deformity or contractures. And they can help protect the joints at times when they are stiff or sore. "Splints can hold your joints in certain positions or they'll stretch them out so they won't get tighter," Kuhns says. Splints are usually made out of plastic or casting material and may be worn overnight or during the day, depending on the person's condition. Sometimes splints are worn at night to prevent deformity, since young people tend to sleep in a curled-up position that can cause joints to stiffen up.

The two most common types of splints created by occupational or physical therapists are finger splints and wrist splints, also known as cock-up splints. Finger splints are intended to help keep the joints in a person's fingers straight if the arthritis is causing them to bend. Wrist splints are used when the wrist is stiff.[7]

Physical or occupational therapists can also create splints for their patients' knees or ankles. Knee splints are made more often than other types of splints and help to straighten an individual's leg. An orthotist (a person who specializes in making orthopedic braces or splints) may also be consulted to design braces. Like splints, braces can also improve function. However, "a splint is generally worn to stabilize your movement whereas a brace gives a weak limb support while being mobile," says Alana Wallace, who wore long leg braces as a child.

Braces can also reduce pain and inflammation and help teens to strengthen their muscles. Braces can be made from plastic, metal, leather, or moldable foam.

Stefanie wears leg braces when she has to walk long distances and she wears splints on her wrists. Kristen also wears splints and braces. She says, "I got knee braces. There are some days when I have to wear them. I wear my splints or my knee braces or my ankle wraps whenever I am really sore and having a really tough time." Because splints can make your skin hot and sticky, Kristen recommends putting gauze on the inside of the splint or wearing a light sock underneath in order to make it more comfortable.

Splints are customized to meet each person's needs and can usually be adjusted, if needed. If you get splints, it is important to have them fitted from time to time to see if a new one needs to be created or if you no longer need them. "[Eric] used to use splints, but now he doesn't have to use them," Cynthia Terry says. "His one leg was longer than the other because of the arthritis . . . and his muscles were atrophied [at that time]."

If your legs are uneven, a physical or occupational therapist can also provide you with a special shoe to help you maintain balance. This is sometimes called a lift, and, like splints, it can sometimes be created on-site or you may need to go to a special clinic. Stefanie said she uses a lift in her right shoe because her left leg is longer. In extreme cases, surgery may be recommended to help even out the limbs. Surgery may also be recommended if splints do not help to correct joint deformities.

Walking Aids

Walking aids may be necessary if progressive joint damage has occurred. Occupational therapists and physical therapists can help patients learn how to properly use walking aids, like crutches, arm braces, walkers, and canes. Walking aids may be recommended during times when a person's arthritis has flared. Patients who are having a flare may need to use crutches "so they don't have to put full weight on their joints," McGee says. In some cases, a walker might be recommended instead.

Crutches prevent you from having to put your full weight on painful joints.

In more severe cases, a wheelchair may be necessary. On days when they have to do a lot of walking or when walking becomes too difficult, both Kristen and Stefanie rely on a wheelchair. "I'm not embarrassed to be in a wheelchair," Stefanie says, noting that using a wheelchair at places like the mall or an amusement park helps reduce the strain on her joints and prevents her from suffering later.

Figure 6.1.   Kristen Delaney at the Des Moines, Iowa, Arthritis Walk in May 2007 with her brother, Matt (age ten), and sister, Katie (age two). Kristen uses a wheelchair if her body is in pain.

**When it's too painful to walk
or you need to walk a long
distance, a wheelchair might
be necessary to get around.**

Scheduling Occupational Therapy Visits

Most people with juvenile idiopathic arthritis are seen by
occupational therapists on an outpatient basis. However, "they
could be seen as an inpatient if they had a very bad flare-up"
and need medical care. According to Slater, "If [a patient is]
typically seeing an OT as an outpatient, the first visit for an
evaluation would probably be close to an hour. For subsequent
visits, depending on what [the patient] needs and [if an OT is]
doing splint monitoring and other types of things, it could last
maybe a half hour, or maybe longer." Ultimately, the length of
an OT session really depends on the patient's needs and where
he or she is being treated.

The amount of occupational therapy visits a patient needs
can vary as well. "One of the things about this type of care is
it's very individualized and it really depends on the patient. If
the patient is having a very acute flare-up, they might just come
in to get some splints to rest their joints and [to learn] some
energy conservation techniques and maybe get some adaptive
equipment," Slater says, noting that OT may be discontinued
once the flare subsides.

"Rheumatoid arthritis and those types of diseases are
chronic diseases—systemic," she explains. "They go up and

down. You have exacerbations and you have periods of time when people tend to do better. So this is the kind of the thing where [occupational therapy] should be more of a disease management type of approach. When you have a flare-up, you might need a few sessions of OT, but you're not going to need it necessarily for four months, three times a week. It's really very individualized and depends on what's going on systemically."

OT may also be prescribed by a physician when adjusting a patient's medication regimen. Again, the number of OT visits needed will vary "depending on how that [new regimen] is working for them, because you know you have to try a whole combination of things and see how that works [and] people can have reactions to medications," Slater says.

Generally, "I wouldn't think kids would need to come for a lot of visits," Slater adds. "[Usually], they come and go. They come for a few sessions and might not need anything for months and years, and then they might have a flare-up and need to come in again."

PHYSICAL AND OCCUPATIONAL THERAPY REHABILITATION PROGRAMS

As mentioned, some teens may require a little extra physical or occupational therapy to help get their joints and muscles in better shape. In such cases, doctors may recommend their patient stay in the hospital for a few weeks to meet with physical therapists and occupational therapists on staff more often.

McGee used to work at Children's Seashore House, a medical rehabilitation center for youth who have chronic illnesses that's operated by the Children's Hospital of Philadelphia. "We had kids come for weeks at a time [for rehabilitation]," she says. Some of the patients were recovering from joint replacements, while others simply needed to strengthen their joints and muscles. These patients usually receive physical therapy treatments twice a day, once in the gym area and once in the pool. Patients also meet with occupational therapists during the day.

While working at Children's Seashore House, McGee saw only a handful of patients with juvenile arthritis. In those cases, the disease had progressed because it had taken a while to diagnose it. Intensive physical therapy was needed because "wherever the arthritis was, that joint might have gotten a bit tighter," she says.

Fortunately, fewer teens are admitted into rehabilitation programs for physical or occupational therapy purposes these days. "It is rarely done. Now things have changed tremendously in the last twenty years because medication is so different," McGee says. "The joint damage is so much less now because of the medication they use."

Choosing a Physical or Occupational Therapist

If your doctor decides you need physical or occupational therapy, ask him or her to recommend a clinic, private practice, or hospital in the area that has a reputation for providing quality care. You might also want to ask friends or family members who have received similar treatment if they would recommend the place where they were treated.

It is also not unreasonable to ask to schedule a consultation or to request patient referrals from places you are considering for treatment. Upon your initial visit, you or your parents should ask how many of the employees are physical therapists versus physical therapist assistants (PTAs). "Physical therapists go to school for five to seven years and receive an advanced degree," Kuhns explains. "PTAs cannot perform initial evaluations on patients and create a plan of care. They don't have the training that's required to diagnose and do all the tests needed for new patients. And although they can provide excellent treatment, in many states they must be supervised by a physical therapist. Once a PT has performed an initial evaluation, a PTA can carry out or change the treatment (or plan of care), provided they get it approved by a PT."

It is also helpful to know if employees are members of the American Physical Therapy Association or American Occupational Therapy Association, since members of these organizations are licensed and receive up-to-date information

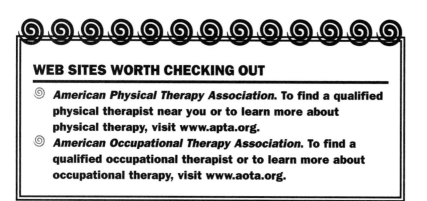

WEB SITES WORTH CHECKING OUT

◎ *American Physical Therapy Association.* To find a qualified physical therapist near you or to learn more about physical therapy, visit www.apta.org.
◎ *American Occupational Therapy Association.* To find a qualified occupational therapist or to learn more about occupational therapy, visit www.aota.org.

about ongoing research and findings in their fields. All PTs and OTs need to be licensed in order to work with patients.

Before working with a physical or occupational therapist, make sure to ask for someone who has experience in working with patients with juvenile arthritis. "You might want to ask how many patients they've seen with this problem before," Kuhns advises.

Once you're matched up with a PT or an OT, he or she will come up with a plan of action to help get your body in the best shape possible. One sign of a good physical or occupational therapist is that he or she will include you in this process. According to Kuhns, "Patients should expect someone who is going to listen to what they want out of therapy and try to accommodate them the best that they can. There should be very good goal setting between the therapist and the patient."

Kuhns also says that patients should begin each visit by updating their PT or OT on their condition, especially if they are experiencing a flare or increased joint pain. A good therapist will adapt the routine in order to help the patient get back on track. Patients should also tell their therapist if they are having difficulty with a certain exercise or task so the therapist can provide assistance or modify the routine.

NOTES

1. Joyce L. Falco et al., *JRA & Me: A Fun Workbook* (Denver, CO: Rocky Mountain Juvenile Arthritis Center at the National Jewish Center and the Arthritis Foundation, 1987), 48.
2. Ibid., 51.

3. Ibid., 47.

4. Arthritis Foundation, *Managing Your Pain* (pamphlet, 2005), 21.

5. Falco, *JRA & Me*, 68.

6. Arthritis Foundation, *Managing Your Activities* (pamphlet, 2005), 6.

7. Ibid., 66.

7 Managing Your Physical and Mental Health

No one ever wants to be told they have a chronic illness.
And if you're like many of those with arthritis, you probably
had a hard time accepting your diagnosis at first—or maybe
you are still trying to grapple with having to adjust to the new
lifestyle that was imposed upon you. Coping with the effects
of a disease like arthritis can be overwhelming—not just
physically, but also emotionally—and this chapter contains
information that will help you begin to deal with those
feelings in the best way possible.

In the first part of this chapter, you will learn about a
number of techniques that can help improve your physical
condition by alleviating pain and reducing fatigue. And who
doesn't want to feel better? The second half of this chapter is
centered on coping strategies and tips you can use to boost your
spirits during times when you are feeling sad or depressed. It's
unlikely that anyone will tell you that living with arthritis is fun
or easy, but learning to manage your physical and mental health
can help you achieve an overall sense of well-being.

PHYSICAL HEALTH

Pain Management

Arthritis pain can be intense, especially during flares
(something you may have already dealt with). It can also
make your heart rate and blood pressure increase and cause
your breathing to become fast and shallow. Pain can even
tighten up your muscles. Whether you experience them

separately or together, these symptoms are draining, both physically and emotionally.

Kristen Delaney says that having arthritis makes her feel elderly, even though she does not look it. "Just by looking at me you would think that I am just an average seventeen-year-old. [But], if you look closely, you would be able to tell that I have arthritis. If someone actually stopped and took the time to look at my hands, they would see that they are red, puffy, and swollen. Most of the time I can't straighten out my fingers because they are so sore and stiff. [My knees] are swollen all the time. In fact, I have a hard time telling what they look like when they are not swollen."

Throughout much of this book, we've discussed ways in which you can help control or prevent the effects of the disease through medicine, diet, exercise, and even surgery. But some days, these things are just not enough. However, you should be happy to know there are a number of other methods that might also help to relieve some of the arthritis pain when nothing else seems to be doing the trick.

First and foremost, "if you're doing something that's stressful to your body, stop and rest," Stefanie Tepley says. She suggests that you think of the pain level you are in at that moment and then decide if you should continue on or stop what you are doing so that you don't regret it later.

Another suggestion for reducing pain and stiffness is to start your day with a warm bath or shower. It's common for

A hot bath can alleviate stiffness.

teens with arthritis to experience morning stiffness. If that is the case, "we usually recommend . . . [you fill the] tub first thing in the morning," Sandra McGee says. Baths filled with warm water are encouraged for teens with arthritis since it allows them to stretch out and do some light exercising. Exercising in the water after waking up can really help to alleviate morning stiffness. Some people with arthritis also have whirlpool bathtubs with built-in jets installed in their homes to provide some added relief.

If you are on a budget or simply pressed for time in the mornings, a warm shower can also help to loosen up joints. "Every morning, I take a hot shower just to get moving. It helps with stiffness," Kristen says. "Some people take baths, [and getting in] a sauna or hot tub would help, too."

During the day or even at night, you may start to notice that your joints are aching or have begun to stiffen up again. If that happens, don't hesitate taking another shower or bath to relieve the stiffness or pain. Or you might try applying some heat or ice to the area for about fifteen to twenty minutes instead. Hot packs or heating pads help to loosen up stiff joints because the heat relaxes muscles and stimulates circulation, whereas ice packs "numb the area and reduce inflammation and swelling."[1] According to the Arthritis Foundation, most teens tend to move better when heat is applied to the joint, but some prefer ice. "I think a hot washcloth works good too," Eric Terry says.

The Arthritis Foundation warns that your skin should be dry and not have any open sores or cuts before you apply heat, ice, or paraffin wax to painful areas. If you have Raynaud's phenomenon, juvenile vasculitis, or poor circulation, you should consult your doctor before treating yourself with heat or ice. After applying a heat or ice treatment, you should make sure the area isn't swollen, have hives on the skin, or seem purplish-red in color, because that could mean the pack is too hot or too cold. For that reason, always wrap the heat or ice in a towel. Furthermore, always wait until your skin has returned to its normal color before applying heat or ice again.[2]

Eric says that he also uses Icy Hot, a topical pain reliever, to help his joints feel better. Kristen agrees with this advice. "I am

157

a big fan of Icy Hot and Biofreeze because your pills and medications can only do so much [to relieve pain]." Biofreeze is a topical analgesic that helps to reduce pain. Allison Davis says it is often used by physical therapists in her office since it can minimize discomfort during exercising and stretching. A word of caution: Do not put topical pain relievers on your skin before applying heat or ice.

Icy Hot and Biofreeze are just two types of topical pain relievers on the market today. There are many other brands of cream or spray-on pain relievers that can be purchased at a local drug store or online and applied to your joints and muscles. Some brands may contain "salicylates, skin irritants, and local anesthetics that relieve pain."[3] According to the Arthritis Foundation, salicylates prevent nerve endings in the skin from detecting pain as strongly, while skin irritants cause users to feel a cold or warm sensation after applying it.

Other topical pain relievers may contain capsaicin. Capsaicin helps to eliminate substance P, which is a chemical in the nerves that sends pain signals to the brain. When applying these products, you might feel a slight, temporary burning or stinging sensation at first. Remember, topical pain relievers only reduce arthritis pain for short periods of time.

ThermaCare HeatWraps are another product you might want to consider using to help reduce muscle and joint pain. The wraps have adhesive on them, so they stick to your skin, providing heat directly to the area for up to twelve hours. Several types of HeatWraps are available, including ones made especially for the wrists, elbows, knees, neck, and back. ACE also manufactures a reusable gel pack that can be heated or chilled and then applied to various areas of the body. Or you might want to try Medibeads Joint Wraps, which are designed to surround larger joints, like the knees. They can be put in the freezer or microwave.

Stefanie has another tip: "The main thing that I've done since I was little . . . is wrap my joints that were hurting with ACE bandages. The warmth, for some reason, you know, wrapping the joints, it isolates it. I can still move [the joint] enough so it doesn't get stiff. Something about the warmth I get from an ACE bandage helps. A heating pad will help too, but it doesn't isolate it as much because I can't wrap it around [the joint]."

There are also a number of home remedies that have proven to relieve arthritis pain in some people. One such remedy is to rub castor oil onto the inflamed joints in the morning and then again at night.[4] Then place a warm washcloth on top of the area. You may find your pain diminishes quickly if you follow this method, or it could take up to four days before you notice a difference. Also, some products, like Castiva Arthritis Pain Relief Lotion, containing castor oil, can be purchased at your local pharmacy.

Other people with arthritis also find relief from pain by drinking grape juice mixed with Certo. It is recommended that you put one to two tablespoons of liquid Certo (or a similar brand of pectin) in eight ounces of purple grape juice and then drink the solution as many as three times a day.[5] This popular method for pain relief can also take as many as four days to begin working.

Massage

Massage has become an increasingly popular therapy for relaxing muscles and reducing stress. In fact, many people incorporate a monthly visit to their local spa or gym for a massage into their regular schedule.

The benefits of massage for someone with juvenile arthritis are that "it loosen[s] up muscles and helps the pain of the arthritis," says Sarah McKeever, a certified massage therapist. "For moderate rheumatoid arthritis, the friction techniques help create heat in the tissues, which is good. However, for acute [or severe] RA, massage is not recommended. But, you can have someone do the 'M' technique, which is basically just very soft touch and motions on certain spots."

Because massage therapists may apply a lot of pressure at times, make sure the person working with you has experience treating people with arthritis. Also, if a certain joint is swollen or painful, do not allow that area to be massaged. If at any

RELIEVING ARTHRITIS PAIN

Here are a few other tips that can help prevent or relieve your arthritis pain:

- During the winter, wear pajamas made of fleece and socks to bed. Doing this will keep you warm at night and help your body move more easily, says physical therapist Sandra McGee.
- The Arthritis Foundation suggests sleeping in a sleeping bag or on a heated waterbed to reduce morning stiffness.
- The Arthritis Foundation also recommends sitting down while doing activities that take up a lot of time. Use chairs that are not low to the ground so it's easier for you to stand up.
- Keep your wrists and elbows bent while sitting in order to reduce pain.[6]
- When lying down, try to keep your body as straight as possible in order to avoid contractures. Also, place a cervical pillow or rolled up towel under your neck instead of a regular pillow so that your neck stays straight and the muscles are not stressed. A down or feather pillow might also do the trick.[7]
- Keep items you often need in easy reach.
- Take your medicine on schedule.
- Remember to change positions often so your body does not get stiff. This is especially important if you are sitting and should be done about every fifteen to twenty minutes.[8]
- Acknowledge your pain. If you are not sure how to assess your level of pain, use a scale of 1 to 10 (1 being very little pain and 10 being extreme pain) to help put it in perspective.
- Change your thoughts. Sometimes it may take a while to get your pain under control, and if you continue to focus on it, the pain will seem more intense. Try thinking about something happy or something that's fun or enjoyable to take your mind off of the pain.

point the massage becomes too painful, feel free to ask the massage therapist to stop or ease up.

Massages can be expensive. So if paying for a massage is out of your budget, consider massaging your own joints or asking a friend or family member to do it for you. "You can do gliding motions on the areas causing pain or put moist heat on them," McKeever suggests.

Alternatively, you might try petrissage or effleurage massages techniques, McKeever adds. Simply put, effleurage is a soothing stroking motion done prior to petrissage, which are movements that use more pressure. "You can absolutely do them on yourself, but if you're in that much pain, you definitely want somebody else to do it," she says. As always, check with a doctor before attempting self-massage or seeing a masseuse.

Pain Management Programs

If you are still having trouble managing the pain caused by your arthritis and want some extra help, look into whether there is a pain clinic or pain management program near you. Staff who are trained in this field will evaluate your condition and recommend some alternatives to the pain management methods you have already tried.

About two years ago, Stefanie's pediatric rheumatologist referred her to the UCLA Pediatric Pain Management Program. "I think that was during the peak of one of my flares. That was a really bad year for me," she recalls. According to the program's Web site, staff create individualized treatment plans that use "state-of-the-art medicine in combination with the regenerative power of complementary therapies to treat children suffering from chronic pain. Patients choose from a variety of healing modalities ranging from acupuncture to art therapy."[9] The ultimate goal is to help patients better manage their symptoms, especially pain.

"I met with the doctor and a physical therapy team and they recommended all kinds of places to go—acupuncture, yoga, pilates," Stefanie says, adding that she also learned pain management techniques, like when to rest her joints.

Dr. Randy Cron says that perhaps the most successful pain program in place is run by Dr. David Sherry at the Children's Hospital of Philadelphia. "He has a 92 percent success rate, which is the best I am aware of," Dr. Cron notes. Through the Pain Management Program, Dr. Sherry specializes in treating musculoskeletal pain amplification syndromes [these are conditions, like fibromyalgia and JA, that involve chronic pain]. According to information provided by Children's Hospital, "The Pain Management Program provides comprehensive inpatient and outpatient evaluation and therapy for children with acute and chronic pain. [Also, a] pain management program physician is available around the clock to provide consultation and therapy for inpatients."[10] Outpatients receive care during their doctor's visits or as part of a daylong therapy treatment program that does not require an overnight stay.

Teens taking part in the program work with physical and occupational therapists for up to six hours a day. Exercise routines are tailored based on the individual's needs; they are intense, and focus on areas that are painful or not functioning properly. While in the program, teens and their parents also meet with a psychologist, since stress is known to cause pain.

Dr. Cron believes "there are similar programs to Dr. Sherry's, which rely on intensive—meaning six hours per day for one to three weeks—aerobic exercise and desensitization, frequently coupled with psychological counseling [that currently exist]. These programs are slowly becoming more prevalent, but they require a lot of staff and a very patient, unique director like Dr. Sherry."

Fatigue

Teens are often expected to be vibrant and full of energy, but having a chronic illness can change that. Juvenile arthritis might cause you to feel tired more than usual because of the stress the disease places upon your joints. If you are depressed over your condition, this can also make you feel tired. Many medications are also known to cause fatigue. If this is the case, your doctor may be able to switch your prescription to something that may not cause you to feel so sleepy. However, if your medication cannot be changed or if the disease continues to cause you to feel tired, here are a few things you can do to help you feel more energized throughout the day:

- Get proper rest. Sleep helps reenergize your body, which enables you to better manage pain. Most young people need between eight and nine hours of sleep each night for optimal growth and functioning. Sleep is also essential to reducing inflammation. Depending on your condition and age, you may need more than eight hours of sleep. And, when possible, take a quick nap during the day to give your energy level a boost.

- Exercise daily. "Exercise is also crucial for maintaining energy levels. Any amount of resistance exercise to build strength makes everyday activities easier [which helps you] save energy. Aerobic exercise also can boost energy levels," Marla Brodsky says. You may feel tired at first, but it will ultimately improve the condition of your body.

- Eat a healthy snack in the mid-morning or mid-afternoon. "One of the big things that helps is to make sure you are eating an anti-inflammatory diet, including whole foods versus high glycemic (or processed carbs) with lots of sugar. When blood sugar stays low, you don't get energy crashes," Brodsky says. She also recommends avoiding sugary candy, cookies, and white flour breads. Instead, try eating nuts, fruit (apples with peanut butter), popcorn, or hummus with tortilla chips or whole grain crackers.

- Keep a positive attitude! Staying upbeat will help you get through the day with greater ease and make even large tasks look more manageable.

- Maintain proper posture because slouching can cause fatigue.[11]

- Pace yourself, otherwise you will tire yourself out much more quickly. And don't take on more than you can handle.

"One of my problems is [recognizing] my limitations because I push past my limitations all the time, which usually causes me a lot more pain than it would have if I had just sat down or taken a break for a few minutes or used the wheelchair like Mom said to."—Kristen, age seventeen

- Ask for help. If your arthritis is preventing you from doing something or it's causing you too much pain, that's okay! Don't be afraid or timid. It's better to ask for assistance than to inflict more damage upon your body.
- Organize your day ahead of time. Planning out your day and grouping similar tasks together will save you time and energy.
- Be creative. Look for simple ways of doing things or use assistive devices in order to minimize wear and tear on your joints.
- Go outside and get some fresh air to reinvigorate yourself. As an extra benefit, sunlight "does provide vitamin D, which is very important for RA and all autoimmune diseases (since) it can help prevent the progression of an autoimmune illness," Brodsky says. "If you can't get into the sun for fifteen minutes per day, then take a vitamin D3 supplement." You should always remember to exercise caution during high temperatures, because excessive heat can cause fatigue. Also, some medications have side effects that are triggered by the sun. Ask your doctor if that applies to you. Remember, it's always a good idea to put on sunscreen and sunglasses when spending time outdoors.

Being tired can cause you to feel irritable or even prevent you from being able to concentrate. So if following these

Wear sunglasses to protect sensitive eyes when outdoors.

suggestions does not seem to alleviate your fatigue, have your doctor test your blood to see if you are anemic. Anemia is often associated with individuals who have arthritis and it can cause fatigue.[12] Appropriate treatment can boost your energy levels, leaving you feeling good as new!

It's also a good idea to keep a daily journal that indicates when you feel tired because it can help you to pinpoint why it's happening. Bring your journal to your next healthcare visit to get your doctor's opinion on whether medication, daily activities, or something else is at the root of the problem.

MENTAL HEALTH

Coping

Being diagnosed with a chronic illness is life changing, and it's *normal* to feel angry, sad, resentful, or scared. In fact, your family and friends may also feel that way. At times, you may even feel that you somehow brought on your illness or you may try to blame your parents for being the reason you got sick— but it is no one's fault. While it's okay to express your emotions from time to time, it is important to remember that your emotions can affect your physical condition. If you are feeling down, it may aggravate your arthritis. In this section, you will learn ways to cope with your emotions so that life won't seem quite so bad after all.

Kimberly Pate of Virginia, Illinois, knows firsthand how difficult it can be to have to adjust to living with a disability or chronic illness like juvenile arthritis. Pate's life was turned upside down when she became a quadriplegic as a result of a broken neck. Today, Pate is a psychotherapist at Cass County Mental Health Agency in Illinois, where she provides counseling to groups and individuals dealing with a variety of issues.

No matter the cause—whether illness or injury—"facing the intrusion of a disability in our lives can contribute to a sense of helplessness," Pate says. "Life with a disability is not something you willingly volunteer or sign up for; therefore, when it presents itself anyway, it can cause you to feel completely out-of-control of your life."

Pate's injury occurred in 1987 when she was a passenger during an automobile accident. "Initially, the onset of my disability caused me to question what I could and could not do," she says. "I was fearful and let several opportunities pass me by. The thought of failing intimidated me. As I began to realize I was limiting myself by not even exploring options, I decided to redefine success. For me, success was no longer about the final results or outcome. Success was having the courage to try."

Thinking Positively

Pate, a national certified counselor/licensed professional counselor, also believes that thinking positively has helped her and others to overcome the challenges imposed by disability or chronic illness. "Something that helped me significantly was the realization that although I may not be able to control the circumstances surrounding my disability, I do have a choice in how I handle those circumstances. Recognizing my ability to decide how to approach life with a disability restored some sense of control over my life," she says. "Understanding the value of mind-set and the influence it has in our lives can be very useful. When you exercise your ability to think positively, it gradually becomes a natural part of who you are."

Kristen McCosh, who turned forty in 2008, also believes in the power of positive thinking. Like Pate, McCosh suffered a spinal cord injury as a result of a diving accident; she was only fifteen years old at the time. Today, McCosh works as an early intervention program consultant at Spaulding Rehabilitation Hospital in Boston, Massachusetts. As part of her job, she counsels both newly disabled individuals and their families. "What I try to tell people is a lot of it, at least half the battle [when dealing with a disability], is your attitude because your attitude is everything. When I feel good, I can take care of anything," she says. She finds herself giving similar advice as well as daily living tips to her friend Lisa Urban, who has juvenile rheumatoid arthritis. Urban, who is thirty, was diagnosed with

JRA at the age of twelve. "[McCosh] helps me out on how to do things and how to do things better," Urban says.

Instead of letting arthritis get the best of you, focus on maintaining a positive outlook. "We can't control the disease, but we can control our response to it," McCosh adds. "If you do control your response . . . that will trickle down in terms of feeling good health-wise, and you'll feel much better mentally. Everyone knows when they don't feel good, who wants to do anything? You don't want to go to work. You don't want to go to school. Just getting your health status quo is going to help you want to do other things."

WISH AWAY THE PAIN

According to the Arthritis Foundation, your body manufactures "chemicals that help block pain signals traveling through the nerves." Endorphins are one of these chemicals. These chemicals are referred to as "morphine-like painkilling substances" and are produced as a result of your own positive thoughts and emotions.[13] So remember to focus on the good in life!

If you find yourself thinking negatively, try to turn your thoughts around into ones that are more positive. For instance, if you are making excuses about why you shouldn't do something—like exercise or go out with friends—think of some reasons why exercising or socializing might benefit you. Positive self-talk can lead to less pain, whereas negative self-talk can do the opposite.[14]

Self-Help Books, Support Groups, Counseling, and Hypnotherapy

Self-Help Books

"Becoming a positive thinker can enhance the quality of our lives. There are numerous methods and self-help books to get you started. Some of the basic [tips] include focusing more on your abilities, surrounding yourself with positive people, and consciously looking for the good in people and situations," Pate says.

McCosh agrees that self-help books are a great way to help you get in the right frame of mind. Since her accident, McCosh has read a number of these types of books, including *The Seven Habits of Highly Effective People* and the *Chicken Soup for the Soul* series, both of which she recommends. Another popular book and DVD that promotes positive thinking is *The Secret*. McCosh also suggests reading medical books and articles about juvenile arthritis so that you keep up-to-date on the latest advances involving treatment and can better manage the disease.

Support Groups

Many chapters of the Arthritis Foundation have established support groups for youth with arthritis and their family members because the foundation believes that "the key to dealing with emotions is to talk about them."[15] Rheumatology centers and hospitals often offer their own specialized support groups for people with arthritis. By attending these meetings, you will be able to express your feelings and learn valuable ways of coping from those who have shared similar experiences. You will also learn ways in which you can adapt

Having support from friends can improve your quality of life.

your lifestyle so that daily living activities become easier and less stressful on your joints. "Social interaction is crucial," Pate says. "Pursuing support groups or activities that involve socialization can add to the quality of life for anyone."

Professional Rehabilitation Mentoring

When McCosh meets with hospital patients, she also recommends that they join a support group after their diagnosis. However, she realizes that not everyone is willing to join a support group. Sometimes patients need time to grieve by themselves at first, while others are just not open to the idea because they are too upset or they prefer to keep their feelings private. That is in part why Spaulding Rehabilitation Hospital established its Early Intervention Program. McCosh likens the program to peer mentoring, explaining that all new patients are visited regularly by a staff member who has been in their shoes. "I see everybody. Everybody gets a peer visit, and most of them love it" because they can have all of their concerns addressed in a private setting, McCosh says.

Other hospitals are beginning to implement similar programs. "I think we are kind of like a national model. I know I didn't have it when I was injured," McCosh says. "Some rehabilitation hospitals are beginning to have peer mentor staff right there in the hospital; it's definitely an emerging field."

Professional Counseling

Sometimes it may not be enough just to attend support groups or to work with a professional rehabilitation mentor. You may need to meet with a licensed professional counselor if the emotional stress of coping with juvenile arthritis or any secondary conditions becomes too difficult to bear. If you feel like you need help coping, your doctor should be able to put you in touch with a professional counselor or psychiatrist.

Counselors and psychiatrists will work with you to help you learn to deal with feelings of anger, sadness, or self-pity. You may also feel resentment toward siblings or other people your age because they do not have a chronic illness and are not restricted in their day-to-day living. "Counseling can provide an opportunity to process those difficult emotions that go along with facing a disabling injury or disease," Pate says. "Identifying your feelings and discussing them is a critical step in healing. When life presents us with an unfamiliar hardship, we may not know how to react. A counselor can help as you try to come to terms with the changes that have taken place."

Another benefit of counseling is that you can express your feelings to someone who can maintain an unbiased view of your situation. "As we know, a disability affects not only the disabled individual, but the family too," Pate says. "This reality may make it difficult to openly share all you are going through with your loved ones. Counseling gives you the opportunity to discuss all the issues with someone who is not directly involved on a daily basis. The freedom to explore the full impact of your disease on your life and your relationships can be an invaluable tool in learning to cope."

Pate says her approach to working with clients tends to resemble a team effort. "Together we explore coping skills that match the needs and personality of the individual. Effective coping skills can be helpful in adjusting to life with a disability [or chronic illness]."

Psychiatrists can also prescribe medication for depression or anxiety, if you need it. There a few reasons why medication for depression and/or anxiety might be prescribed to a teen with JA, including the following:

1. **Psychotherapy is a process that takes time. If a teen's symptoms of depression or anxiety are severe, medication might be prescribed to provide relief more quickly.**

2. **Some severe symptoms of depression and anxiety may hinder the therapeutic process; therefore, medication may be prescribed in conjunction with therapy. When symptoms are alleviated, individuals are better able to participate in therapy and produce effective results.**

3. **Some disorders are the result of a chemical imbalance in the brain, which can be corrected with the proper medication.**

Hypnotherapy

Hypnosis has been shown to have therapeutic effects, and, for some people, hypnosis is useful in helping to alleviate pain. If this is something that appeals to you, you will need to visit a licensed professional psychologist or counselor who is trained in hypnosis and can guide you through the process. Hypnosis does not work on all patients. However, those who are able to be hypnotized enter into a trancelike state that enables them to relax. A counselor or psychologist can also teach you a few self-hypnosis techniques to use when warranted.

Peer Support

While McCosh encourages patients to meet with the hospital's psychiatrist, she still feels that they can benefit more from peer mentorship. Seeing a psychiatrist is "not always relevant. They can listen, but they can't [always] understand like a peer could," she says. Along those lines, McCosh recommends people with juvenile arthritis look into joining groups like Partners for Youth with Disabilities (PYD). "It's kind of like a Big Brothers/Big Sisters [organization] for people with disabilities," she says. PYD runs a mentoring program that pairs up youth and adults with disabilities. Mentors work to empower youth toward reaching their full potential. PYD organizes various support group meetings, including one for parents of youth with disabilities and another for youth with special needs, and leadership or career development groups for young people. For more information on Partners for Youth with Disabilities, visit www.pyd.org.

Dr. Marisa Klein-Gitelman also suggests participating in activities hosted by your local chapter of the Arthritis Foundation. She said many of the chapters have special events specifically for teens and children who have juvenile arthritis and their families. Events range from walkathons to family fun days to informative meetings.

Eric, Stefanie, and Kristen have all been involved with the Arthritis Foundation for years. The first time the Terry family joined in on one of the foundation's activities was when their local chapter invited individuals with arthritis and their family members to a Washington Nationals baseball game. "The whole family went and we had a nice outing. That was our first time talking to other kids [with JA] outside the doctor's office," Cynthia says.

Since then, the Terry family has taken part in many other activities hosted by their local chapter, including their holiday parties, golf tournaments, and the annual Arthritis Walk. "We became very involved with the walk," Cynthia says, noting that they have participated in several already and raised

Figure 7.1.   Eric Terry at his second Arthritis Walk. It was his first time being the local hero in the Prince William County Arthritis Walk.

thousands of dollars for the foundation. Because of their efforts, Eric has been invited to speak at the chapter's fund-raising gala and even appeared in a video ad campaign sponsored by the national foundation.

Becoming involved with "the Arthritis Foundation actually was really good for me because I don't feel like the only one that has arthritis," Eric says. "Just seeing other people with it actually makes you feel kind of bad, but it makes you feel kind of happy too because it doesn't make you feel like the only one."

"The benefits of the Arthritis Foundation are just support for Eric alone and just support for us," Cynthia adds. "We found other parents whose children are going through the same thing."

Aside from organizing annual Arthritis Walks and various other events, many chapters also host special summer camps for youth with juvenile arthritis. "Sometimes kids like to talk to other kids about specific things," Dr. Klein-Gitelman says. Signing up for camp is a great way to meet other children who are going through similar experiences. Plus, it can be a lot of fun.

Stefanie said she first learned about the Southern California Chapter's summer camp when she was thirteen years old. "My rheumatologist, Dr. McCurdy, told me about Camp Esperanza," she says. Camp Esperanza, which is the Spanish word for "hope," was established in 1985 especially for children ages eight to seventeen who have arthritis or related diseases. For a number of years, participants have stayed at the YMCA's Camp Harold F. Whittle in the San Bernardino Mountains near Big Bear, California, for five days. The chapter runs several camp sessions for different age groups.

"I actually went [to the camp] for five years," Stefanie says. "It was my first overnight camp experience. I was nervous, but they have doctors that are available 24/7 for you. A lot of the times, they are the doctors that the kids go see [for their routine care]. Also, all the counselors either suffer from arthritis or a similar illness, so they have lots of experiences with it. You feel like it's sort of a big family. You talk to them about what's going on and they understand."

Camp Esperanza is free to attend, aside from a small registration fee. Campers get to participate in a whole host of

Figure 7.2.   Stefanie Tepley (fourth from left) with fellow campers at Camp Esperanza in Big Bear Lake, California, getting ready to go for a wagon ride around the camp.

activities, ranging from swimming to canoeing to arts and crafts. "I actually got to go horseback riding," Stefanie adds. Counselors also organize various team building activities and theme days as well.

The foundation's Greater Southwest Chapter, which serves Arizona, New Mexico, and part of Texas, hosts two camps. Children and teens who take part in Camp Cruz stay at accessible camps in either Arizona or New Mexico for six days. Campers, who are between the ages of seven and sixteen, enjoy participating in various activities from archery to kayaking to team challenges. There is also a counselor-in-training program for individuals who are seventeen or eighteen and have attended the camp previously.

In addition, the Greater Southwest Chapter also runs Camp Imagine Life without Arthritis (ILA). As part of Camp ILA, children and members of their immediate family go on a weekend excursion to an area camp. The purpose of Camp ILA is to give families of children or teens with JA the chance to connect with other families so that they can share their experiences or get advice.

The Greater Southwest Chapter also has plenty of other initiatives, including the Angels Program, an ongoing effort "to work with physicians and rheumatologists [in order] to provide information and support to newly diagnosed youth and families and youth who are in the hospital," says Mendoza.

You can contact the Arthritis Foundation to find out what programs your local chapter offers and decide what interests you.

GOAL SETTING

Another way of getting your life back on track after being diagnosed with arthritis is to set goals for yourself. "I am big into [creating] action steps and goals," McCosh says. Action steps are literally a step-by-step outline of what you will need to do in order to reach your goals. Writing down your action steps will help make reaching your goals more manageable and less overwhelming.

"What I always tell everybody is to set both short-term and long-term goals," McCosh says. "Everybody always wants to get healed; that can be a great long-term goal, but don't give up on the short-term goals."

One example of a short-term goal could be your rehabilitation program. If you are undergoing physical or occupational therapy for several weeks, ask yourself what you want to get out of it and what skills you want to gain. McCosh says, "I tell [patients] when they [return] home, they are on their own, so [they should] to try to make use of this time—take the most that they can from the professionals that are there to help."

Depending on the type or severity of your arthritis, your goals could be as vast as increasing the distance you can walk to finding ways of making your morning routine before school or work easier. "In order to achieve the goals, I try to help [patients] plan out action steps. It's all very action based, my approach," McCosh says. "I am not a wallower. I am not someone who sits there. When I see a problem, I say, 'Okay, what can I do to solve it?' That's just my personality, but I think it helps because if I stay active and busy, my mind won't be dwelling on everything I can't do."

Life goes on in spite of arthritis, Dr. Patience White says. "Don't have it your [sole] focus." She, too, believes you should still have goals and continue to pursue your dreams. And even if you've had arthritis for years, setting goals can help you to lead a healthier life or accomplish things you've only imagined.

PHYSICAL ACTIVITIES

"Physical and emotional health can also be achieved through physical activity," Pate says. In previous chapters, we have discussed the benefits of exercise in terms of how it can improve your overall physical health. But it's also important to note that engaging in physical activity can improve your mental health as well.

"There's so much stress out there today anyway, never mind having a disability. One thing I find that really helps is physical activity," McCosh says. "One of my best friends has arthritis. She's ambulatory, but she has a tough time with her knees and climbing stairs. The doctor recommended an exercise routine for her and we try to do that together, even if it's just going for a walk. Because just to get out, to see people, to take some time for yourself, to exercise or do yoga—that's important for maintaining good mental health."

There are plenty of activities you can do by yourself or in a group. "So many sports and activities have been made accessible to individuals with disabilities. Adaptive equipment has paved the way for inclusion in areas once unheard of," Pate says. "Participation in group sports provides additional opportunities to interact with others. Also, competitive challenges can be stimulating and rewarding. [Physical activity] is also an excellent way to relieve stress." The list of activities you can choose from is endless. But keep in mind that you need to choose an activity that isn't too stressful on your joints. When in doubt, ask your doctor.

VOLUNTEERING

One surefire way to help better yourself is to start by helping others first. Consider getting involved with community service

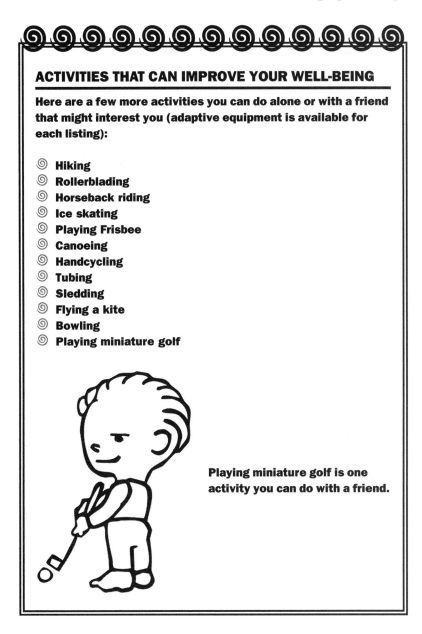

ACTIVITIES THAT CAN IMPROVE YOUR WELL-BEING

Here are a few more activities you can do alone or with a friend that might interest you (adaptive equipment is available for each listing):

- **Hiking**
- **Rollerblading**
- **Horseback riding**
- **Ice skating**
- **Playing Frisbee**
- **Canoeing**
- **Handcycling**
- **Tubing**
- **Sledding**
- **Flying a kite**
- **Bowling**
- **Playing miniature golf**

Playing miniature golf is one activity you can do with a friend.

activities and nonprofit organizations, like the Arthritis Foundation. You may want to follow in the footsteps of Amanda, Eric, Kristen, and Stefanie by helping to organize your local Arthritis Walk or some other foundation event. By volunteering with the foundation, you will get to meet other people like yourself while working to raise funds and awareness for a cause that's important to you.

"I've done a lot of work with the foundation," says Kristen, who became familiar with the organization's mission when she was selected as a youth honoree at its fund-raising event called the Jingle Bell Run several years ago.

Although she did not keep up her involvement with the organization, she got involved again about two years ago. At the time, Kristen was thinking about her personal experiences and all the struggles she had gone through and the issues with having arthritis in our society, and she wanted to help in some way. She said, "What if I could teach others how to better themselves? Someone could learn from my bad experiences how to make their lives better for their future."

Kristen contacted the foundation's North-Central Iowa Chapter and agreed to help organize its annual walk in 2006. The staff even asked her if she'd like to be a youth honoree again. "I was in the newspaper to promote the walk," Kristen says, adding that she also got to be on the radio. "I formed my own team named 'Kristen' to raise money. Last year, our main goal was to raise awareness in the area. And that was still our goal this year." Staff at the foundation "were apparently impressed with my speaking skills . . . and they asked me to come be a guest speaker at their [fund-raising] dinner. It was really neat because I went up there and spoke to over three hundred people at this black tie event. I went up there and told my own personal story; I didn't sugarcoat anything . . . and I got a standing ovation."

After she finished her speech, Kristen noticed that some people in the audience were crying, and a few even came over to shake her hand and told her she had inspired them. "For the first time in my life, I realized that other people do care [about children and teens with arthritis]. Before that, no one really listened or understood to the full extent of my words," she says.

Since then, the chapter asked Kristen to be its youth representative at an arthritis advocacy summit in Washington, D.C. At the summit, she encouraged government officials to support the Arthritis Prevention, Control, and Cure Act, which would improve the lives of the millions of Americans living with arthritis. "It is actually not a new bill. It just has to keep getting reintroduced [in Congress]," Kristen says.

Figure 7.3.   Kristen Delaney in Washington, D.C., for the Arthritis Foundation's Advocacy Summit in February 2007. She is resting while waiting to see Sen. Chuck Grassley of Iowa.

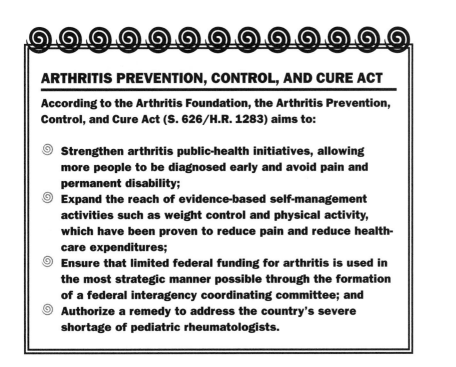

ARTHRITIS PREVENTION, CONTROL, AND CURE ACT

According to the Arthritis Foundation, the Arthritis Prevention, Control, and Cure Act (S. 626/H.R. 1283) aims to:

- Strengthen arthritis public-health initiatives, allowing more people to be diagnosed early and avoid pain and permanent disability;
- Expand the reach of evidence-based self-management activities such as weight control and physical activity, which have been proven to reduce pain and reduce health-care expenditures;
- Ensure that limited federal funding for arthritis is used in the most strategic manner possible through the formation of a federal interagency coordinating committee; and
- Authorize a remedy to address the country's severe shortage of pediatric rheumatologists.

More recently, Kristen was selected as a National Arthritis Walk Honoree and had the chance to share her story in *Arthritis Today* magazine. While Kristen clearly enjoys raising funds and awareness for the Arthritis Foundation, perhaps you would prefer to join another type of organization that has nothing to do with arthritis so that you are able to "forget" about your disease for a while. If you are not sure what community service projects are taking place in your area, ask friends or family members if they can recommend something you might like. Or look online or in your local newspaper. Newspapers often run stories about nonprofit organizations and include contact information if volunteers are needed. By giving of your time, you will feel better about yourself and you will see that there are many other people who have problems, too.

"With the severity of my disability, a large part of my day goes into ensuring my physical needs are met. It is easy to become fixated on managing the various aspects of my disability," Pate says. "I think it is helpful to invest time in helping others in some capacity. As a psychotherapist, my job involves focusing on my clients and the issues they are facing. I believe we can gain a fresh perspective by 'getting out of ourselves' and realizing everyone faces challenges in life."

Kristen adds, "Don't focus on the things that you can't do. Focus on the things that you can do. You have to move on and try to find other things that you can do and things that you like to do."

SELF-ACCEPTANCE

Reading self-help books, joining support groups, setting goals, and engaging in physical activities are all excellent ways to help you learn to cope with having juvenile arthritis. But truly being able to manage your mental health comes down to one thing—self-acceptance. And this means falling in love with *yourself*.

"I think a lot of it is a matter of just saying this [disease] is a part of me—at least at this point of my life," Dr. Harry Gewanter says, adding that adjusting to life with juvenile arthritis is like jazz. "The essence of any song is rhythm. And the person with juvenile arthritis has a melody. It just takes a while to learn what the melody is."

To find your inner melody, Dr. Gewanter recommends that you begin by learning to recognize your strengths and weaknesses and then try to make the best of it. As an example, he says, you might not be able to become a professional football player, but you could be a coach.

In a way, we are all disabled, Dr. Gewanter adds. "Nobody can do everything." He suggests that those with arthritis concentrate on finding ways to adapt or cope in order to help them overcome their limitations. And he believes that the Juvenile Arthritis Alliance, a council of the Arthritis Foundation, can help. The alliance is devoted to improving the quality of life for those who suffer from juvenile arthritis. If you decide to become a member, you will receive up-to-date information on JA and take part in its support groups, which can help you learn to come to grips with your condition.

While self-acceptance certainly begins within, McCosh also believes that it has something to do with how you present yourself. "I always try to look good. I feel better if I look good. I try to do my hair, put on makeup, and wear something cute because I'll feel better," she says. "If I'm just laying around with messy hair, I'm not going to want to see anyone or do anything, so I try to maintain positive self-esteem [by looking presentable], and that helps me with stress, too, because when I feel negative about myself, I definitely feel more stressed." She also says it's important to always have faith in yourself and in life. "I really believe that where we are [in life] is where we are meant to be. In a lot of ways, it just involves faith that things will work out. You do all you can [to live well] and the rest of it, you just have to let it be. Only worry about what you can control."

MANAGING STRESS

It's not uncommon to feel overwhelmed or frazzled when you're trying to keep up with your everyday activities and dealing with a chronic illness on top of it. But if you allow yourself to become too stressed out, it will put a strain on your body and affect your overall physical health.

There are many ways stress can manifest in your body, but the following are a few common signs to look out for:

- **Muscle spasms**
- **Headaches or jaw clenching**
- **Nausea or vomiting**
- **Sweating**
- **Dry mouth or problems swallowing**
- **Difficulty concentrating**
- **Change in appetite**
- **Increased anger or frustration**
- **Diarrhea or constipation**
- **Insomnia**
- **Crying**[16]

If you are experiencing any of these symptoms or feel stressed in other ways, consult your physician or rheumatologist. He or she may recommend you get counseling or possibly even prescribe medication to calm your nerves. There are also other things you can do to alleviate stress before it builds up so much that it affects your health.

One way to cope with stress is to prioritize. Take care of what you feel is most important first and try not to worry as much about minor tasks or issues at hand. If you are not sure what to tackle first, evaluate what will happen if you do not complete a specific task by a certain time. Then plan out your schedule according to which tasks carry the most weight. Remember to ask for help and, if possible, extra time when you need it.

Also, keep in mind that "the disease is not under your control. You can't stress out about it, but you can worry about the things that are under your control," McCosh says.

What you can concentrate on are things like completing schoolwork or taking your medicine on schedule. "You can't fix the disease, but you can keep up with [things like] your medical appointments. You can do your best. The rest, you just have to have faith and a lot of that comes from the meditation, I think," McCosh adds.

Meditation is another excellent way to cope with stress. There are many different meditation techniques, but in most cases, people focus on either a particular phrase (something positive) or serene place in order to help them relax. "I meditate all the time," McCosh says. "Meditation, I think is really just trying to get in touch with your body. [It's about] just really trying to relate your mind and your body [in order to] get everything to relax your mind. Sometimes it's more difficult to get your mind to relax than your body."

You can learn to meditate by taking classes at your local health and wellness center or by purchasing instructional books or tapes. Or, for starters, try this simple meditation technique:

Begin by lying down in a quiet place. Then envision being in your favorite place—somewhere serene. Think about what it looks, feels, and smells like to be there. If your favorite place is outside, play a CD of sounds heard in nature, like the ocean. Then let your body become limp. Breathe slowly and deeply. As you continue to relax, your mind and body will feel better. Make sure to do this every day.[17]

It has often been said that laughter is the best medicine, so why not enroll in a laughter therapy program or laughter club? Steve Wilson, cofounder of the World Laughter Tour, and his partner, Karyn Buxman, have worked to establish laughter clubs and programs around the world because they believe laughter is a great way to improve your mental health. "It is now indisputable that laughter plays a role in healing, staying healthy, controlling stress reactions, and maintaining emotional balance," Wilson said in a press release issued by Robert Wood Johnson University Hospital in Hamilton, New Jersey. Laughter has been known to reduce pain, relax muscles, alleviate headaches, burn calories, and benefit the immune system in a variety of ways.

Many of the activities listed throughout this chapter, like exercise or joining a support group, are also excellent ways of managing stress. But if nothing's piqued your interest yet, here are a few more suggestions:

- Crafting or other hobbies, like knitting or painting, can be very relaxing. Often, local craft stores offer or know of classes you can take to get a basic understanding of the craft.

- Going for a walk. Just getting out for some exercise can help you blow off some steam—and it doesn't cost a dime!

- Joining a local theater group can help you learn to express your emotions in a positive way. Or, if you only like to sing, maybe you'd rather join a choir. Kristen says she likes to take part in school plays, musicals, and the choir. "I express myself through my voice. Music is a huge part of my life. For me, it's my relief. It really is my expression," she says. "When I relax, I sort of escape into a different world, away from the pain. The pain is still there, but singing and (public) speaking, they are my passion. They are the two things I love to do."

- Writing your feelings in a journal is great way to release your emotions.

- Using a punching bag to take out your aggressions can be therapeutic both physically and mentally.

- Getting a pet, like a dog or cat. Dogs are sometimes brought into hospitals to visit with patients because they can be therapeutic and help cheer people up.

Kristen Delaney feels singing is a way to relieve stress.

Pets can help boost your spirits.

◎ Turning to your trusted friends for advice whenever you feel overwhelmed. Don't be embarrassed or feel like you have to handle tough situations on your own.

FOSTERING OPEN COMMUNICATION

"The biggest problem of all this is the isolation. Nobody wants to be different than anybody else, especially teenagers," says Dr. Gewanter. But keeping quiet and hiding your feelings will only make things worse. It's important to have a support system of people you can confide in. Fostering open communication with your family, friends, and health-care workers is the best way to help them to understand your needs, and this will enable them to better assist you whenever you need it.

"Learning to cope when witnessing your child experience daily pain was most difficult," says Stefanie's mother, Kathy Tepley. "As a parent, you want to take that pain away, but in the case of JRA that is not always possible and does not help the young person learn the necessary techniques to assist them through daily life. We found that having a strong [connection with] doctors, educators, church, family, and friends helped us accomplish the necessary support system to assist Stefanie with her day-to-day normal functions."

Talking to Family and Friends

In Kristen's case, opening up about her condition hasn't been easy. "I don't like to let people know I have arthritis [because]

185

not everybody is open-minded and not everybody is willing to accept that somebody could have a disease that could affect their lives so much," she says.

When Kristen was in elementary school, her classmates would often ask her why she was limping or walking "funny," she recalls. "I would try to explain to them it's different for me to run [or walk] because it hurts," Kristen says. "As a younger kid, some kids thought they didn't want to hang out with me anymore because they were afraid they were going to catch [my] arthritis or that it was going to be passed on like a cold. For me, that was really hard as a first- or second-grader, because I had made good friends with that person, but they changed their minds in a split second when they found out I have arthritis."

Now that she is a teenager, Kristen's classmates realize they cannot catch her illness, but she still finds that there are times when her peers don't understand the nature of the disease. For instance, Kristen's classmates occasionally get upset when she says she cannot play tag football or that she has decided not to participate in a school dance. "Sometimes my peers think I am blowing them off, but I am really not . . . it's just that I am sore," she says.

It's also difficult for Kristen when her friends don't include her in activities because of her arthritis. "They think that I will hold them back if they hang out with me," she says.

In addition, Kristen has found that some adults don't realize what it means to have arthritis. "I've had a lot of people question why I can walk one day but not another," she says. "A lot of it has to do with the weather, like if it's rainy or snowing. During the winter is when I'm at my worst, because it's cold and really hard on my joints."

Unfortunately, facing adversity is not uncommon when you have a disability. "There will be times that others will reject an individual with a disability due to their own ignorance. I think it is important to keep in mind that their rejection is about their limitations rather than ours," Pate says.

After her diagnosis, McCosh says she was afraid to ask friends or family members for assistance because it would seem as if she was dependent upon them, but she soon realized that being up-front about her disability is the best thing to do and denying it only makes things harder. "You have to be realistic about your needs and communicate about them honestly," she says.

For example, if McCosh plans to go for a walk with a friend, she suggests taking a trail that is wheelchair accessible. Other times, she recommends an accessible theater when she and a friend want to go see a movie. Whenever she makes a recommendation, McCosh tries to do it casually and has found that people always respond favorably. "There's never been an issue," she says.

McCosh says that her family members and caretakers now have a good understanding of all of her needs and are there to help her whenever she requires assistance. To make it easier on them, McCosh makes a special effort to tell them in the morning what she will need for the rest of the day. "I try to go organize it in my mind, what I need for set up [for the day], because then they don't feel like they are waiting on me hand and foot," she says.

A WORD OF ADVICE

Always remember to surround yourself with positive people who are willing to offer you support and encouragement when you need it.

McCosh finds that most tasks take longer to accomplish when you have a disability, so planning ahead also cuts down on the time it takes to get things done.

At first, it may be embarrassing to have to express your needs to others, but opening up about your situation does get easier with time. "It just becomes part of who you are," McCosh says. "I never hide the fact of what I need, but I don't focus on it. I don't dwell on it. I always try to be honest about my limitations, even if it's with a new friend." Urban adds, "if [you] need help, ask people for help. Always be open and up front with people."

Despite her past experiences, Kristen is also learning that it can be beneficial to talk about your condition with others. "Over the past few years, I have been coming out of my shell because the world does need to know people have arthritis and how it affects people every day," she says.

DOCTOR'S VISITS

Like many teens, Amanda doesn't like going to the doctor's office. She doesn't want to answer questions about her condition during the visit and she especially hates having blood work done. Sometimes she even says she feels fine when she really doesn't. You, too, may feel resentful or scared, and become snippy or even withdrawn when you go in for a checkup. It's not uncommon to have anxiety when you're unsure of what lies ahead.

If you find that you typically "clam up" when you get to your doctor's office, you might want to write up a list of concerns ahead of time. This is something Dr. Alexander Carney also recommends. "When you worry, you forget to ask all those questions. That's why preparing ahead of time is the best policy," he says.

On your list, include any health problems you are having, like additional pain or drug side effects. "Letting doctors know how well you're functioning [is important] so they can adjust your medicine" or make other changes in your treatment plan, says Dr. Klein-Gitelman. Never try to hide health problems you are experiencing, because that could result in serious damage down the road.

If going to the doctor's office causes you anxiety, you might want to consider having a parent or friend go along with you. He or she can provide you with emotional support and remind you to mention issues you want the doctor to know or address. And he or she can help you remember any advice the doctor gives you. Kristen's mother always accompanies her to visits. At times, however, her doctor tends to direct health-related questions toward her mother instead of her. "I've expressed to him several times that it's my body

ADVICE ON DATING WHEN YOU HAVE A DISABILITY

Dating can cause anyone to feel nervous, anxious, or even a bit unsure of him- or herself at first. And having a disability, like juvenile arthritis, might even intensify these feelings of self-consciousness. On top of that, you might find yourself wondering if or when you should tell your date you have arthritis and explain how it affects your body. Or you might not know how to respond when your date asks you to join in an activity that is too challenging for you. Other times, you might be unsure about how to tell your date that your arthritis or your medication is causing you to feel irritable and that you are not up for socializing at that time. Questions or situations like these may be a bit awkward or difficult emotionally, but never allow them to prevent you from the wonderful experiences that dating offers.

To make things easier when dating, you may need to explain some details about your condition that your date might not be familiar with. Don't cringe! If you are open and honest with your dates, it will turn out better than you think. Always make your date comfortable with asking you any questions he or she may have about your disability. In the end, you would rather your date ask than to make any wrong assumptions about you. Open communication is always the best way to go.

So far, "my only serious boyfriend has been Griffin, and I told him [about my arthritis] on our first date," Amanda White says. "He was extremely supportive and always has been ever since. I didn't have many reservations, because almost everyone at my school knows about it and he knew already as well. The only thing we have to work around is if I am having a bad day; I might be in a bad mood or not want to go out, but he is always extremely nice and great about it."

However, sometimes, a romantic interest or partner might not be so understanding—or, perhaps, you may have reservations about discussing your physical limitations. Tiffiny Carlson, who began using a wheelchair as a result of spinal cord injury at the age of fourteen, knows firsthand that the dating game can sometimes be uncomfortable when you have a disability or chronic illness. Over the past few years, Tiffiny, who resides in Minneapolis, Minnesota, has shared her experiences and offered up plenty of advice in dating articles and columns she has written for a variety of disability Web sites and publications, including BeautyAbility.com, Lovebyrd.com, Disaboom.com, Nerve.com, the United Spinal Association's *Action* magazine, and *New Mobility* magazine. Here, she shares some special advice for you.

TIPS ON DATING WITH A DISABILITY

Just entering the tumultuous dating arena and you happen to be disabled? If so, follow these never-fail suggestions:

- If you're doing the online dating thing, make sure you tell all perspective dates *right away* about your disability. Better yet—put it in your profile. Keeping it a

(continued)

ADVICE ON DATING WHEN YOU HAVE A DISABILITY (*Continued*)

secret until you feel "the time is right" is never a good idea. You'll come across as untrustworthy. Put yourself in their shoes: Wouldn't you want to know?

- Grab a friend and take him or her out clothes shopping with you. When starting to meet possible mates, it's always essential to look your best. Up-to-date clothes, a fresh haircut, and, if you're a woman, a new makeup look, can all help you snag *the one*.
- Remember not to put all of your eggs/hopes in one basket (aka man or woman). It may be scary to finally be out there meeting new people, but don't limit your opportunities by only meeting one or two people, then stopping. Schedule as many dates as possible in the beginning, if you can. Remember, dating is a numbers game; the more people you meet, the better your chances will be!

Are you embarrassed about your disability? Think nobody will want you? I can say from personal experience that no matter what your disability may be, that's simply not true. Here are some tips on keeping your ego afloat, instead of sinking like a rock:

- Always look your best. Staying groomed will help you feel über-attractive.
- Read up on disabled people out in the world—online, that is. (Google "dating and disability"; you'll find hundreds of Web sites about people who are either dating, married, having kids, or all of the above.) There are thousands upon thousands of disabled folks breaking the status quo, and so can you.
- Try writing a list of why you're a worthy mate. Make sure you jot down at least twenty things.

And lastly, if you've finally scheduled the date but you're not sure about where to go or what to do, here are some universal date ideas:

- Dinner and a movie. Both are sitting-down activities and they're always enjoyable.
- Art museums. Art can be enjoyed by most everyone, no matter their ability.
- Live music. Another pleasurable (and definitely my fave) sitting-down activity.

Looking for more dating advice? Check out my bimonthly column on Lovebyrd.com for fresh dating and disability articles, and for an archive chock-full of dozens of other helpful related articles.

and I can advocate for myself, but there is still a large communication gap," she says. So if you bring a friend or relative with you to the doctor's office, make sure you let the doctor know at the start of the visit whether or not you want the individual included in the discussion.

If you have concerns or are worried about a new treatment plan or something else the doctor suggests, make sure to let him or her know. It's possible something can be done to make things less stressful for you. Keep in mind that doctors are there to help you and they only want to do what's best.

"We found through the resources at Gillette Children's [Specialty Healthcare] in St. Paul, Minnesota; CHOC [Children's Hospital of Orange County, California]; UCLA's Pediatric Rheumatology Department; and the UCLA Pain Program, many great resources for Stefanie's daily care plan," Kathy says. "[Through them], we found alternatives to fun activities, learned to recognize when to say when [is enough] and not overdo activity, when to medicate, and that a good home [care] program and proper diet and exercise is so very important."

On the other hand, if you feel that your general practitioner or rheumatologist isn't providing you with quality care, or you simply don't mesh well with him or her, then ask your friends,

WEB SITES WORTH CHECKING OUT

- *American Academy of Pain Management.* To find a pain management professional or program near you, visit www.aapainmanage.org.
- *American Self-Help Group Clearinghouse.* To find a local support group that's appropriate for you, visit www.mentalhelp.net or call (973) 989–1122.
- *American Academy of Child and Adolescent Psychiatry.* To find a psychiatrist who treats children and adolescents or for more information on psychiatry, visit www.aacap.org.
- *American Psychological Association.* To find a psychologist in your area, call (800) 964–2000 or visit http://locator.apa.org.

family, or local Arthritis Foundation chapter to recommend someone you might like better.

NOTES

1. Arthritis Foundation, *Managing Your Pain* (pamphlet, 2005), 16–17.

2. Ibid., 16–17.

3. Ibid., 12.

4. Peter Gott, "Home Remedies," *Sharon (PA) Herald*, April 24, 2007, www.sharonherald.com/community/local_story_113143138 .html.

5. Ibid.

6. Arthritis Foundation, *Managing Your Activities* (pamphlet, 2005), 4.

7. Ibid., 5.

8. Ibid., 6.

9. UCLA Pediatric Pain Program, "Who We Are," www.mattel .ucla.edu/pedspain/whoweare.php.

10. Children's Hospital of Philadelphia, "Pain Management Program: Overview," www.chop.edu/consumer/jsp/division/ service.jsp?id=26662.

11. University of Washington Department of Medicine Orthopaedics and Sports Medicine, "Fatigue," www.orthop .washington.edu/uw/livingwith/tabID__3376/ItemID__85/ PageID__109/Articles/Default.aspx

12. Ibid.

13. Arthritis Foundation, *Managing Your Pain*, 4.

14. Ibid., 6.

15. Arthritis Foundation, *Arthritis in Children*, 25.

16. American Institute of Stress, "Effects of Stress," www.stress .org/topic-effects.htm?AIS=0e7a9fd84b78de49776a7e14b5412a3e.

17. Joyce L. Falco et al., *JRA & Me: A Fun Workbook* (Denver, CO: Rocky Mountain Juvenile Arthritis Center at the National Jewish Center and the Arthritis Foundation, 1987), 125.

8

Moving Forward: Adapting Your Life

Being diagnosed with juvenile arthritis can turn your life upside down—or so it may seem. Fortunately, there are plenty of ways to adapt your style of living so that your life can be as normal as possible once again. The information provided in this chapter will show you how to do just that.

No matter where or how you spend your time—at home, at work, at school, or at play—there are many things that can be done to make your life easier. In this chapter, you will find tips that are sure to save you time and effort. If you are a student, you will also learn about the many ways your school can accommodate your disability. Be sure to also check out appendix A at the end of this book, which includes a comprehensive list of assistive and adaptive devices that make daily living easier. Also be sure to read the section at the end of this chapter for advice on what you will need to know when transitioning from a pediatric to an adult rheumatologist. But first, we'll begin with an overview of government programs and nonprofit organizations that were created to help teens like you obtain funding or other health-care needs so that they can continue living the best life possible.

GOVERNMENT PROGRAMS AND NONPROFIT GROUPS

There are many federal and state programs and agencies in place today that can help you and your family cover the costs of medical care, assistive devices, modified vehicles, and even

BIOGRAPHY OF JULIETTE RIZZO

From covering and coordinating national news stories as a journalist to being selected by an organizing committee of the Atlanta Olympic Games to carry the Olympic Torch through downtown Dallas, Juliette Rizzo has proven that personal dreams and goals are within reach for people with disabilities when the appropriate supports are in place. Rizzo, of Maryland, may have juvenile rheumatoid arthritis, scleroderma, and fibromyalgia, but she hasn't let these medical conditions prevent her from leading a full life.

In 2005 Rizzo was named Ms. Wheelchair America. Her platform, "Power through Participation: Illuminating Opportunities for People with Disabilities," centered on encouraging individuals with disabilities to find their identity through involvement in and personal contributions to community life.

Her advocacy on behalf of those with disabilities didn't start there, however. In the past, Rizzo helped the U.S. Surgeon General roll out the first Call to Action for Improving the Health and Wellness of People with Disabilities in America. She also appeared on *The CBS Early Show* as the national spokeswoman for National Women's Health Week and helped to raise awareness of the effects of scleroderma on the *Today* show.

In 1999 Rizzo was asked by renowned disability leader Judith E. Heumann (also cofounder of the independent living movement for people with disabilities), then assistant secretary of the Office of Special Education and Rehabilitation Services, to relocate to Washington, D.C., where she served as director of communications and media support services in the office, which is part of the U.S. Department of Education.

She later served as communications director to Assistant Secretary Robert H. Pasternack and even assisted with the development of a national disability-specific media and outreach list for the White House under President George W. Bush's New Freedom Initiative for persons with disabilities. Presently, Rizzo is director of exhibits and events planning in the Department of Education.

In 2008 Rizzo was honored as one of Maryland's Top 100 Women for her achievements and community service—a first for a woman with a disability. For years, Rizzo has served as a volunteer for numerous organizations and committees. Among them, Rizzo serves on the Governor's Commission on People with Disabilities in Maryland. She is also the National Arthritis Foundation's National Public Relations Chair for Arthritis Walks nationwide. "While I have benefited from the services of so many organizations, it is in giving back and serving others, especially through the Arthritis Foundation, that I have found a purpose for my pain . . . and my life work," she says.

schooling. (Not all programs, however, are available in every state, and the services offered may vary.) Staff at many of these same institutions are also on hand to field any disability-related questions you have or help you overcome any problems you encounter. If you are unfamiliar with the type of programs and organizations out there, here is brief list of where you can turn for assistance.

GOVERNMENT PROGRAMS

U.S. Social Security Administration

Individuals with disabilities, including juvenile arthritis, might be eligible to receive social security benefits, which can include health insurance coverage and monthly stipends that can be used to cover medical or living expenses.

One type of benefit you might be eligible for is Supplemental Security Income (SSI). Individuals with disabilities, including teens and children, can receive SSI if they have a limited income.[1] "Children with disabilities, depending on the severity of the disability, are eligible for SSI benefits," says Ranita Wilks, who works as an independent living skills/peer counseling specialist at Independence, Inc. in Lawrence, Kansas. "However, eligibility is also based on the parent's income and resources. For example, if Mom and Dad have resources of $200,000, this would make the child ineligible to receive benefits—unless the medical cost for the child exceeded the financial limits of the household." To see if you meet the financial requirements for SSI, contact a representative from your local Social Security office.

If you do qualify to receive SSI, it is likely that you will also be given Medicaid coverage. "Basically, [Medicaid] is a state program for individuals who have limited income or are considered indigent. Many children without insurance from parents are eligible for Medicaid," Wilks explains. As a side note, some teens and children who do not meet the financial guidelines for SSI may still be able to receive Medicaid benefits if their medical expenses are high.[2] Funded by both the state and federal governments, Medicaid is managed by the state.

According to Javier Robles, deputy director of New Jersey's Division of Disability Services (DDS), Medicaid is a federal program that is funded with matching state tax dollars. "The match is usually based on how wealthy the state is. For example, a wealthy state like New Jersey is a 50/50 match. Whereas, a state that is not so wealthy, like Louisiana, may have a 75/25 match," he explains.

Another benefit you may be eligible to receive is Social Security Disability Insurance (SSDI). "Social Security Disability Insurance is payable only to individuals who have worked and paid into the system, and who meet the medical requirements under Social Security guidelines for disability benefits," Wilks says. This can include teens who have been employed.

After you have received SSDI benefits for twenty-four months, you will also become eligible to receive Medicare.[3] "Medicare is a federal program for adults [or teens] who are disabled or retired. It is payroll tax funded and also funds Social Security. No state funds are involved," Wilks says.

Wilks also notes that individuals "needing personal care attendant services through the state waiver program HCBS [Home- and Community-Based Services] must meet the eligibility criteria for Medicaid. If they are Medicaid eligible, the waiver program will cover the cost for in-home care. If not, the individual must pay out-of-pocket for care." To find out if you are eligible, check with your state Medicaid agency for criteria.

What to Do If You Are Denied Benefits

"If an individual applies for SSI or SSDI and is denied, he or she has the option to appeal. The individual should receive a denial letter, which will give them the time frame and procedure for appealing SSA's decision of denial. The individual should gather any additional information that would support their claim, which might include any medical support and/or school records, and provide that information to SSA," explains Lillie Lowe-Reid, MEd, who works for Disability Rights, New Jersey and is project director of Protection and Advocacy for

Beneficiaries of Social Security. Because the process can be confusing, teens should seek the assistance of a parent or guardian when making an appeal.

For more information or to find your local Social Security office, call (800) 772–1213 or visit www.ssa.gov. "Centers for Independent Living should be able to assist individuals with understanding the above mentioned information," Wilks adds. (Centers for Independent Living will be discussed below.)

Government Health Insurance Programs for Children

Children age eighteen and under who are not already medically insured may be eligible for health insurance at little or no cost, even if their parents or grandparents are employed. Eligibility requirements are based on income. Even if your family does not qualify for Medicaid due to their income, you may still be eligible for this program. The insurance program, which varies by name depending where you live, covers doctor visits, hospitalizations, and prescriptions, among other medical expenses.[4]

Each state also receives "funds to provide rehabilitation and other services for disabled children under the age of 16 who qualify."[5] For more information on this or about your state's health insurance program for children and teens, call (877) 543–7669 or visit www.insurekidsnow.gov.

Health Insurance for People with Disabilities Who Work

People with juvenile arthritis and other disabilities who are employed may also be eligible to receive Medicaid health insurance through their state's Medicaid Buy-In program. The program may be referred to by different names depending where you live. For example, in New Jersey it is called NJ WorkAbility, while in Oregon it is known as the Employed Persons with Disabilities Program. According to Robles, the Buy-In program resulted mostly from the passing of the Work

Incentives Improvement Act of 1999. "The national movement toward Medicaid Buy-In programs has given states the ability to provide health insurance to one of the most vulnerable working groups—people with disabilities," he says. Eligibility varies from state to state, so you will need to consult your state's Medicaid office for specific information.

Vocational Rehabilitation

If you have specific career goals but need assistance to achieve them or require guidance in defining a career goal that is consistent with your abilities and interests, you might want to meet with a counselor from your local vocational rehabilitation office to see how he or she can assist you in the process of obtaining employment. Presently, many states have a division (or office) of vocational rehabilitation. Depending on where you live, the vocational rehabilitation program may fall under the state's Department of Labor, Department of Education, or Department of Human Services.

"I feel that we provide job search assistance and then, once hired, job coaching, as the most frequently utilized services," notes Renee Balke, supervising counselor at the Division of Vocational Rehabilitation Services (DVRS) central office in Trenton, New Jersey. According to the New Jersey DVRS Web site, some of the services vocational rehabilitation counselors can provide you with include:

- *Vocational counseling and guidance.* Clients are given assistance with handling job search issues that impact employability. They also receive job maintenance strategies and help in developing skills needed to be successful in a work environment.
- *Placement services.* Counselors help clients develop job leads. You may also be eligible for on-the-job training (OJT), supported employment (SE), or time-limited placement and coaching (TLPC).
- *Job-seeking skills.* Counselors provide assistance in helping clients with tasks such as resume writing, preparing for interviews, and other activities related to the job search.

◎ *Supported employment.* You may be able to work with an SE provider who can assist you in searching for employment, applying for appropriate positions, and preparing for interviews. An SE can also provide on-the-job coaching to help you understand your duties. Once the coaching session concludes, the SE will follow up to ensure everything is going well.

◎ *Time-limited placement and coaching.* Supported employment services are similar to those stated above, but do not include follow-up meetings.

◎ *Job accommodations.* Counselors can recommend changes or modifications to a work environment that would enable you to work more independently, effectively, and safely.

◎ *Skills training.* Counselors can assist you with applying to vocational, technology, trade, or business schools. If you need special accommodations or help with financing, your counselor may also be able to help in those areas.

◎ *College training.* If a college plan is agreed upon and you choose to attend a two- or four-year degree program, your counselor can guide you through the application process. Counselors may also be able to help secure special accommodations and financial aid for tuition and books.

◎ *Physical restoration.* So that you are able to hold a job, counselors can arrange for you to receive any necessary adaptive equipment or physical, occupational, speech, or cognitive therapy. In addition, you might be eligible for prosthetic/orthotic devices, special shoes, eyeglasses, and other items that can improve your overall productivity in the workplace.

◎ *Emotional restoration services.* You might also be eligible to receive short-term counseling if you have mental health problems or have issues centered around getting and keeping a job.

◎ *Mobility equipment.* Counselors can work with you to acquire mobility devices, if needed, including items like wheelchairs or scooters.

◎ *Driver training.* If you need to drive to work, counselors can arrange for you to meet with a special driving instructor who will assess your driving ability and determine whether you need special modifications installed in a vehicle so that you can drive. A counselor can also arrange for you to receive driving lessons from the instructor, who, in most states, is known as a driver rehabilitation specialist.

 Vehicle modification. Should your vehicle need to be adapted with special equipment, counselors will provide you with a list of vendors who are able to modify the vehicle. Financial assistance toward the cost of modifications is also available, depending on your income. Vehicle modifications will be discussed in more depth below.

Home modifications. If your home needs to be modified so that you can get to work or even work from home, counselors can assist in that process. An example of a home modification would be a stairlift, which can transport you up or down stairs. Again, financial assistance is available when making modifications.[6]

In order to qualify for vocational rehabilitation services, you must have a "physical or mental impairment that is a substantial impediment to employment," according to the NJ DVRS Web site. In New Jersey, counselors work with both adults and students. For those in school, NJ DVRS offers a program for individuals who are looking to transition from school to work. "As for the age requirement to receive DVR assistance, you need to be fourteen to receive technical assistance, but you must be out of high school in order to begin receiving cost services or job search assistance. There is no maximum age to receive services, as long as the person is interested in working," Balke says.

If you are currently a student and are interested in working with a DVRS counselor, someone from your school district should arrange for a referral for services. However, the initial request for services can also be made by you, your parents, or even a counselor or caseworker.

Once you've met with a DVRS counselor, you will both "work on the plans in the transition part of the Individual Education Plan . . . or guidance plan," according to the DVRS Web site. Once you are ready, you and your counselor will develop an Individualized Plan for Employment (IPE), which highlights the steps and services you will need to get and maintain employment. After that, your counselor will continue to work with you until you are settled in a job.

"DVRS records are confidential," says Ferne Allen, supervising counselor at the DVRS office in Westampton, New Jersey. "Information is given out only with the participant's written consent, if required by law or for the safety and protection of the participant or others." Also, should a situation arise, "an appeal process is available to resolve any disagreements or concerns one may have regarding agency services," she says.

Modified Vehicles

"It would sure help out a lot if I had some kind of [vehicle] adaptations, because most days I can't drive my car because I'm too sore—and that's really frustrating, being seventeen and not being able to drive anywhere," says Kristen Delaney. "Plus, being young, my car isn't in the greatest condition to begin with, so the gears are sticky, the steering wheel is extremely difficult to turn, and putting the key in the ignition and twisting that key is terrible. It brings big pain every time I turn it on. It's even difficult just to climb in and out of my little '93 Saturn. [But] I don't have the money [to adapt my car], and I don't know where to find these modifications or what they even look like."

If you're like Kristen, then meeting with a vocational rehabilitation counselor is a good place to start. As discussed above, depending on your income, a counselor may be able to get you funding toward the purchase of modifications for a vehicle, if you are deemed unable to operate a regular car and need to drive in order to get to school or work.

"There are many options for the equipment needed to adapt a vehicle. The first step, however, is to have an evaluation and driving instruction with a certified driver rehabilitation specialist," says Craig Phillips, general manager of Accessible Vans & Mobility (AVM) in Cinnaminson, New Jersey. Driver rehabilitation specialists will evaluate your muscle strength,

JA AND DRIVING

By Kelly Rouba

I was diagnosed with a severe form of juvenile rheumatoid arthritis in 1982. At the time, I was just two years old. Because I was only treated with baby aspirin for many years after being diagnosed, the disease took quite a toll on my body. In fact, I began relying on a wheelchair to get around outside my home by the time I had reached middle school.

In spite of my physical limitations, my parents always supported my endeavors and I became especially creative at finding unique ways to accomplish my goals. As I approached "driving age" and watched all my friends begin taking driving lessons, I had no doubt that I would soon be joining them. So it came as a surprise when my parents said they didn't think I was capable. But it seemed they might be right when a driver evaluator who worked with people with disabilities at a local rehabilitation center didn't think she could accommodate me.

Fortunately, luck was on my side, and a wonderful counselor at our local office of the Division of Vocational Rehabilitation Services arranged for me to go through another driver evaluation program at a rehabilitation center in Pennsylvania called MossRehab, which had plenty of adaptive equipment to meet my special needs. Within no time, I was out cruising the streets in my neighborhood—and I got my license on the first try, too!

For the next ten years, I drove a modified van with a lift and a raised roof to accommodate my wheelchair. I also had extensions put on my gas and brake pedals so that I could reach them, because the arthritis has stunted my growth. The driver's seat also turned sideways so I could easily transfer from my wheelchair. In addition, the steering wheel was smaller in size and sat flat on the steering column (not upright); the mechanics even made it so there was little resistance when turning the wheel. Once situated, I hit a special panel of buttons on my right that operated the functions on the dashboard, because the horizontal steering column made it difficult to reach the dashboard.

In 2008 I finally got a new van. Due to some improvements in technology, I now drive a van with a lowered floor, a foldout ramp, and an upright steering wheel that is still small in size. I still have a seat that turns and pedal extensions, but I no longer need that special panel of buttons because I can reach the dashboard. While technology has certainly come a long way over the past ten years, I will never forget how much I loved getting my first set of "wheels" and the independence it gave me.

range of motion, coordination, reaction time, vision, and decision-making abilities, among other things.[7] If the specialist feels you are capable of driving, he or she will give a list of necessary vehicle modifications to your DVRS counselor.

AVM, which has several locations in New Jersey, New York, Delaware, and Pennsylvania, is just one of many vendors nationwide that modify all types of vehicles to meet customers' special needs. Some of the more common vehicle modifications requested by driver rehabilitation specialists include:

- *Hand controls.* If you have minimal strength in your legs, lever-like hand controls that operate the brake and gas pedals can be mounted by your steering wheel. Controls can even be ordered with foam grips and wrist supports so that you have better leverage and don't tire as easily while driving. Hand controls that resemble a game system joystick are also available and can be used not only for giving the car gas and applying the brake, but also for steering.

- *Custom steering wheels and steering columns.* There are a variety of special steering wheels available for use, including ones that are smaller in size and others that resemble a metal disk and are mounted flat (like a plate) on top of a horizontal steering column. Zero-effort steering is also available, which means there is little resistance when turning the wheel.

- *Steering controls.* Spinner knobs, hooks, or foam pin grips can be attached to your steering wheel so that you are able to get a firm grasp on the wheel, Phillips says. "When people are taught to drive, they are trained to use two hands to keep control of the vehicle. When one hand is responsible for a hand control, proper grip is a problem. A spinner knob would give the client more control of the steering wheel with one hand."

- *Foot controls.* A left-foot accelerator can be installed if you have trouble using your right leg. Also, a pedal guard can be installed to prevent you from accidentally hitting the right accelerator.

- *Pedal extensions.* If you are of short stature and have trouble reaching the gas and brake pedals, extensions of four to twelve inches can be mounted on the pedals so they are within your reach.

⊚ *Extension controls.* Handle-like extensions can also be applied to the parking brake, turn signal lever, and gearshift to make for easier reach and use.

⊚ *Voice control systems.* Simply put, upon speaking a command, the voice control system will carry it out. "Voice scan is a control system [designed] to operate primary and secondary controls. Primary controls include turn signals, horn, headlights, and cruise control. Secondary controls include power windows, HVAC controls, power locks, and fan speeds," Phillips says. "We can set it up to [operate] almost everything on the dashboard area as well as the mobility equipment if necessary. And if a client does not want to listen to the voice of a narrator speaking, we can change it to tones, like keys on a piano, instead."

⊚ *Command consoles.* Depending on your needs, command consoles can carry out virtually any function in your vehicle with just a simple touch of a button. Functions range from shifting gears to opening a window to turning on the radio.

⊚ *Lift or ramp.* If you use a wheelchair, a lift or foldout ramp can be installed so that you can easily get into the vehicle. You also have the option of driving from your wheelchair or transferring into the driver's seat.

⊚ *Transfer seat.* Driver's seats can be made to swivel, go back and forth, or even go up or down, depending upon your needs when transferring or driving. Some seats even extend outside the driver's side door if the driver needs easier access.

⊚ *Key adapter.* This device provides you with better leverage when starting your car.

"As you know, there is always tailoring of the equipment to meet the clients' needs to get them as comfortable driving as possible," Phillips says. "I have had prescriptions of driving aids that have been the same from one client to another, but yet after the custom tailoring to the vehicle, the completed jobs were very different. Most of the clients that also have limited movement in their necks will need additional visibility. So, in this case, we add mirrors to the vehicle to increase visibility."

Once you've met with a driver rehabilitation specialist, it is likely that DVRS will provide you with a list of approved vendors in your area that can make the necessary modifications to the vehicle you purchase. Companies like AVM are growing in number around the United States. When selecting a vendor, make sure the company is a member of the National Mobility Equipment Dealers Association (NMEDA) or a similar organization that ensures vendors follow standards for modifying vehicles.

If purchasing a modified vehicle proves too expensive for you, most communities offer accessible transportation at modest fees for individuals with disabilities. Accessible transportation options may include your local bus system or door-to-door transportation services that can accommodate even those who use a wheelchair or walker. If you request a personal transportation service, there may be a long waiting period before you get picked up due to the high volume of people reliant upon those services.

Unfortunately, if you are on a tight schedule or may get called into work unexpectedly, "the best option is to contact your local advocacy center and see what other funding resources are available" so that you can get your own vehicle modified, Phillips says. Your health insurance company may even cover vehicle modifications. And nowadays, many vehicle manufacturers offer special rebates to individuals purchasing modified vehicles.

Division of Disability Services

Many counties and states have a government office, department, or commission that you can contact to learn more about the variety of services (many of which foster independent living) and medical or financial aid that are available for people with all types of disabilities. According to Robles, "Most people call the New Jersey Division of Disability Services seeking information on housing, transportation, and employment—in that order."

However, no matter what the need, DDS staff are trained to handle all inquiries either by providing appropriate solutions or by referring the person with a disability or his or her family member to another agency that can address the matter at hand. DDS also publishes a free annual guide called *Resources*, which identifies most of the programs and services for people with disabilities who live in the state. You can contact your local office to get a copy of this guide.

Tom Shaw, director of the Mercer County Office for the Disabled in New Jersey, says that services offered on the county level also tend to vary depending upon where you live—if you have a local office or commission for the disabled. Offices typically offer a variety of services that promote independent living among people with disabilities, which can include:

- Information about and referral to various service providers
- Technical assistance
- Consumer advocacy
- Improving accessibility
- Information about the Americans with Disabilities Act (ADA)
- Therapeutic and educational services
- Occupational training and employment services
- Information on housing
- Recreational programming

Some county offices also arrange personal care assistance for individuals who need help with daily-living activities like grooming or light housekeeping. If this is a service you need, contact your county or state office to apply. If you are unsure whether your county or state has a Disability Services Department, contact your state's Department of Human Services or your governor's office.

NONPROFIT GROUPS

Arthritis Foundation

Throughout this book, a lot of information has been provided about the Arthritis Foundation's efforts to run programming, ranging from support groups to exercise classes, for individuals of all ages who suffer from arthritis. Established in 1948, the foundation also strives to create awareness of the disease and to raise funds for "the prevention, control, and cure of arthritis and related diseases."[8] To this end, the foundation supports research initiatives, hosts informational conferences, and pushes for the approval of public policies that would benefit people with arthritis. Staff from the foundation can also help you get in touch with other local health-related programs and services that you might need.

The New Jersey chapter of the Arthritis Foundation even has staff who give talks about juvenile arthritis at schools. If you are shy or don't like talking about your disease, perhaps you can ask someone from your local chapter to give a JA presentation at your school. This way, your classmates will learn about juvenile arthritis and better understand how it affects you. "Our school program includes an interactive lesson that will teach your students all about arthritis, including the fact that over three hundred thousand children in the United States have arthritis and how it affects them during school," says Andrea Mueller, who is a community manager for the chapter.

According to Yvonne Mendoza, the Greater Southwest Chapter has a similar program, called Arthritis Parents: Learning, Understanding, and Sharing (A-PLUS). A-PLUS was designed and developed by parents of children and teens with JA to help promote arthritis awareness in schools by educating staff and students about the effects of the disease. Furthermore, the Arthritis Foundation has a guide for teachers called *When Your Student Has Arthritis*, which can help to enlighten faculty about the disease if your chapter doesn't offer in-school programming. This guide can be ordered online at www.arthritis.org.

To learn more about the disease, many families also attend the foundation's annual National Juvenile Arthritis Conference. At the conference, you and your parents will be able to sit in on a variety of educational workshops that explore the latest medical advances in relation to the treatment of juvenile arthritis. These conferences are often attended by experts in the field of rheumatology, many of whom also give lectures at the event.

The conference also features fitness programs and educational sessions geared toward children, teens, and young adults. At the conference Amanda White attended with her mother, Diane, these ranged from tai chi to a workshop on alternative therapies to a panel discussion called "Future College and Career Planning." During some of the sessions, young people learn how to live a healthy lifestyle as well as ways to improve their communication skills with parents, teachers, and peers. And those who attend are able to meet with other youths who share similar experiences and may even be able to give you ideas on adapting your lifestyle. Sometimes, other children or teens with JA can become lifelong friends and provide support during times when you feel alone.

Events hosted by the Arthritis Foundation are usually open to anyone, but if you decide to become an official member (for a small donation), you will receive informative newsletters and *Arthritis Today* magazine, which shares useful tips, medical information, and personal stories about people who have learned to manage their arthritis.

Also, as mentioned earlier, the Juvenile Arthritis Alliance is a national council of the Arthritis Foundation. "[It's] a community of people who are interested in children with arthritis," Dr. Patience White says. You might want to consider getting involved with them or joining in on juvenile arthritis programs hosted by your local chapter of the Arthritis Foundation. "All chapters have a strong focus on JA-related programming," says Kimberly Thompson-Almanzor, former community manager with the New Jersey chapter of the Arthritis Foundation.

"The benefits of getting involved are being empowered to take more control of your arthritis or your child's arthritis, and to do so while networking with people who are going through the same struggles. Something like that is most powerful when you're volunteering or participating in programs with other families in the area."—Kimberly Thompson-Almanzor, former community manager with the New Jersey chapter of the Arthritis Foundation

Centers for Independent Living

Every state has Centers for Independent Living (CILs). Run mostly by people with disabilities, CILs are grassroots nonprofit organizations devoted to advocating for the rights and inclusion of individuals with all types of disabilities. Staff also work with people with disabilities to prepare them for living independently. Services offered at CILs are free and fall under four categories: information and referral, peer support, independent living skills training, and individual and systems advocacy.[9] The following is a breakdown of each subdivision:

- *Information and referral*. If you have a disability-related question, staff should be able to provide you with an answer or refer you to someone who can. CILs also make sure that "people with disabilities have access to information needed to achieve or maintain independence in their community."[10]

- *Peer support*. According to information on the National Council on Independent Living's Web site, "to preserve their integrity as grassroots organizations, CILs implement peer support to achieve objectives set by the disability community itself."[11]

- *Independent living skills training*. CILs rely on staff and peers in the community to provide training for people with disabilities so that they are able to live on their own. These individuals can give clients "information about affordable and accessible housing programs, accessible modifications to housing, funding for accessible modifications, and Fair Housing Rights," Wilks says. Staff can even help clients apply for benefits, like Social Security, and state social services programs. "Also, [we receive] a lot of requests for assistance with finding employment, applying for funding to start a small business, applying for vocational rehabilitation services, budgeting, transportation training, and finding health-care resources." Your local CIL might also be able to help make arrangements if you need personal care services on a daily basis. "This depends on what state the CIL is in and its funding sources," says Norman Smith, chair of the New Jersey Statewide Independent Living Council. Also, some CILs provide funding toward transportation or the purchase of a modified vehicle.

⊚ *Individual and systems advocacy.* **This includes providing "information about employment rights under the ADA and the Human Rights Commission, [as well as] information about reasonable accommodations, and how to file a complaint," Wilks says. Staff at your local CIL can even provide disability awareness training, or they can serve as an advocate when it comes to improving accessibility in your community or defending the rights of a person with a disability.**

CILs "are mandated to do advocacy as their primary mission and reason for being," Smith says.

Every CIL within a state is governed by a Statewide Independent Living Council (SILC), which creates a State Plan for Independent Living that contains goals and funding measures. Members of the state council also promote the development of their CILs by providing training for staff members, keeping them up-to-date on current disability-related issues and outlining plans to expand services. For more information or to find your local Center for Independent Living, visit www.ncil.org or call the National Council on Independent Living at (202) 207–0334.

Easter Seals

Established more than eighty-five years ago, Easter Seals is a nonprofit organization that "provides rehabilitative and therapeutic services to children and adults with disabilities [along with] a variety of support services to their families such as information on funding, community resources, and informational support groups," says Linda Rogers, vice president of programming for Easter Seals Arkansas.

In addition to Puerto Rico, Easter Seals is in every state with the exception of Mississippi. Although the services and programs offered vary from state to state, here is a general list of what Easter Seals provides:

⊚ *Medical rehabilitation.* **Through medical rehabilitation, professionals aim to prevent, diagnose, or treat individuals with disabilities so they are able to live more independently.**

Professionals also work with patients to restore loss of function. Medical services are typically funded by Medicare, Medicaid, or other state programs or public funding sources, as well as private insurance. To receive treatment, clients often go to an Easter Seals outpatient center, Easter Seals Child Development Center, or one of their adult day programs. Easter Seals also offers educational and prevention programming. In addition, Easter Seals Outpatient Therapy Services provides PT, OT, and speech therapy to children from birth to school age, as well as support services for their families.

◎ *Physical therapy.* By providing physical therapy services, Easter Seals hopes that it will preserve, maintain, or restore loss of function in individuals with disabilities that affect their mobility. Therapists also work to decrease pain and swelling. After an evaluation, physical therapists design an exercise treatment plan. During visits, therapists may introduce patients to mobility devices, like walkers or braces. They also often provide information on safety, health, and fitness. Services may be provided at an Easter Seals' outpatient clinic, Child Development Center, adult day program center, home, school, or elsewhere.

◎ *Occupational therapy.* Occupational therapists work to restore or increase function for individuals with mobility impairments so they are able to perform daily-living activities with greater ease. Patients may learn how to use assistive devices or be required to wear splints to preserve function. If you attend school or have a job, occupational therapists can also recommend ways to make certain activities easier for you to do. Services can be provided in the same locations as physical therapy, above.

◎ *Early intervention.* Related services promote cognitive, social, emotional, communicative, adaptive, and physical development in young children so they are able to better function or cope as they age. "These services are covered for children ages zero up to age three years," says Ellen Harrington-Kane, assistant vice president of autism and medical rehabilitation for Easter Seals, Inc. Overall, "there are fourteen core services and each child is assessed to determine [his or her] need."

- ◎ *Workforce development.* "Employment provides the opportunity to participate as a member of a community," Harrington-Kane says. "Easter Seals job-training and employment services help people with disabilities learn skills to successfully enter the workforce, or to return to work after an illness or injury." Easter Seals also helps individuals with disabilities like juvenile arthritis learn ways to adapt their work environment in order to make tasks easier. All of these services are available to those who are newly diagnosed and are looking to reenter the workplace. For example, according to Rogers, Easter Seals Arkansas "provides center-based services to adults, ages twenty-one years or older, or [those who] graduated from public school and who have a developmental disability. Each adult has individual goals and objectives, which are worked on in a classroom/training setting. The adults may work on jobs at the center or in the community."

- ◎ *Adult development services and adult day services.* Easter Seals adult day services offer choices for young adults with disabilities like arthritis who need a safe, supervised social daytime setting. Easter Seals adult daytime care services provide younger adults with disabilities appropriate support and a chance to live satisfying lives in their communities. Whether through birth conditions, accidents, or chronic illness, many young adults and their families benefit from Easter Seals adult day services. Some young adults join Easter Seals adult day programs as they transition from school to community-based services. Center-based adult day services provide therapeutic programming for individuals eighteen and older who have a physical disability or social or cognitive impairment and need some assistance with activities of daily living, like bathing, dressing, or eating. Programs also offer a break for family caregivers.

- ◎ *Camping and recreation.* Because statistics show that people with disabilities are not as likely to socialize as those who don't have a disability, Easter Seals runs a variety of on-site recreational programs and community outings to promote fun and foster independence. Examples of some recreational activities include holiday parties, picnics, and fishing trips. Easter Seals also has 140 accessible camping sites nationwide where youth can visit for the day or stay

overnight, and they even offer weekend and after-school programs. Activities range from boating to swimming to arts and crafts.[12]

There is no income requirement necessary to receive any of the services listed above. Also, "we do assist people in applying for funding options under Medicaid and state funding to help with payment for services," Rogers says. For more information on Easter Seals, call (800) 221–6827 or visit www.easterseals.com.

ADJUSTING AT SCHOOL

If you are of school age, it's important to know that the law dictates that all children with disabilities, including juvenile arthritis, have a right to receive a free appropriate public education. In fact, Section 504 of the Rehabilitation Act, which is a civil rights law, "bans discrimination against disabled persons in programs that receive federal funds and allows for accommodations to be made in school programs."[13] The Americans with Disabilities Act also requires private schools to be accessible. To ensure that you have the best experience possible while attending school, it's best that you and your parents or guardians schedule a meeting with school officials to discuss any special needs you have in order to see how they can be met during school hours.

A federal education law known as the Individuals with Disabilities Education Act (IDEA) requires public school districts to evaluate students to determine whether they are eligible to receive special education services. Depending on which state you live in, these evaluators may be referred to by various group

AMERICANS WITH DISABILITIES ACT HOTLINE

If you have questions relating to the Americans with Disabilities Act or would like to request informational materials, call (800) 514–0301. This toll-free information line is operated by the U.S. Department of Justice.

"When a student is diagnosed with arthritis, yes, they should notify the school, especially the school nurse and guidance counselor. With written information from the physician, [staff] can implement a plan to accommodate the student."—Linda Dandrow, nurse, Ponaganset High School, Rhode Island

names. For example, in New Jersey they are part of the Child Study Team, whereas in New York they are known as a Committee on Special Education (CSE) team.

After students are evaluated, a determination is made as to whether they are eligible for services and, if so, an Individualized Education Program (IEP) is developed. "The term IEP is utilized nationally. It differs from a Section 504 Accommodation Plan [in that] an IEP is a document that states what services and supports will be provided to a student who is eligible for special education services and it is required by the IDEA. A 504 Accommodation Plan also states what supports or services a student will receive, but it is for a student who does not meet the criteria of eligibility for special education services and it is required by Section 504 of the Rehabilitation Act of 1973," explains Carolyn Hayer, director of parent and professional development for the Statewide Parent Advocacy Network in New Jersey.

"The primary difference between the two is IDEA provides for special education services above, beyond, or different than what everyone else gets and it is based on the unique and individual needs of the classified student. Section 504 provides for access to general education services—the same program that everyone else has, but if a disability limits or prevents access, then 504 provides the services needed for the student to gain access; it does not provide for more or different educational programming. This is an important distinction for teens and young adults because IDEA covers students through age twenty-one and not beyond; Section 504 covers for a lifetime. The biggest impact is on students with disabilities who may want to attend college. There is no IEP for college students; however, they can have a 504 Accommodation Plan," says Hayer.

Whether you qualify for assistance under the IEP or Section 504 Accommodation Plan, such an arrangement can include anything from allowing you extra time to get to classes to providing an aide to assist you in moving from class to class if you have a wheelchair or need help carrying books. Or, if hallways are crowded, an aide or even a classmate might be assigned to walk with you to prevent you from getting bumped or knocked into.

If you need additional time when it comes to taking tests or doing assignments, that can be incorporated into the plan too. "I have extra time on tests . . . because when I'm taking a test, [my hands] cramp up," says Allyson Shapiro, who attends a private school. She also plans to ask for additional time to take her SATs.

Sometimes teachers will even give you an extra set of books—one set for school and one for home—so you don't have to carry a heavy book bag every day. However, if you do have to carry heavy textbooks or class projects, remember to use your bigger joints to bear the weight.

School staff also need to know which students have disabilities in case of an emergency. "You could always have fire drills and bomb scares, so you've got to think of that and design an evacuation plan accordingly," says Linda Dandrow, a school nurse. At the school where she works, there is a wheelchair on both floors of the building in case of an

Carry textbooks using your bigger joints to bear the weight.

emergency. If a student with a disability has difficulty walking at times, he or she is allowed to borrow the wheelchair. Allyson's school has an elevator that is typically off-limits to students, but she was granted permission to use it so she doesn't have to climb steps.

If your arthritis is severe, you might not necessarily have to take physical education classes, provided you have a doctor's note, Dandrow notes. "I don't take gym," Allyson says. "I had to get out of it [because of my arthritis], so I had my doctors [write a] note."

Depending on your condition, a doctor might write a note that excuses you only from certain physical activities so that you can still partake in the class and get some exercise. Also, some schools will make arrangements so that students with disabilities receive what is known as adaptive physical education in a private or small group setting. "We do have a physical therapist who comes in to work with some students," Dandrow adds.

Some teens with juvenile arthritis, like Allyson, have eliminated certain foods from their diets in order to keep inflammation down. When creating a plan with school officials, make sure to let them know if you have any special dietary needs or allergies. Depending on the type of school you attend and "how specialized the diet is, the student might have to bring their lunch in from home," Dandrow says. "We have several students on special diets and they bring their own food. I have a microwave that one student heats his meals in. Our school kitchen provides nourishing food and does not use peanuts because of allergies, but because of having to prepare large quantities for students, staff do not prepare specific, individualized meals."

Aside from making the school aware of your dietary needs, you must also inform them about any medication you will need during the day or at times when your arthritis flares up. "Then the parents have to deliver the medicine to the school along with a doctor's note saying how much to take and when," Dandrow says. "In Rhode Island, only a nurse can pass out medication, so they would have to get to my office to take it.

Students are not allowed to carry it around on their own and take it on their own." You should ask your school for its policy on taking medicine during school hours, since it may vary.

Most often, Dandrow finds that students take their medicine at home at breakfast and again at dinner, so they might only need to take one dose at lunchtime. "What the kids usually do is come down on their lunch period so they are not interrupting an academic setting," Dandrow says. However, students are always allowed to come to the nurse's office for medicine when they are having a problem, like a flare or a headache.

ADVOCATING FOR ASSISTANCE AT SCHOOL

Sometimes it may take a bit of effort to get your school to accommodate your needs. Therefore, you will need to learn to advocate for yourself. However, don't hesitate to turn to organizations, like the ones listed below, for guidance.

Parent Training and Information Centers

Each state has a Parent Training and Information Center (PTI), which is governed by the National Technical Assistance Alliance of Parent Centers. The national office can provide you with information on IDEA, special education, and other disability-related topics. For more information or to contact your local PTI, visit www.taalliance.org.

Association on Higher Education and Disability (AHEAD)

To learn about this association, which is committed to the full participation of persons with disabilities in postsecondary education, visit www.ahead.org.

Kids as Self Advocates (KASA)

This national advocacy group teaches youth about their rights, provides peer support, and training, and advocates for inclusion in schools, communities, and places of employment. For more information, visit www.fvkasa.org.

When it comes to getting an education, the Arthritis Foundation recommends meeting with school officials on an annual basis in order to update any changes in terms of what accommodations you need. You might want to do this before the beginning of each new school year to make the transition into a new grade level go as smoothly as possible.

When Amanda was officially diagnosed with JIA, "it was pretty late in her freshman year, so I only talked to her dean so that her final exams were taken care of in terms of giving her more time to take the test. Her sophomore year, I became the best of friends with the school nurse and she communicated to Amanda's teachers what her needs were," says her mother, Diane. In fact, the school nurse even provided faculty with informational materials on juvenile arthritis.

"During Amanda's junior and senior years, I met with all of her teachers to explain the disease. In hindsight, I should have done this at the beginning of her sophomore year as well. Because of the lack of physical symptoms, I am not sure her teachers understood what she was going through," Diane adds.

The Whites' decision to send Amanda to a private school was ultimately because staff were willing to meet her needs without having to develop an IEP for her, as is required in public schools. "That was the advantage of a private school; they were able to be more flexible with her. The public school wanted to classify her [as a student with special needs] in order to give her extra time for assignments, tests, time off for doctor visits, etc. And they would have also provided additional

PLANNING AHEAD

Always plan ahead the night before in terms of what you will need for the next day—whether it's clothes or making sure your homework assignments are completed and packed in your book bag. Getting ready for school in the mornings usually requires extra time when you have a mobility impairment, since it often takes longer to do things.

services that we didn't think were necessary, such as an aide to carry her backpack or take notes. We chose a private school to keep Amanda mainstreamed," Diane explains.

"The private school we chose allowed extra time [for tests and assignments] and the teachers provide extra help for all of the kids pretty regularly," says Diane. "Amanda has taken advantage of that time with teachers when necessary. I also e-mail all of her teachers and the nurse whenever she has a flare-up and Amanda learned to advocate for herself as time went on."

No matter if you attend a public or private school, don't be afraid to express your needs. There is no reason to struggle through the school day, which can cause your work to suffer.

Getting Through the Day

Even if you're not involved in extracurricular activities, the regular school day can seem very long, especially if you have arthritis. And since most of the day is spent sitting at your desk, it's easy to become stiff rather quickly. When your body is inactive, you may also feel restless. So to help you get through the school day—or work day, for that matter—here are a few tips:

- Maintain proper posture. Keep your back straight and your feet flat on the floor. Use a footrest if your feet are dangling or your back feels strained.

- Sit on a cushion to avoid getting pressure sores from sitting constantly.

- Volunteer to write on the blackboard or to hand out papers whenever possible so you get a chance to loosen up your joints.

- Eat a healthy breakfast to get yourself energized for the day ahead. At lunch, eat something healthy to reenergize your body. If you buy lunch, carry your tray using your forearms or ask someone else to bring it to the table for you.

- If you are allowed to go outside during lunch or at other times throughout the day, go out for some fresh air instead of staying inside.

◎ When you get home, have a healthy snack and unwind a bit before beginning homework.

◎ Go to bed early so you are refreshed when morning comes.[14]

HOMESCHOOLING AS AN ALTERNATIVE

The onset of juvenile arthritis can be a painful experience for many teens. Sometimes the disease itself flares up or the medications prescribed to treat it present complications. In either case, there are times when some teens with arthritis become too ill to physically attend school. If that happens, a teen's physician can write a letter to school administrators requesting that he or she temporarily receive schooling at home or even in a rehabilitation setting, Dandrow says.

Some families may choose to have a child homeschooled permanently. In this case, Stefanie's mother says, a doctor's note is not necessary. "You do not need a doctor's note to homeschool your children," Kathy says. "Some districts, due to political reasons and losing tax dollars, will try and make the withdrawal of a student difficult, but you do not have to get permission to remove a specific student from his or her school. A parent has the right to choose what school, whether private or public, to utilize for a formal education. However, some counties try to get involved when a child or teen is being removed from a public school. [If that is the case], making sure that the family has [selected] a good [homeschool] program that is accredited is helpful before withdrawing the child from the public school so that proof of enrollment can be presented at the time of removal."

Kathy decided to take Stefanie out of public school and enroll her in an independent study program after they moved to California. She made this decision because she didn't feel their local public schools could accommodate her daughter's special needs, and getting through the school day became too difficult for Stefanie. "[It] would exhaust her sitting at a desk with thirty-five to forty students, and the daily routine did not make her a productive student," she recalls.

"[A]t the age of seven, when Stefanie tried [attending] the California public school and they ended up having three to four recesses each day, with the heat and sun, it did not appeal to Stefanie's daily function," Kathy says. "It was determined she needed an alternative type of learning environment. Not only did they not provide the 'special education' as established in Minnesota, but [the school system] could not provide a conducive environment for her limitations. Even [when we lived] in Minnesota, having her bundle up in a snowsuit and sit on the bus for an hour and a half every day was limiting to her. The bus driver would honk her horn so we could go out and carry Stefanie off the bus if she couldn't get her body to work after the long ride."

Moreover, at times, "Stefanie would miss school due to pain, fatigue, and illness and the school would not accept the absences. Their absence policies did not cater to children with health issues, which was very discouraging for Stefanie," Kathy says.

In 1997 Stefanie began the independent study program and received instruction in her home and at a local academic center. "It was determined early on that the public schools Stefanie attended were not set up for a student with her form of limitations," Kathy says. "It took us a few steps to determine the appropriate independent learning program for Stefanie. We chose the Alexandria Academy, which has students all over the United States. Dr. Stacey McEnnan was an amazing educator in making school for a homebound student fun and successful. Her program offered the alternative to public education for Stefanie."

According to Kathy, "With the independent study program, she could learn in any environment we selected. [The program consists of] one or two two-hour sessions with her teacher and one day each week for two and a half hours of an honors class with other students. Stefanie could also choose [to do] activities at the library, museums, and other sources because she wasn't having to attend a public school five days per week."

If you are having difficulty attending school because of your arthritis, you and your parents might want to look into the availability and types of homeschool or independent study programs near you. There are many different programs to select from. "We chose the independent study program because the curriculum catered to the needs of the student," says Kathy.

Kathy and Stefanie feel that homeschool or independent study programs are usually very accommodating toward individuals with special needs and that they are individually geared to the needs of those students. "Homeschooling is not for everyone, but for a young person living with a disability, homeschooling can be the answer," Stefanie says. "It helped me focus on subjects that were not my strongest and go further on ones I was dying to learn more about. Having a strong support system is the key, though."

Kathy adds, "I also believe that depending on the program, a student can be empowered with this type of experience. Depending on the teacher and the program, the students end up having a more successful and positive educational experience. I know that we did."

TRANSITIONING TO COLLEGE

If you're nearing the end of your high school years, you are probably starting to think about going to college. While it is exciting to imagine what lies ahead, transitioning from high school to a college campus can be overwhelming.

Amanda and Kristen know the feeling. In 2008 both girls toured several colleges to see which would be the best fit for them. According to Amanda's mother, Diane, nearby "access to a hospital and rheumatologist, as well as access to a nurse for Amanda's injections" were major factors in determining which colleges she applied to.

Amanda says she also looked at the reputation of the local hospital and rheumatologist. "I am definitely looking forward to [being treated at] better medical facilities. Hopefully, if I attend a school with a hospital nearby, I won't have to drive [far] like I do now to see my rheumatologist. Also, I am happy that most colleges have good workout facilities. Right now, I have to drive thirty minutes to get to my gym." Amanda eventually decided to attend the University of Richmond in Virginia.

When deciding what college to attend, having a reputable hospital and rheumatologist nearby are certainly two things to consider. What type of gym or exercise equipment the school has on-site are some other things to keep in mind so that you are able to continue your workout routine. Here are a few other things to check out when touring colleges that interest you:

- **How large is the campus?** Many colleges have buildings spread out over a vast area, and you may be required to walk long distances to get from one class to another. At some city colleges, you need to take a bus to get from one academic building to another. If you are interested in a college that has a large campus, find out if your classes will be concentrated in one building or if they can be scheduled close to each other.

- **What is the student/teacher ratio?** Some colleges hold classes with many students, and it's easy to be overlooked. If you have special needs, consider attending a college that has smaller class sizes, making it easier for professors to become familiar with their students.

- **What is a typical schedule like for a first-year student?** Find out if freshmen have some flexibility in planning their schedule. Since colleges usually hold classes from early in the morning into the night, you want to be sure you're not running to classes sporadically. Some schools will allow students with disabilities to set up their schedules before other students; this way, you can schedule your classes together and at times that are the most convenient, based on your needs.

- **Are you required to live on campus?** Some colleges require students to live on campus during their first year. If you have special needs or must visit your doctor routinely, this might not be an option for you. However, you can inquire as to whether an exception could be made for you.

- **Is the college considered a "commuter" or "suitcase" school?** Many colleges have a large number of students who come to campus only when they have a scheduled class, or who stay during the week and then head home on weekends. You might find commuting easier if you have certain needs that would make living away from home difficult. If you are interested in commuting, you might want to consider schools that have a lot of commuter students so that you don't feel as if you are missing out on college life.

- What kind of health care is available? If you decide to live on campus (especially at a college far away from home), it's important to know whether health care is available on-site and what hours it's available. You never know when an emergency might arise.

- Is there a buddy system? Some colleges pair new students up with an upperclassman. This person can make suggestions that might help you adjust to college life more easily, and let you know where to get assistance if you need it.

- Perhaps most important, does the college have a Disability Services Department? While it may go by another name, depending on the school, many colleges have a department dedicated to meeting the needs of students with disabilities. Before touring a college campus, ask to meet with someone from Disability Services. Explain what accommodations you will need and see if they can be met. Make sure to get this signed in writing, as some colleges don't always come through, despite what they promise.

Stefanie began attending Santa Monica College (SMC) in California in 2007. She encountered a few obstacles in the beginning, but found that staff from Disability Services were quick to help smooth things out. "The first major issue was during the enrollment process, due to the large campus and many administrative buildings on different ends of this vast campus," her mother says. "This amazingly huge campus continues to provide a challenge for Stefanie. During the enrollment process, being sent to and from many different buildings due to inaccurate information was frustrating and energy depleting for her. However, always up for a challenge, the Disability Services department made up for the challenges that she encountered during the enrollment process. We are very, very blessed to have the staff that SMC has."

Stefanie agrees. "Everyone within the college's disability program has been very helpful. I started out with a meeting and they were able to provide me with a slip to give to each one of my teachers to sign so I could take all of my tests at a different location allowing me with time and a half," she says.

Aside from having arthritis, Stefanie is also dyslexic, and Disability Services was willing to accommodate her needs stemming from that as well. "The women I met with [from Disability Services] provided me with many recommendations and helpful solutions for my first semester. Most of the things at the disability center helped me with my dyslexia," she says. "I was also able to go to a facility where someone could put my textbooks on tape. The disability center has classes and programs I can use at their facility as well."

TIP

If you are not yet in college and plan to pursue higher education, there are many scholarships out there for people with disabilities. Ask your guidance counselor to help you determine what is available, or search the Internet to learn more.

The help from Disability Services staff members made Stefanie's transition from being homeschooled to attending college go quite smoothly. "I believe that Stefanie's first semester success was mainly because of the Disability Services department, wonderful teachers, and the program of SMC," says Kathy.

TRANSITIONING FROM A PEDIATRIC TO AN ADULT RHEUMATOLOGIST

"I just switched from a pediatric rheumatologist to a regular rheumatologist," says Kristen. Because she had to drive about four hours away to see her pediatric rheumatologist in Omaha, she and her mother decided to starting seeing an adult rheumatologist in her own town.

"I actually didn't want to switch, because I liked my pediatric rheumatologist . . . [but] I was just old enough and I knew I was getting to the point where I was going to have to switch to a regular rheumatologist anyway," Kristen says. She plans to visit her new doctor about once a month.

According to Dr. White, by the age of seventeen, individuals with juvenile arthritis should be managing their own health care. She feels that switching to an adult rheumatologist at that time allows for more age-appropriate and preventative care.

Dr. Randy Cron also believes that those with arthritis should start to take control of their own health care around the end of their teenage years, if they are physically and emotionally ready. "This depends on the individual child. Some are mature enough to transition at eighteen years and some are not. Some transition at twenty-one years and beyond, but this is not ideal for all involved. The sooner the better if a child is able to manage their own care, including knowing [about] and taking their own medicines. Teenagers who go off to college away from home should definitely transition to an adult rheumatologist near their campus."

Shaun-Marie Robbins was closer to Kristen's age when she transitioned. "I switched to an adult doctor when I was fifteen. At that point, I didn't need any sort of treatment," says Shaun-Marie, who was in remission at the time. "I had anti-inflammatories on hand in case of any flare-ups, but I had them few and far between."

One of the best times to transition to an adult rheumatologist is when your condition is stable, as Shaun-Marie did. However, if you feel your current rheumatologist is not managing your care well, you might need to switch to another doctor, whether a pediatric or adult rheumatologist, sooner.

Tips on Finding a Rheumatologist

Depending on which state you live in, rheumatologists can be hard to come by. In a number of states, "it is very hard to find a rheumatologist, but even more difficult for youth to find a pediatric rheumatologist," Kristen says.

Figure 8.1. Dr. Alexander Carney with author Kelly Rouba, former Ms. Wheelchair NJ, at the 2007 Mercer County Arthritis Walk. Dr. Carney, who practices rheumatology in Mercerville, New Jersey, manned the Arthritis Answers booth at the 2007 and 2008 walks.

Recently, Kristen had the opportunity to view a map pinpointing office locations of all the adult and pediatric rheumatologists in the country. "If you look at the map, there are very few pediatric rheumatologists, especially on the west side of the United States. A lot of people have to drive out-of-state to get to a rheumatologist, especially a pediatric rheumatologist," she says. Dr. Marisa Klein-Gitelman adds, "We see several hundred patients as a group. There are not that many pediatric rheumatologists in Chicago."

According to the Health Resources and Services Administration, which falls under the U.S. Department of Health and Human Services, "multiple studies have demonstrated that the number and distribution of pediatric rheumatologists in the United States is not sufficient to provide patient care to all children with rheumatic diseases. At a minimum, the number of pediatric rheumatologists needs to increase from the current number of 192–200 to a minimum of 331–337 to achieve comparable provider to patient ratios across the States."[15]

ADVOCACY MATTERS: VOLUNTEER SPIRIT
By Lauren Danker, tenth grader

Excerpted from Arthwritings, Arthritis Foundation, Maryland Chapter, 2006. Copies of this newsletter can be obtained at www.arthritis.org/chapters/maryland.

Every time I attend an arthritis event, I am reminded of how many other people share my disease. In addition to adults, there are lots of children that are stricken with arthritis. Many were misdiagnosed or not given treatment initially, leading to many months or years lost. Some kids need to travel great distances just to have appointments with their rheumatologists, which makes me realize how fortunate I am to have one just minutes away. The medications are expensive and I've talked to kids that don't have insurance to cover all the costs.

Much needs to be done—we need more doctors to specialize in pediatric rheumatology and more money for research. Our government can and should help and that's why 250 of us headed to Washington, DC. In my AP government classes, we learned about the difficult process for bills to become laws (over 4,000 bills are introduced in every two-year Congress). Since the Arthritis Foundation has introduced H.R. 583 and S. 424, I thought I'd help spread the word to my representatives that this bill needs to get passed. (The last bill passed for arthritis was 1979.) We need more funding to continue to develop drugs like Enbrel (the one I take) and to help support medical students considering rheumatology as a specialty.

If you are not yet seeing a rheumatologist or if you want to switch to a different doctor or simply get a second opinion on your condition, you might start by asking your primary care physician or a representative from the local chapter of the Arthritis Foundation to refer you to a rheumatologist. Kathy says the Arthritis Foundation is a great resource because staff know the reputation of area rheumatologists.

You can also find a qualified rheumatologist by visiting the American College of Rheumatology's Web site at www.rheumatology.org. Once there, click on "Find a Rheumatologist" and conduct a search by location.

BOOKS WORTH READING

Taking Arthritis to School, by Dee Dee L. Miller and Tom Dineen
Toolbox of Hope—For When Your Body Doesn't Feel Good, by
   Deva Joy Gouss
Juvenile Arthritis, by Judith Peacock
*Nicole's Story: A Book about a Girl with Juvenile Rheumatoid
   Arthritis*, by Virginia Tortorica Aldape and Lillian S. Kossacoff

NOTES

1. Arthritis Foundation, *Arthritis in Children* (pamphlet, 2004), 28.

2. Ibid., 28.

3. Ibid., 29.

4. U.S. Department of Health and Human Services, Insure Kids Now, www.insurekidsnow.gov.

5. Arthritis Foundation, *Arthritis in Children*, 30.

6. State of New Jersey, Department of Labor and Workforce Development. "Services for Individuals for Disabilities." http://lwd.dol.state.nj.us/labor/dvrs/disabled/DisIndex.html.

7. National Highway Traffic Safety Administration, U.S. Department of Transportation, *Adapting Motor Vehicles For People With Disabilities* (pamphlet, July 2002), 4.

8. Arthritis Foundation, *Arthritis in Children*, 31.

9. National Council on Independent Living, "Centers for Independent Living," www.ncil.org/about/CentersforIndependentLiving.html.

10. Ibid.

11. Ibid.

12. Easter Seals, "The Story of Easter Seals," www.easterseals.com/site/PageServer?pagename=ntl_wwa_we_are&s_esLocation=wwa.

13. Arthritis Foundation, *Arthritis in Children*, 28.

14. Joyce L. Falco et al., *JRA & Me: A Fun Workbook* (Denver, CO: Rocky Mountain Juvenile Arthritis Center at the National Jewish Center and the Arthritis Foundation, 1987), 89–91.

15. U.S. Department of Health and Human Services, *The Pediatric Rheumatology Workforce: A Study of the Supply and Demand for Pediatric Rheumatologists*, http://bhpr.hrsa.gov/healthworkforce/reports/ped_rheumatology/6.htm.

9 Looking Toward the Future

If you're like many people living with a chronic illness, you want to know when there will be a cure—or at least more advanced treatment options that will make you feel better more quickly. In fact, it's a subject that's probably never far from the forefront of your mind.

"There are a whole host of things people [with arthritis] worry about," Dr. Patience White says. "They worry about their future; they worry about which drugs they have to take. The good news is, we have a lot of excellent treatments. People with arthritis do extremely well and can lead normal lives."

As discussed in chapter 4, that wasn't always the case. Fortunately, a lot of progress has been made in terms of treating the disease. "Today, the treatments are very different than they used to be and have clearly made a difference in the [well-being] of someone with arthritis," Dr. White says.

Well, maybe not *so* long. Currently, there are many scientific researchers affiliated with universities, drug companies, and research facilities worldwide who are working diligently to find better treatments and even a cure for juvenile arthritis. "I think we're looking at an unbelievably bright future for children who have arthritis," Dr. White says.

RESEARCH GROUPS

While there are numerous entities spearheading arthritis-related research, here are just a few of the key players, aside from drug companies.

Dr. Stanley Cohen, associate director of the Division of Rheumatology at University of Texas Southwestern Medical Center–University Hospitals, wrote in an article that "the last decade could be characterized as the 'Golden Age of Rheumatoid Arthritis (RA) Therapeutics.' Based on discoveries from the 1980–90s, therapies such as the TNF inhibitors were developed that targeted proteins that are critically involved in the ongoing joint inflammation. The treatment shift has been described as a shift from 'empirical' therapies that we, as rheumatologists, borrowed from other specialties, such as methotrexate, to the era of 'targeted' therapies based on a better understanding of the immune system abnormalities occurring in RA."[1]

"If you look at the advancements in medicine, the past five years alone have been amazing. But medicine still has a long way to go so we can live pain free."—Kristen, age seventeen

National Institute of Arthritis and Musculoskeletal and Skin Diseases (NIAMS)

The NIAMS is one of a number of institutes governed by the National Institutes of Health, which is an agency of the U.S.

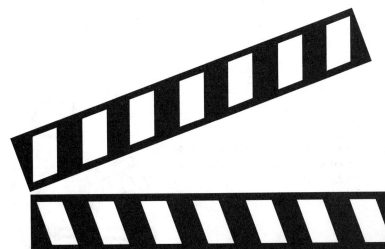

WAKING UP—A DOCUMENTARY ON JUVENILE ARTHRITIS

Recognizing that little programming on JA exists, Agency New Jersey, a photo agency that covers news, current events, and issues locally and globally happening in or related to New Jersey, has begun filming a full-length documentary in an effort to fill that void and create awareness of the disease. Tentatively called *Waking Up*, it will give viewers an inside look at the disease by focusing on what youth with JA deal with on a daily basis. Viewers will see stories, including personal struggles and triumphs, that bring this issue to light in a very human and profound way. They will also learn about the work and research being done to treat the disease while seeing the widespread effects of the individuals and various organizations fighting to educate and comfort those with juvenile arthritis.

Through this documentary, Agency New Jersey hopes that people will begin to understand what it is like for those living with JA. Families dealing with JA will also see that they are not alone in their struggles and that help is out there. For existing and potential donors, the filmmakers hope that the documentary will show the need for funding. For legislators and voters, *Waking Up* will show the immediacy and importance of JA and give it a human face, thereby increasing awareness in those who have control over state and federal budgeting and funding. For more information on the documentary or on Agency New Jersey, visit www.agencynewjersey.com.

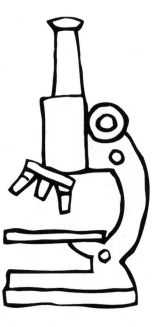

Scientists are working hard to find new treatments for juvenile arthritis.

Department of Health and Human Services. NIAMS was established in 1986 thanks to the successful lobbying efforts of the Arthritis Foundation, which continues to urge Congress for additional funding in support of NIAMS on an annual basis. To date, NIH is the largest supporter of arthritis research.[2]

NIAMS is headquartered in Bethesda, Maryland. Its mission is "to support research into the causes, treatment, and prevention of arthritis and musculoskeletal and skin diseases, the training of basic and clinical scientists to carry out this research, and the dissemination of information on research progress in these diseases."[3] Presently, NIAMS "supports and conducts basic, clinical, and epidemiologic research [as well as] research training at universities and medical centers" nationwide.[4]

Since its inception, NIAMS and the Arthritis Foundation have worked together on a number of initiatives. In February 2005 the foundation signed a memorandum pledging nearly $500,000 "to fund new genetic research that could revolutionize the way in which rheumatoid arthritis is diagnosed and treated."[5] Furthermore, NIAMS has been working in conjunction with the North American Rheumatoid Arthritis Consortium (NARAC), which is a group of researchers looking to identify the genetic factors that contribute to rheumatoid arthritis. So far, NARAC and other researchers "have identified a genetic region associated with increased risk of rheumatoid arthritis."[6]

Genetic research, however, is just one of a long list of initiatives NIAMS has undertaken. To learn more about NIAMS or current research findings and studies, visit www.niams.nih.gov/Research.

American Autoimmune Related Diseases Association, Inc. (AARDA)

Founded in 1991, AARDA is a national health agency devoted to eradicating autoimmune diseases like rheumatoid arthritis, lupus, Crohn's disease, scleroderma, Sjögren's syndrome, Raynaud's phenomenon, and uveitis, among many others. In order to advance its mission, AARDA conducts educational programming on various diseases and provides funding towards research.

Because autoimmunity is the second cause of chronic illness, AARDA "supports basic autoimmune research, which will have impact on multiple autoimmune diseases by identifying the mechanism that initiates the autoimmune response which triggers all autoimmune diseases."[7]

Among its research-related initiatives, AARDA spearheaded and provided funding toward the establishment of the Autoimmune Research Center at Johns Hopkins University Medical Center. Since its founding, the association has supported research initiatives at the center, as well as at other research institutes.

Furthermore, AARDA advocates on behalf of all individuals suffering from autoimmune diseases at both the state and federal level. AARDA also offers patient services, which include providing health information and referrals, to those in need.

AARDA, which is headquartered in Detroit, Michigan, is a certified member of the National Health Council. The association relies on public donations and grants to carry out much of its work. For more information about AARDA's services or on current research, call (800) 598–4668 or visit www.aarda.org.

Arthritis National Research Foundation (ANRF)

In 1970 "a corporate board of community individuals came together to provide grants to further research in arthritis," says executive director Helene Belisle. The organization they governed became known as the Arthritis National Research Foundation, which continues to have as its sole focus the funding of arthritis-related research projects.

Based in Long Beach, California, ANRF now comprises a board of directors, an advisory board, and a scientific advisory board. All year long, board members and volunteers, many of whom are researchers or have a form of arthritis, help to secure funds so that grants can be awarded on an annual basis to highly qualified researchers associated with nonprofit research facilities, universities, and hospitals throughout the country. In fact, "ninety-one cents of every dollar raised directly supports research," Belisle notes.

Each year, ANRF funds between twelve and twenty research projects. In 2007 they awarded a total of $650,000 to thirteen scientists. Moreover, since the year 2000 ANRF has awarded more than $4.3 million in grants to support arthritis research. And "95 percent of the scientists ANRF has funded over the years have remained in the arthritis research field," Belisle adds.

All ANRF grant recipients work on projects aimed at preventing, treating, or curing rheumatoid arthritis, osteoarthritis (the breakdown of joint tissue caused by wear and tear, which comes with aging), and other related autoimmune diseases. However, in order to receive funding in support of its initiatives, researchers must be selected by ANRF's scientific advisory board, which comprises world-renowned doctors and research scientists. During the selection process, members of the board conduct a rigorous peer review of all grant applications to ensure that recipients are, indeed, performing cutting-edge arthritis research under optimal lab conditions at nonprofit research universities and facilities. "Our grant review process is the same every year," Belisle says. "We want to fund the top people working at the top places on a project that has the best hope for the future."

To learn more about the Arthritis National Research Foundation and projects it funds, call (800) 588–2873 or visit www.curearthritis.org.

Childhood Arthritis & Rheumatology Research Alliance (CARRA)

Since it was established, the Arthritis Foundation has given more than $320 million toward research.[8] One research group the foundation supports is the Childhood Arthritis & Rheumatology Research Alliance. Comprised of pediatric rheumatologists from North America, CARRA aims to "foster, facilitate, and conduct high quality clinical research in the field of pediatric rheumatology" in order to improve the health of those children living with rheumatic diseases.[9]

CARRA is made up of several committees, which are governed by a steering committee with members from ten pediatric rheumatology research centers located in the United States and Canada. According to CARRA's Web site, the organization's vision is to "provide mechanisms whereby:

1. **All children with rheumatic disease have an opportunity to enter protocols of high clinical relevance and impact.**

2. **Translational and basic scientists working in the area of pediatric rheumatology are facilitated in the acquisition of biologic specimens and clinical data through the alliance."[10]**

To carry out its objectives, CARRA established, beginning in 2001, "a multi-center network of pediatric rheumatology research centers across North America that is working together on investigations. Such collaboration increases the number of children who participate in studies and reduces the research time it takes to reach valuable conclusions."[11] Most of the research is centered on juvenile arthritis, pediatric lupus, juvenile dermatomyositis, scleroderma, vasculitis, and chronic musculoskeletal pain.

Aside from getting financial support from the Arthritis Foundation, CARRA has received funding from the American College of Rheumatology; the National Institute of Arthritis and Musculoskeletal Skin Diseases; numerous pharmaceutical companies, including Amgen and Pfizer; and several other foundations.[12]

For more information on CARRA, call (650) 736–4364 or visit www.carragroup.org.

Centers for Education and Research on Therapeutics (CERTs)

The objective behind the establishment of the Centers for Education and Research on Therapeutics was not only to foster research, but also to provide education that "will advance the optimal use of drugs, medical devices, and biological products."[13] In addition, CERTs also have as their mission:

◎ **Managing risk by improving the ability to measure both beneficial and harmful effects of drug therapies;**

◎ **Advancing strategies to ensure that therapies are used only when they should be in order to prevent adverse effects; and**

◎ **Informing policymakers about the state of clinical science and the effects of current and proposed policies.**

All CERTs are run by the Agency for Healthcare Research and Quality (AHRQ), which operates in conjunction with the Food and Drug Administration. While most funding CERTs receive comes from AHRQ, they also rely on public and private donations to continue their mission.

As of 2008, there are fourteen CERTs nationwide, in addition to a coordinating center:

◎ **University of Alabama at Birmingham (UAB)**

◎ **Kaiser Permanente's Center for Health Research in Portland, Oregon**

- Duke University in Durham, North Carolina
- Harvard Pilgrim Health Care in Boston, Massachusetts
- Brigham and Women's Hospital in Boston
- The Critical Path Institute in Tucson, Arizona
- Cincinnati's Children's Hospital Medical Center in Ohio
- Vanderbilt University in Nashville, Tennessee
- University of Chicago in Illinois
- University of Illinois at Chicago
- University of Texas M.D. Anderson Cancer Center in Houston
- Rutgers, The State University of New Jersey in Camden
- University of Iowa in Iowa City
- Weill Medical College of Cornell University in New York

According to a press release issued by the University of Alabama at Birmingham, in 2007 the U.S. Department of Health and Human Services bestowed a "$41.6 million funding award . . . to expand the CERTs program through the Agency for Healthcare Research and Quality."[14]

For more information on CERTs, visit www.certs.hhs.gov.

Metroplex Clinical Research Center (MCRC)

Headquartered on the campus of St. Paul Medical Center at the University of Texas Southwestern in Dallas, Metroplex Clinical Research Center was founded in 1984 and now has four satellite offices that serve about 1 million patients.

MCRC has nine board-certified rheumatologists on staff, along with certified and trained coordinators, recruitment specialists, regulatory specialists, and laboratory technicians. The center's medical directors are Dr. Stanley B. Cohen and Dr. Roy M. Fleischmann.

Since its establishment, MCRC "has completed more than 800 Phase I through IV clinical studies in a variety of therapeutic areas, including rheumatology, osteoporosis, and musculoskeletal pain."[15] MCRC has also partnered with a host of pharmaceutical companies, including Amgen, Biogen, and Centocor, on various initiatives.

For more information on the Metroplex Clinical Research Center, call (214) 879–6737 or visit www.mcrcdallas.com.

The National Institutes of Health (NIH) Pediatric Rheumatology Clinic

Located in Bethesda, Maryland, the NIH Pediatric Rheumatology Clinic "is a specialty-care medical facility dedicated to evaluating and treating children with pediatric rheumatic diseases who are enrolled in clinical trials." The facility is divided into two parts: a health information resource center and a medical clinic. At the health information resource center, individuals can obtain a variety of information about arthritis and other rheumatic diseases—from symptoms to managing the illness. The clinic was established to help researchers and doctors better understand what causes juvenile rheumatic diseases in an effort "to diagnose, treat, and ultimately prevent these diseases" in the future.[16] Aside from serving as a site for clinical trials, the Pediatric Rheumatology Clinic also offers training for rheumatologists.

To receive medical care at the clinic, patients should be referred by their current rheumatologist, pediatrician, or health-care provider. Medical staff at the clinic are qualified to diagnose and treat children with arthritis, periodic fever syndromes, lupus, and other rheumatic diseases. At the first visit to the clinic, the child will be "examined by medical staff, which includes pediatric rheumatologists, pediatricians, nurse practitioners, research nurses, and doctors in training to become specialists." Depending on the outcome of the exam, some patients may be prescribed medicine and asked to schedule additional appointments for follow-up care, which can include testing or even physical therapy. While under care at the clinic, the patient's regular health-care providers will be kept up-to-date on their treatment and progress.[17]

Furthermore, once a child or teen becomes a patient at the clinic, he or she will have opportunities to participate in clinical trials if he or she meets the necessary criteria. Some studies conducted at the clinic are done to evaluate new treatments or diagnostic tests, whereas others may look at the symptoms or progression of the disease while they are under what is considered to be routine care. Those patients who agree to partake in a clinical trial receive medical care, which includes exams and necessary testing, at no cost.

CLINICAL TRIALS

There are plenty of opportunities to participate in clinical studies designed to test treatments or simply to learn more about autoimmune diseases. Like Kristen Delaney, you too may decide you'd like to partake in a clinical trial someday. If you meet the necessary eligibility requirements, you may be compensated financially or offered various other perks for your time and efforts.

According to MCRC's Web site, clinical trials, which are sometimes referred to as research studies or protocols, are conducted in four phases:

Phase I studies test, for the first time, new investigational (or study) drugs on humans. A small group of volunteers are recruited so researchers can evaluate best dosage practices and potential side effects.

Phase II studies require even more volunteers so researchers can determine the effectiveness of the investigational drug, how the body utilizes the medication, and whether any side effects result after use.

Phases III and IV studies also require larger groups of volunteers and usually compare the investigational drug with a commonly used drug or a placebo, which is an inactive substance.[18]

All legitimate clinical trials are approved and monitored by an Institutional Review Board (IRB) in order to ensure that the rights of participants are protected. Before you participate in a clinical trial, you should be briefed on the study (including any potential side effects that could result) so that you can make an educated decision on whether you'd like to be a part of it. It's always a good idea to consult your rheumatologist beforehand to make sure he or she feels it is safe and won't jeopardize your health. If you do ultimately agree to participate after knowing all the facts, this is known as giving "informed consent."[19]

In some trials, participants may simply be observed by researchers so they can see how the disease affects them. In other studies, volunteers may need to follow certain procedures, like taking medicine at specific times. Either way, volunteers will be evaluated by a research or health-care team at the beginning and end of the study, as well as during several points in between. Testing may also need to be done at various points.[20]

As time progresses, the individuals running the study should still keep you apprised of important details. Know that you may terminate your participation at any point.

To find out about pending clinical trials, check out Web sites run by any of the groups discussed above, like MCRC, NIAMS, or CARRA. "You can also access the ClinicalTrials.gov Web site (http://clinicaltrials.gov), a registry of federally and privately supported clinical trials conducted in the United States and around the world. ClinicalTrials.gov gives you information about a trial's purpose, who may participate, locations, and phone numbers for more details," says Richard Clark, science writer/editor for the NIAMS Office of Communications and Public Liaison, NIH, in Bethesda, Maryland.

RESEARCH AND CLINICAL STUDIES

To learn more about upcoming research studies or to express interest in participating, call (800) 411–1222 or visit http://clinicalstudies.info.nih.gov.

STAYING UP-TO-DATE ON RESEARCH BREAKTHROUGHS

To keep current about the latest findings in research, visit the Web sites of organizations like CARRA and ANRF. The Arthritis Foundation also keeps a running list of discoveries in research and explanations that can be accessed at ww2.arthritis.org/research/summaries/Summaries_default.asp. Visitors to the site are invited to sign up to receive research updates via e-mail. This is something ANRF offers as well.

There is another option for those who want to stay informed. "To discover what research is being done for children with arthritis, you can consult the CRISP database at www.crisp.cit.nih.gov. CRISP [Computer Retrieval of Information on Scientific Projects] is a searchable database of federally funded biomedical research projects conducted at universities, hospitals, and other research institutions. The database is searchable on a variety of fields, including key words," Richard Clark says.

Keep in mind that new treatments that come on the market aren't always approved for use in teens or children. Additional testing is required before teens and children can use these treatments.

RAISING FUNDS FOR A CURE

In spite of all the work that is being done, "we still need to raise funds and continue to advocate for arthritis awareness," Dr. White says.

A WEB SITE WORTH CHECKING OUT

National Center for Complementary and Alternative Medicine (NCCAM) Clearinghouse. **Touted as the federal government's lead agency for scientific research on complementary and alternative medicine, NCCAM conducts scientific research on study practices and products that are not considered to be conventional in order to share their findings with the public and medical professionals alike. To read up on research findings or to participate in a clinical trial, call (888) 644–6226 or visit www.nccam.nih.gov.**

To date, the Arthritis Foundation is the largest private nonprofit organization funding arthritis-related research initiatives.[21] Much of this money comes from corporate and individual sponsors. ANRF, AARDA, and CARRA also rely on donations to help fund research projects. If you want to help but have a tight budget, consider volunteering at a fund-raiser. Not only can you take part in organizing the event, but you can also help rally public support.

NOTES

1. Stanley B. Cohen, "Treatment of Arthritis/2008," *LoneStarthritis*, January 2008.

2. Arthritis Foundation, *Arthritis Answers* (pamphlet, 2000), 23.

3. National Institute of Arthritis and Musculoskeletal and Skin Diseases, "Mission Statement," www.niams.nih.gov/About_Us/Mission_and_Purpose/mission.asp.

4. Wikimedia Foundation, Inc., "National Institute of Arthritis and Musculoskeletal and Skin Diseases," Wikipedia, http://en.wikipedia.org/wiki/NIAMS.

5. Arthritis Foundation, "Partners," www.arthritis.org/partners.php.

6. National Institute of Arthritis and Musculoskeletal and Skin Diseases, "Researchers Identify Genes That Increase Rheumatoid Arthritis Risk," Press release, October 4, 2007, www.niams.nih.gov/News_and_Events/Press_Releases/2007/10_04.asp.

7. American Autoimmune Related Diseases Association, Inc., "AARDA Facts," www.aarda.org/aarda_facts.php.

8. Arthritis Foundation, *Arthritis in Children* (pamphlet, 2004), 31.

9. Childhood Arthritis and Rheumatology Research Alliance, "Mission Statement," www.carragroup.org/content_dsp.do?pc=mission.

10. Childhood Arthritis and Rheumatology Research Alliance, "Fact Sheet," www.carragroup.org/content_dsp.do?pc=fact.

11. Ibid.

12. Ibid.

13. Centers for Education & Research on Therapeutics, www.certs.hhs.gov.

14. University of Alabama at Birmingham Center for Education and Research on Therapeutics, "Musculoskeletal Center Wins $3.8 Million Research Grant," press release, October 19, 2007.

15. Metroplex Clinical Research Center, www.mcrcdallas.com/index_professional.aspx.

16. National Institute of Arthritis and Musculoskeletal and Skin Diseases, "NIH Pediatric Rheumatology Clinic," www.niams.nih.gov/Health_Info/Pediatric_Diseases/default.asp

17. Ibid.

18. Metroplex Clinical Research Center, "About Clinical Research," www.mcrcdallas.com/clinical_research_pt.aspx.

19. Metroplex Clinical Research Center, www.mcrcdallas.com/index_professional.aspx.

20. U.S. National Institutes of Health, "Understanding Clinical Trials," ClinicalTrials.gov, www.clinicaltrials.gov/ct2/info/understand.

21. Arthritis Foundation, *Arthritis Answers*, 23.

Appendix A: Assistive Devices

Several assistive or adaptive devices have already been mentioned throughout this book, but here is a more comprehensive list of other items that can save you time and help to prevent joint pain—many of which have been recommended by the Arthritis Foundation.

HOME

These items can all be used to make daily living activities easier around your home. Some might also be helpful to have at school or work.

Grooming

- ◎ *Dressing stick.* Those who find it hard to bend over or have trouble reaching will find that this product comes in handy when dressing. The stick is lightweight and has two different hooks at one end for pulling on clothes.
- ◎ *Elastic shoelaces.* If you have difficulty reaching down to tie your shoes, these laces are thicker and easier to handle compared to regular ones.
- ◎ *Sock aid.* Place your sock on the flexible sock trough and use the straps to pull it on your foot. A similar device is also available for stockings.
- ◎ *Long-handled shoehorn.* This makes slipping on shoes easier because you don't have to bend over.

- *Shower and bath chairs.* If you have trouble standing or fear that you may fall while showering, consider purchasing a shower or bath chair. Shower chairs come in a few different styles. One form is a plastic board that mounts on your bathtub and can easily be removed. The other resembles a plastic chair that can be placed in your tub. If you are looking to soak your joints in warm water and have difficulty sitting down in the bathtub (or getting back up), you may want to invest in a bath chair. These are usually more expensive than shower chairs because they run on a hydraulic system (not electricity) that enables the chair to lower to the bottom of the bathtub. They are not permanently attached to the tub and can easily be removed.

- *Grab bars.* These can be installed inside the shower and by the toilet in order to help you get up from a seated position or steady your balance.

- *Long-handled sponges.* Limited range of motion in your shoulders or elbows may make it difficult to reach your feet, neck, or back when bathing. Long-handled sponges help you clean those hard-to-reach places.

- *Toilet paper aids.* Although it may be embarrassing to discuss, those who have arthritis in their arms may find it difficult to wipe after going to the bathroom. If this is the case, you can purchase a toilet paper aid, which allows you to wrap toilet paper around a long-handled device for easy reaching.

- *Raised toilet seats.* If you have difficulty getting up from a seated position, an elevated toilet seat may make it easier and reduce strain on your knees at the same time. Carrying cases are also available if you need to transport the seat.

- *Electric toothbrushes.* Those with limited dexterity might find it easier to brush their teeth with an electric toothbrush, since electric power moves the bristles for you. One such toothbrush is the HydraBrush Express, which is fully automatic and made by Oralbotic Research, Inc., a sponsor of the Arthritis Foundation. Electric toothbrushes also usually have bigger handles for easy gripping. Foam tubes are also available that can be applied to regular toothbrushes to improve grip.

◎ *Extended brushes and combs.* Those with limited range of motion or pain in their shoulders will find these long-handled brushes and combs helpful.

◎ *Hair dryer stand.* Hair dryers can be heavy and strain your joints when you hold them for a while. This flexible stand allows you to dry your hair hands-free.

◎ *Easy-grip nail clippers.* These are much easier to use than traditional nail clippers: Simply squeeze the wide, soft-grip handles with mild pressure to cut your nails.

Dining

◎ *Enhanced utensils.* Cutlery with enlarged, soft rubber grips for easy handling can be purchased, or an occupational therapist can make special grips for you.

◎ *Automatic jar opener.* If you have trouble gripping, just push a button on this device and it will open jars of any size.

◎ *Can opener.* Use an automatic can opener to save energy in your wrists.

◎ *Bottle opener.* There are a variety of inexpensive tools that make it easy to twist caps off of bottles. Some tools also have a feature that allows you to pry up soda can tabs with ease.

Miscellaneous

◎ *Stairlifts.* If climbing stairs is difficult or impossible, you can have a stairlift installed. To get up or down steps, you sit on a chair that is powered by a nearby electrical outlet so that it can ride up the stairs. Some lifts have batteries that keep a charge even if the power goes out. Lifts that hold wheelchairs are also available.

◎ *Rollout/pullout cabinets.* Whether you are short in stature, use a wheelchair, or simply have trouble extending your arms, you can use cabinet shelves that can be pulled out and lowered for enhanced accessibility.

- *Personal pager/call for help system.* With a personal pager, you can push a button to let the person who has the receiver know you need help. More advanced devices, like the call for help system, are also available to allow users to reach 911 and up to five other telephone numbers of their choosing when an emergency occurs, simply by pressing a button on a pendant worn around the neck. A prerecorded message is then sent to those emergency contacts, who can then speak to the person in need via a speakerphone.

- *Reacher or grabber.* One of the best tools around for anyone who has trouble reaching things is a reacher. At the end of this aluminum stick is a gripper that opens and closes when you squeeze the handle at the other end. You can use a reacher to pick things up or even to aid you in dressing. Most reachers have a magnet by the gripper so you can pick up metal objects. Some reachers can even be folded up and put in a backpack or briefcase.

- *Pill bottle opener.* This device attaches to bottle caps, providing you with extra leverage so they twist off easier. Many pharmacies will substitute regular pill caps with easy-open tops upon request.

- *Universal Elastic Cuff (U-cuff).* Kristen McCosh recommends using a Universal Elastic Cuff if you have limited dexterity. "I don't have any actual hand function. I don't have a grip," she says. "This product is a cuff that goes on your hand to help you hold a fork, or a toothbrush, or things like that."

- *Doorknob turner.* This plastic handle fits over most doorknobs and enables easy entry simply by pushing down on it.

- *Lamp switch enlarger.* This plastic device is placed on top of lamp switches to make it easier to turn them on. Similar devices can be put on oven knobs. Another option is to consider buying a lamp that turns on simply by tapping the base or pulling a small chain.

- *Lap desk.* If your body aches from sitting at your desk, try using a lap desk or lap board. Lap desks have a stable cushion-like base and a hard flat surface to write on—allowing you to take your work to a comfortable couch or bed.

- *Seat belt extension.* Reaching back for your seat belt can be difficult and even cause strain on your muscles. This lightweight device attaches to your seat belt and juts out several inches so you don't have to reach back as far.

◎ *Car door opener.* This device has a key holder at one end to help you unlock the door and a handle at the opposite end for lifting door handles. It also has a padded handle to make gripping easy.

◎ *Push-button umbrella.* Trying to open a regular umbrella can be a real hassle. Instead, you can use one that opens and closes just by pushing a button.

SCHOOL

These products can also be used at home or work.

◎ *Voice recorder.* Voice recorders can come in handy on days you are having difficulty taking notes. Always make sure school officials know that you plan to use the device first.

◎ *Pen and pencil grips.* Special rubber grips can be placed on your pen or pencil to make writing easier. You can also purchase writing instruments that are thicker or curved in such a way that it alleviates pressure on your wrists and fingers. One unique item called Pen Again has a Y-shaped handle that fits your hand's natural writing position. It is comfortable and improves handwriting.

◎ *Book bags on wheels.* Using a book bag that has an extended handle and rolls on wheels will eliminate muscle and joint strain from having to carry heavy loads. If you have a wheelchair, you can purchase a specially designed book bag that fits over the handles.

◎ *Bookstand.* Prevent neck strain by placing your books upright in a bookstand. A special strap keeps pages open.

WORK

◎ *Modified mouse.* If you have trouble using a mouse, look for one that resembles a joystick. You can also try a mouse that has a trackball on top; gently moving the ball with your finger automatically moves the cursor. Or you might want to purchase a laptop that has a touchpad, which enables you to move the cursor by lightly touching the pad with your finger. As a last resort, you might look into getting a mouse that you control with your feet or by way of head- or mouthgear.

- *Voice-activated software.* Many companies manufacture software that types the words you speak. Having voice-activated software on the computer can be very helpful for people who have pain in their hands and wrists.

- *Speakerphone/headset.* Holding a telephone for long periods of time can be draining on your arms and wrists. If you find this is the case, try using a speakerphone. Or, if your conversations need to be kept private, buy a headset that can be plugged into your hand receiver (if it has that capability). You might also consider purchasing a cordless headset phone so you can put the headset over your ears and clip the dialing unit to your pants.

- *Rolling briefcase.* Avoid straining your arms, wrists, and shoulders by using a briefcase or laptop case that rolls on wheels.

- *Pillbox.* Put your regular medicine in a pillbox if you need to take it during work hours. You can also take some extra pain medicine along in case of a flare-up.

- *Automatic door opener.* If the doors at your office building or home are heavy and tough to open, you can have an automatic door opener installed. With a simple touch of a button, the door will open automatically.

PLAY

- *Playing card holder.* If you have limited range of motion in your fingers, or your wrists tire easily, fan your cards out in this device.

- *Video game controls.* Those with limited dexterity can purchase special controls or buttons for video game systems or computers.

- *Bionic Tennis Glove.* Manufactured by Hillerich & Bradsby Co., this special glove maximizes grip strength and reduces hand fatigue.

- *Accessible playgrounds.* Fully accessible and interactive playgrounds are becoming more and more common. These

COMPANIES THAT SELL ASSISTIVE DEVICES

There are numerous companies that manufacture or sell assistive or adaptive devices. The list of products now on the market continues to grow. Here are just a few companies that offer a wide selection of items that will make daily living easy for you.

Aids for Arthritis
(800) 654–0707
www.aidsforarthritis.com

Allegro Medical
(800) 861–3211
www.AllegroMedical.com

Amazon.com

Arthritis Supplies
(877) 750–0376
www.arthritissupplies.com

Independent At Home
(800) 996–5481
www.IndependentAtHome.com

Remember—prices may vary, so be sure to shop around!

special playgrounds have games and play stations for those in wheelchairs. They are also made with soft surfaces and materials to avoid injuries.

- *Adaptive sports.* As discussed in chapter 5, many sports have "adapted" versions that can be enjoyed by people with physical impairments. Adaptive equipment is available for those interested in fishing, boating, and tennis—to name just a few. Fishing rods, paddles, and rackets can be fitted with Velcro straps or loops to aid in gripping. In addition, special seating systems are available for individuals who have difficulty getting into small boats and rafts.

Appendix B: Research Initiatives

According to both the Arthritis Foundation and the Arthritis National Research Foundation, significant progress has been made in the areas of arthritis-related research over the past few years. "It has [progressed] in a number of areas because technology has improved so much," Helene Belisle explains. "And, because of the mapping of the human genome, scientists are able to conduct genetics-based studies with greater accuracy now."

Aside from exploring the role genetic factors play in relation to the disease, scientists also have been able to make improvements in diagnosing and monitoring disease activity. In addition, researchers are continuing to work on regrowing joint cartilage from stem cells in an effort to relieve pain and promote function. One ANRF grant recipient is even testing a drug that would re-train the immune system to function properly.[1]

"Overall, the work has just exploded. And I think technology has a lot to do with it—the ability to look at things from a molecular level," Belisle says. "There are so many treatments on the horizon that would be helpful for individuals with JA, and they may not necessarily come only from the field of arthritis research."

Traditionally, scientists conduct research in one of four areas: causes, treatments, education, and lifestyle influences.[2] Following is a summary of initiatives in several of those areas.

RESEARCH INITIATIVES

Biologic Agents (or Response Modifiers)

As of December 2007, two more biologic agents made it to phase III trials, several others are in phase II trials, and one has been submitted to the FDA for approval. Here is a list of the latest biologic agents presently in clinical trials as reported by *Arthritis Today* magazine.[3]

- Baminercept (BG 9924) entered phase II trials in 2007. This weekly injection is used to treat rheumatoid arthritis, Crohn's disease, and lupus. The drug works by targeting lymphotoxin-beta, a molecule on the surface of cells that incites the inflammatory process. The molecule was discovered by ANRF Scientific Board Chair Carl F. Ware, Ph.D., and blocking its signals can help restore the immune system. Patients with arthritis who were treated with the drug had significantly less swelling of their joints. Side effects range from headache to flulike symptoms. Baminercept may also benefit individuals with multiple sclerosis. [Author's note: In 2009, Baminercept was pulled from production due to lack of positive results.]

- In phase III trials as of 2007, Certolizumab pegol (Cimzia) is used to treat rheumatoid arthritis, Crohn's disease, and psoriasis. A monthly injection, this drug targets TNF-alpha and has been found to reduce pain, swelling, and stiffness sooner than other TNF inhibitors. Another benefit is that Cimzia may be safe for pregnant women since "it doesn't cross the placenta during pregnancy and is not evident in breast milk."[4] Side effects include increased risk of infection.

- Denosumab (AMG 162) entered phase II trials for RA as well as phase III trials for osteoporosis in 2007. The drug targets "RANK ligand, a protein involved in the development of bony erosions," and is given via injection twice a year. It is beneficial because it slows "the rate at which bone erodes in people with RA."[5]

- Golimumab (CNTO 148), which is in phase III trials as of 2007, can be used to treat rheumatoid arthritis, ankylosing spondylitis, and psoriatic arthritis. Like Cimzia, it targets TNF-a and is an injection given once a month. Benefits include less pain, inflammation, and swelling, as well as fewer skin and nail problems.

- Ofatumumab (HuMax-CD20) is also in phase III trials as of 2008. It is an intravenous infusion that reduces the number of B cells. While it may be of benefit to individuals with Crohn's disease or Wegener's granulomatosis, the focus is currently on helping people with RA who have not responded well to methotrexate and other biologic agents. Those who've tried Ofatumumab have noticed less joint swelling and tenderness. Side effects include site reactions, rashes, shortness of breath, and a sore throat.

- Tocilizumab (Actemra) was submitted to the FDA for official approval in 2007. It is an intravenous infusion that can benefit those with RA and systemic juvenile idiopathic arthritis. Tocilizumab targets interleukin-6 (IL-6), which is an inflammatory protein. Those tested found that the drug, when taken with methotrexate, alleviates pain and stiffness. Side effects may include infections and possibly "an increase in blood cholesterol and liver enzymes."[6]

Other new biologic therapies being developed include "monoclonal antibodies, receptor inhibitors, and peptide vaccines—all of which are designed to modify the immune response in a precise manner."[7]

Immune-Modulation Therapy Research

According to Dr. Gale A. Granger, "Important progress has been made in beginning to understand some of the genetic mechanisms that are involved in the start of the disease. This has led to the development of a possible vaccine, which is being [studied in] clinical trials to test the safety of this new approach. One of the ANRF fellows developed this."

The vaccine Dr. Granger is referring to was developed by Dr. Salvatore Albani. It is an immune modulation therapy (which is not the same as an immunosuppression therapy) that revolves around a synthetic peptide called dnaJP1.

The new treatment developed as a result of Dr. Albani's "work on the immune system's T cells, which trigger inflammation to kill and clear infections from the body. [Dr.] Albani reasoned that if the immune system of RA

257

Figure B.1.   Dr. Salvatore Albani, professor of medicine and pediatrics and director of the University of Arizona Arthritis Center.

patients could be altered, T cells might be less likely to cause chronic inflammation."[8]

In order "to prevent T cells from attacking the body, Dr. Albani sought to develop a vaccine therapy that could 'reeducate' the diseased immune system in RA patients to prevent rampant inflammation." He then centered his efforts "on a protein called dnaJP1 that is used by T cells to help initiate the inflammation process."[9]

By giving dnaJP1 to individuals with rheumatoid arthritis via a vaccine, Dr. Albani confirmed that it was able to prevent a T cell attack that would have caused inflammation. "In essence, we reeducated the immune system T cells in RA patients to be tolerant of the dnaJP1 amino acid sequence that would usually trigger inflammation," Dr. Albani notes.[10]

This form of immune modulation ultimately prevented a T cell attack against the body's own tissue. Dr. Albani says the vaccine is vastly different from other treatments on the market in that it "leaves the patient's natural immune responses intact."[11]

The vaccine has passed through Phase II clinical trials and was found to be safe and well tolerated by patients, who experienced an improvement in rheumatoid arthritis symptoms of swollen joints, tenderness, pain, and mobility.

Autoantibody Research

Autoantibodies are a type of protein created by the immune system that work against one or more of the other proteins in the body. "It is clear that autoantibodies directed at self tissues can cause damage in the joints and tissues of patients with RA," Dr. Granger says. "Studies are beginning to reveal how antibody production is controlled, which could lead to the ability to inhibit autoantibody production, and it could also lead to new therapies."

WHAT ELSE IS NEW IN THE WAY OF RESEARCH?

Aside from the initiatives discussed above, scientists are working on plenty of other projects in an effort to better treat or even cure arthritis. Take a look at a number of the research projects sponsored by some of the groups mentioned previously.

Arthritis National Research Foundation Initiatives

According to literature provided by ANRF, 2007 grant recipients worked on the following projects:

- *Beyond TNF: A Newly Discovered Cytokine May Provide New Target for RA Therapy; Investigator: Christopher Benedict, PhD, La Jolla Institute for Allergy and Immunology, San Diego, California.* Dr. Benedict is studying a newly discovered cytokine network that is a close relative of TNF and may contribute to the initiation and/or severity of RA. Using mouse models, he hopes to generate information about neutralizing this new network that could lead to new clinical treatments for RA.

Autoimmune Disorder Target: DRAK2; Investigator: Martina Gatzka, PhD, University of California, Irvine, California. Dr. Gatzka has been studying autoimmune diseases, including the body's natural surveillance mechanisms, since 2005. In particular, she is studying a surveillance mechanism that keeps T cells (or T lymphocytes) from going awry, which is called DAP-related apoptotic kinase-2 (DRAK2). Her research applies cutting-edge immunological and molecular biological methods to investigate how a DRAK2 modulates T cell activation and tolerance in a mouse model of rheumatoid arthritis, collagen-induced arthritis (CIA). Identifying strategies to specifically block and eliminate self-reactive T lymphocytes is key to the development of efficient new therapies for these immune mediated diseases.

Are You Susceptible to RA? It May Be in Your Genes . . . ; Investigator: Alyssa Johnsen, MD, PhD, Joslin Diabetes Center, Boston, Massachusetts. As we know, rheumatoid arthritis is caused by a complex set of environmental and genetic factors. However, only a small number of the genes that increase a person's risk of developing RA have been identified, thus far. Discovering additional genes that control RA would help us understand what causes the disease and how to treat or even prevent arthritis more effectively. In 2005 Dr. Johnsen began using a unique group of mice to help find the genes controlling inflammatory arthritis. Once she treats the mice so that they develop arthritis, Dr. Johnsen can then correlate the presence of a particular DNA sequence at a specific location on the genome with the severity of the arthritis. This will identify the location of the genes that are controlling arthritis in these animals. Given the similarity of the mouse model with human RA, it is likely that these genes also play a significant role in the human disease. Finding how genes control susceptibility to RA will enhance our understanding of how the disease works and will potentially identify new targets for pharmaceutical development.

From Stem Cells to Cartilage Repair; Investigator: Audrey McAlinden, PhD, Washington University School of Medicine, St. Louis, Missouri. According to Dr. Granger, "There is also research [being done] on stem cells, which is at an early stage. There are serious questions and problems to overcome, but this approach may lead to new methods for the treatment and prevention [of rheumatic diseases]." Articular cartilage is an essential component of our joints, providing a lubricating, low-friction, gliding surface. This tissue contains no blood supply and so displays a limited capacity for self-regeneration. Strategies to promote articular cartilage growth are very important given the high incidence of osteoarthritis (OA) in the aging population. In OA, articular cartilage tissue degrades, resulting in severe joint pain and debilitation. A promising method of treatment involves the use of adult mesenchymal connective tissue cells (MSCs). These cells can be differentiated to become cells of cartilage, bone, adipose, or other tissues. Dr. McAlinden's study tests an innovative approach to induce cartilage cell production from adult MSCs isolated from both fat tissue and bone marrow. Her aim is to differentiate MSCs into the type of cartilage cells called chondrocytes, which are found only in articular cartilage of our joints. By using virus technology, Dr. McAlinden hopes to be able to select from the desired chondrocyte necessary to promote articular cartilage repair. Results of this study would also benefit people with rheumatoid arthritis.

◎ *Growth Factors in Cartilage Cells: A Novel Therapy; Investigator: Chuanju Liu, PhD, New York University School of Medicine, New York, New York.* The molecular mechanisms controlling cartilage formation, and specifically those relating to osteoarthritis, are still unclear. It is believed that specific growth factors and surrounding matrix proteins play critical roles in controlling cartilage formation and the progression of osteoarthritis. Dr. Liu's research in 2006 led to the discovery of granulin/epithelin precursor (GEP), a novel growth factor in cartilage and a therapeutic target in arthritis. The primary focus of Dr. Liu's ANRF study is to determine the role of GEP in the differentiation and metabolism of cartilage cells. He hopes this study will enhance our understanding of growth factors in cartilage and their application to the treatment of arthritis.

◎ *Lupus Therapy without Toxicity; Investigator: Hee-Kap Kang, PhD, Northwestern University, Chicago, Illinois.* This is the second year ANRF has funded Dr. Kang's work. Dr. Kang has developed a therapy to repair a cell defect that may cause lupus. To test this therapy, Dr. Kang's lab is studying the effects of injecting a specific peptide into a lupus-prone mouse. The peptide therapy appears to be beneficial without any toxic effect so far, and thus might be very important in maintaining tolerance in lupus patients after remission has been induced by more toxic immunosuppressive agents. Even apparently healthy subjects and family members of lupus patients who might be at risk of developing lupus (as predicted by genetic and biomarkers) might benefit from the peptide therapy.

- *Understanding Bone Loss in RA; Investigator: Sougata Karmakar, PhD, University of Massachusetts Medical School, Worcester, Massachusetts.* As we know, rheumatoid arthritis is a chronic, debilitating disease that affects the joints in patients and may result in bone loss. The structural integrity of bone is maintained by the coordinated actions of two cell types, the bone-forming osteoblast and the bone-resorbing osteoclast. In rheumatoid arthritis, there is an imbalance in the activities of these two cells, resulting in bone loss that leads to joint deformity and pain. Dr. Karmakar has been studying bone morphogenetic protein (BMP) in arthritic mice, hoping to demonstrate that an antagonist of BMP inhibits osteoblast maturation and function at bone erosion sites in RA joints, which results in impaired bone formation. Understanding these mechanisms will allow for the identification of novel targets to augment bone formation at erosion sites, a necessary step to preserving joint function in RA.

- *A New Model for Treating Scleroderma; Investigator: Edwin Chan, MD, New York University School of Medicine, New York, New York.* In 2006 Dr. Chan identified a molecule called adenosine, which plays an important role in dermal fibrosis (or thickening of the skin). Adenosine binds to a specific receptor on the surface of the cell to produce the scarring effect. By blocking these cell surface receptors, Dr. Chan has substantially reduced fibrosis in animal models, thereby providing a new model for treatment. His ANRF-funded study will explore the way adenosine alters fibrosis in the skin. He hopes that the results from this work will lead to therapeutic options to treat and prevent scleroderma.

- *Understanding the Defective Immune System; Investigator: Ziaur Rahman, MD, PhD, Thomas Jefferson University, Philadelphia, Pennsylvania.* The immune system develops antibodies to use against viral and bacterial infections. When antibodies attack the body's own tissue, it leads to the development of autoimmune diseases, such as systemic lupus erythematosus. In its later stages, SLE can lead to multi–organ system failure and death. When a healthy immune system does *not* attack its own tissues, it is called tolerance. Patients with SLE show a loss of this tolerance. To date, we have come to understand this disease process through mouse models that develop human SLE-like diseases. Using these mouse models, Dr. Rahman has been investigating how this tolerance functions and how autoantibodies are produced when this tolerance is defective. This study will identify the genes involved in this defective tolerance process and help develop effective diagnostic and treatment approaches for systemic autoimmune diseases.

◎ *Genetic Factors in Lupus; Investigator: Amr Sawalha, MD, University of Oklahoma Health Sciences Center, Oklahoma City, Oklahoma.* Systemic lupus erythematosus is a chronic, relapsing autoimmune disease that affects multiple organs including the skin, joints, lungs, kidneys, and brain. The disease is at least nine times more common in females than males. There is evidence for both genetic and environmental factors implicated in the pathogenesis of lupus; however, the exact pathogenesis of the disease is not completely understood. Using a mouse model, Dr. Sawalha is studying a specific gene that is over expressed in the T regulatory white cells of female, but not male, mice. The goal of these studies is to provide new insights into mechanisms causing lupus, and to identify new approaches to the treatment of this sometimes fatal disease.

◎ *T Cells: Using Your Own Cells to Fight Lupus; Innvestigator: Brian Skaggs, PhD, University of California, Los Angeles, California.* Antibodies produced by immune cells in lupus patients inappropriately bind to many different self-molecules, leading to the tissue destruction throughout the body seen in the disease. Not surprisingly, patients and researchers are frustrated that there has not been a new FDA-approved lupus therapy regimen in more than thirty years. This underscores the urgent need for new, innovative lupus therapies. Work by many labs in 2006, including Dr. Skaggs's lab, has demonstrated that a particular immune cell, the regulatory

T cell, can be activated by multiple mechanisms to attack the autoimmune cells that cause lupus and render them ineffective. These exciting studies are tempered by our lack of understanding as to how we could manipulate these "good" immune cells to destroy the "bad" autoimmune cells. Dr. Skaggs's laboratory has identified a novel way to turn on the "good" regulatory T cells in a mouse model of lupus. He is studying how regulatory T cells work by deciphering the intracellular networks necessary to activate these cells. Regulatory T cells have the potential to be a novel, safe method of controlling—and hopefully curing—lupus and other autoimmune diseases.[12]

CARRA Initiatives

According to information available on both CARRA and the Arthritis Foundation's Web sites, the following are recent juvenile arthritis studies supported by CARRA.[13]

Juvenile Idiopathic Arthritis Studies

Long-Term Outcome of Two Cohorts of Children with Juvenile Rheumatoid (Idiopathic) Arthritis. "Beth Gottlieb, MD, MS, at Schneider Children's Hospital [in] New Hyde Park, New York, is leading a long-term study of two groups of children with juvenile rheumatoid arthritis, [who were] recruited from twenty-three centers in the United States and Canada. The first group includes 473 children enrolled in 1996–1999 and who are assessed annually to record their disease progression, medication use, laboratory and radiographic parameters, and functional status. With funding from the Arthritis Foundation, the researchers began in 2001 to enroll a second study group of newly diagnosed JRA patients. This new group includes children diagnosed in the era of the new biologic response modifier treatments, which will provide important data on how different medications affect the long-term outcome in children with JRA."[14]

Other JIA studies supported by CARRA include:

🎐 *Multicenter Prospective Registry of Infliximab Use for Childhood Uveitis.* **Principal Investigators: Egla Rabinovich, Duke University Medical Center, and Deborah Levy, Children's Hospital of New York–Presbyterian**

🎐 *Immune Tolerance after Severe Immunosuppression and Stem Cell Rescue for JIA.* **Principal Investigators: Yukiko Kimura, Hackensack University Medical Center, and Carol Wallace, University of Washington**

🎐 *Safety and Effectiveness of Rilonacept* for Treating Systemic Juvenile Idiopathic Arthritis in Children and Young Adults.* **Principal Investigator: Norman T. Ilowite, MD, Montefiore Medical Center**
*Rilonacept is an IL-1 inhibitor.

🎐 *Early Aggressive Therapy in JIA.* **Principal Investigators: Carol Wallace, University of Washington; Dan Lovell and Ed Gianinni, Cincinnati Children's Hospital Medical Center, Ohio**

Systemic Lupus Erythematosus Studies

🎐 *Atherosclerosis Prevention in Pediatric Lupus Erythematosus (APPLE); Principal Investigators: Laura Schanberg, Duke University, Durham, North Carolina, and Christy Sandborg, Stanford University, California.* **"This twenty-three center clinical trial will test the safety and benefits of using atorvastatin, a cholesterol-lowering drug to prevent atherosclerosis or hardening of the arteries in children with lupus. 'Atherosclerosis, which can result in heart attacks and premature death, occurs earlier and more commonly in people with lupus,' said Laura Schanberg, MD, from Duke University in Durham, North Carolina. We are hopeful that this research will result in more effective ways to prevent cardiovascular disease and improve the quality and lifespan of children and young adults with lupus."[15]**

🎐 *Nitric Oxide Metabolism in Statin-Treated Pediatric SLE; Principal Investigator: Marc Levesque, Duke University Durham, North Carolina.* **Dr. Levesque "will measure nitric oxide levels in the blood of the APPLE trial participants. It is believed that the premature hardening of the arteries in lupus** may be due to overproduction of chemicals like nitric oxide that cause inflammation and damage in blood vessels. This study will help determine if atorvastatin reduces overproduction of nitric oxide and inflammation in children with lupus."[16]

Towards Evidence-Based Practice Guidelines for Use of Steroids in Children with SLE; Principal Investigator: Hermine Brunner, Cincinnati Children's Hospital Medical Center, Ohio. Dr. Brunner received two grants to conduct this study, which is now complete. In one study, the purpose was "aimed at clarifying how steroids should be used in the treatment of pediatric lupus. Steroids are a mainstay of treatment, but they have serious side effects and there is considerable variation in how steroids are used." Overall, the study looked at various treatments and how they impacted the patient in terms of side effects, quality of life, and even financially. Dr. Brunner also ran "a second multi-center study . . . aimed at developing better tools to measure the effectiveness of new drugs in pediatric lupus clinical trials. More sensitive and standardized measures of disease activity would make it easier to do clinical trials of new lupus drugs."[17]

Effects of Puberty on Childhood Onset Systemic Lupus Erythematosus and the Development of Antiphospholipid Antibodies; Principal Investigator: Kathleen O'Neil, Children's Hospital of Oklahoma, Oklahoma City. Dr. O'Neil "is conducting an observational, multi-center pilot study to examine the possible role of female sex hormones in systemic lupus erythematosus. The study will examine disease activity in girls aged eight-twelve whose lupus began before puberty [in order] to define which hormones are important in exacerbating disease activity during puberty, and what the immune effects of hormone changes in puberty are. If a hormone trigger to lupus activity is identified, it may be possible to modify hormone activity in children when their disease is particularly active, perhaps decreasing the toxicity of the strong medications needed to control very active lupus."[18]

Other SLE studies supported by CARRA include:

Meaningful Outcome Measures for Pediatric Lupus Trials. Principal Investigator: Hermine Brunner

- *The Role of Maternal Microchimerism in Pediatric SLE.* Principal Investigator: Anne Stevens, University of Washington, Seattle, Washington

- *Towards Improved Biological Markers for Lupus Renal Disease.* Principal Investigator: Hermine Brunner

Juvenile Dermatomyositis Studies supported by CARRA

- *Study of Microchimerism in Juvenile Dermatomyositis; Principal Investigator: Ann Reed MD, Mayo Clinic, Rochester, Minnesota.* Dr. Reed "is studying how the transfer of a mother's cells to her fetus might result in the development of juvenile dermatomyositis (JDMS), a multi-system autoimmune disease. Preliminary data shows that the mother's genetic makeup can facilitate the transfer and/or persistence of maternal cells in the blood of the fetus and that these maternal cells appear to play a direct role in the JDMS disease process."[19]

Other Juvenile Dermatomyositis studies supported by CARRA include:

- *Towards Standards of Care for Juvenile Dermatomyositis.* Principal Investigator: Brian Feldman, University of Toronto, Toronto, Ontario.

- *Rituximab* for the Treatment of Refractory Adult and Juvenile Dermatomyositis.* Principal Investigator: Ann Reed

*Rituximab rids of B cells.

CERTs Initiatives

One of the latest CERTs initiatives comes out of the University of Alabama at Birmingham (UAB) Center for Education and Research on Therapeutics. According to a press release from UAB, the center was awarded a "$3.8 million grant renewal from the U.S. Department of Health and Human Services for research into inflammatory, arthritic, and musculoskeletal diseases and their treatments."[20]

Through use of the grant, the UAB CERTs will "continue its often-cited research on the safety and effectiveness of new therapeutics for these diseases. The UAB CERTs works diligently to move these new therapeutics into the clinical-testing phase for potentially widespread use. Additionally, the renewal funds will help UAB CERTs continue its work at reducing treatment disparities among minority communities where musculoskeletal diseases are a problem." As a side note, the musculoskeletal system encompasses bones, joints, muscles, and tendons.

UAB CERTs will also work toward "the development of more effective policies for treating these diseases, and educational programs for physicians who see musculoskeletal patients through their own medical practice." Previously, "CERTs also led a worldwide push to better understand how existing musculoskeletal treatments should be used within the framework of newer therapeutic discoveries for conditions like arthritis and osteoporosis."[21]

For more information on each of the CERTs and their past, present, and future research projects, visit www.certs.hhs.gov.

Metroplex Clinical Research Center

"In our clinical research unit, we continue to work with a multitude of newer 'targeted therapies' that have a potential for greater efficacy and safety," Dr. Cohen said in his recent article. "We are also working on 'small molecules' that can be delivered as pills that might be as effective as biologic therapies and significantly less expensive. On another front, significant research into the genetics of rheumatoid arthritis may allow us to tailor our therapies based on a particular genetic/biomarker profile, which should save significant time and resources in identifying optimal care for an individual patient."[22]

Here are a few brief descriptions of MCRC's clinical studies as listed on its Web site in 2008.[23]

Rheumatoid Arthritis Study

MCRC is conducting a research study of an investigational medication to see if it can help control RA, alleviate signs and symptoms, and maintain physical function. Participants are over the age of eighteen, have been diagnosed with RA for at least six months, and have not responded to at least one disease-modifying antirheumatic drug.

Rheumatoid Arthritis Treated with Methotrexate Study

An investigational medication is being tested in a medical research study to evaluate its effectiveness for rheumatoid arthritis symptoms. Patients will be considered for this study if they are taking methotrexate but are not benefiting as much as they or their doctors feel they should be. They will remain on methotrexate and add the study medication to their therapy.

Rheumatoid Arthritis/Osteoarthritis Study

MCRC is conducting a research study of three approved medications commonly used to treat pain associated with RA and osteoarthritis in people who also have, or are at high risk for, heart disease.

Psoriatic Arthritis Study

The center is currently looking for individuals who have been diagnosed with psoriatic arthritis for more than three months and are over the age of eighteen. In addition, participants must have failed to respond to at least one disease-modifying antirheumatic drug.

Lupus

MCRC initiated a one-year clinical research study evaluating individuals with lupus to determine if there are particular genes that are associated with disease flare-ups. Those who have been diagnosed with systemic lupus erythematosus and have had active disease symptoms in the last twelve months may qualify to participate in the study.

Past Research Studies

While it's clear that ANRF has awarded grants for scientists working on various arthritis-related research in the past, JA research certainly hasn't been neglected. "We do try to fund at least one juvenile arthritis project each year," Belisle notes. According to information she provided, here are a few of the JA-related projects ANRF has funded over recent years:

- Salvatore Albani, MD, PhD, then Director of the Center for Pediatric Rheumatology at UCSD, was a 1992 and 1996 grant recipient for *New Therapy in Clinical Trials to Correct the Immune System.*

- Elizabeth Mellins, MD, Professor of Pediatric Rheumatology at Stanford University Medical Center, was a 1998–1999 grant recipient for *On-going Molecular Studies of JRA.*

- Anne Stevens, MD, PhD, Professor of Pediatric Rheumatology at University of Washington Children's Hospital Research Center, was a 2000–2001 grant recipient for *Study of Maternal Cells Passed from Mother to Child.*

- Randy Cron, MD, PhD, Children's Hospital of Philadelphia, was a 2002–2003 grant recipient for *Genetic Study in Autoimmunity.*

- David Leslie, MD, Children's Hospital Boston, was a 2004–2005 grant recipient for the study *Molecular Model of Kawasaki Disease, the Leading Cause of Acquired Heart Disease in Children.*

- Hulya Bukulmez, MD, Case Western Reserve University, was a 2006–2007 grant recipient for the study *JRA's Effect on Children's Growth.*

Furthermore, ANRF provided grants to researchers who made the following scientific breakthroughs:

- Discovery of cytokines, including TNF, which can cause the tissue destruction seen in those with idiopathic arthritis

- Discovery of a receptor that neutralizes TNF before it gets to cell tissue, which led to the development of Enbrel

NOTES

1. Arthritis National Research Foundation, "Studies May Yield New, Better Therapies," October 3, 2007.

2. Arthritis Foundation, *Arthritis Answers* (pamphlet, 2000), 23.

3. Arthritis Foundation, "Drugs in the Pipeline: Meet the Next Generation of Biologics," *Arthritis Today*, December 2007, www.arthritis.org/drug-pipeline.php.

4. Ibid.

5. Ibid.

6. Ibid.

7. Arthritis Foundation, *Arthritis in Children* (pamphlet, 2004), 17.

8. Tom Gilbert, "New RA Therapy: Immune Reeducation vs. Immunosuppression," The Doctor Will See You Now, May 2004, www.thedoctorwillseeyounow.com/news/arthritis/0504/ra.shtml.

9. Ibid.

10. Ibid.

11. Ibid.

12. Arthritis National Research Foundation, "Studies May Yield New, Better Therapies."

13. Childhood Arthritis and Rheumatology Research Alliance, "Current Studies," www.carragroup.org/content_dsp.do?pc=fact.

14. Arthritis Foundation, www.arthritis.org.

15. Ibid.

16. Ibid.

17. Ibid.

18. Ibid.

19. Ibid.

20. University of Alabama at Birmingham Center for Education and Research on Therapeutics, press release, October 19, 2007.

21. Ibid.

22. Stanley B. Cohen, "Treatment of Arthritis/2008," *LoneStarthritis*, January 2008.

23. Metroplex Clinical Research Center, "Current Research," www.mcrcdallas.com/mcrc/current_reserach_pt.aspx.

Bibliography

ARTICLES

Advameg Inc. "Leg Lengthening/Shortening." *Encyclopedia of Surgery: A Guide for Patients and Caregivers.* www.surgeryencyclopedia.com/La-Pa/Leg-Lengthening -Shortening.html.

American Autoimmune Related Diseases Association, Inc. "AARDA Facts." www.aarda.org/aarda_facts.php.

American College of Rheumatology. "Ankylosing Spondylitis." www.rheumatology.org/public/factsheets/as.asp.

American Institute of Stress. "Effects of Stress." www.stress .org/topic-effects.htm?AIS=0e7a9fd84b78de49776a7e 14b5412a3e.

Arthritis Foundation. *Arthritis Answers*. Pamphlet, 2000.

———. *Arthritis in Children*. Pamphlet, 2004.

———. "Arthritis in Children, Teens and Young Adults." www.arthritis.org/juvenile-arthritis.php.

———. "Arthritis Foundation Aquatic Program." www.arthritis .org/aquatic-program.php.

———. *Arthritis Information: Practical Information—Where to Turn for Help*. Pamphlet, n.d.

———. "Bracing: One Treatment Option for Arthritis." www.arthritis.org/bracing.php.

———. "Diet & Nutrition." www.arthritis.org/juvenile-arthritis -nutritiondiet.php.

———. "Drugs in the Pipeline: Meet the Next Generation of Biologics." *Arthritis Today*. December 2007. www.arthritis.org/drug-pipeline.php.

——. "Exercise Overview." www.arthritis.org/juvenile -arthritis-exercise.php.

——. "Humira Approved for JRA." *In the Pipeline*. February 2008. www.arthritis.org/pipeline1.php.

——. "Introduction to Exercise." www.arthritis.org/exercise -intro.php.

——. *Juvenile Arthritis Fact Sheet*. 2008.

——. "Juvenile Arthritis." www.arthritis.org/disease-center .php?disease_id=38&df=effects.

——. "Juvenile Arthritis—Other Types and Related Conditions." http://ww2.arthritis.org/conditions/ DiseaseCenter/ja_other.asp#JPA.

——. "Juvenile Arthritis Treatment Options." www.arthritis .org/disease-center.php?disease_id=38&df=treatments.

——. "Juvenile Psoriatic Arthritis." http://ww2.arthritis.org/ conditions/DiseaseCenter/juvenilepsoriaticarthritis.asp.

——. "Juvenile Spondyloarthopathy." http://ww2.arthritis.org/ conditions/DiseaseCenter/juvenilespondyloarthopathy.asp.

——. *Managing Your Activities*. Pamphlet, 2005.

——. *Managing Your Pain*. Pamphlet, 2005.

——. "Partners." www.arthritis.org/partners.php.

——. "Sjögren's Syndrome." *Arthritis Today*. July/August 2007. www.arthritis.org/sjogrens-syndrome.php.

——. *Strengthening Exercises*.

——. "Take Control with the Arthritis Foundation's Life Improvement Series Programs." www.arthritis.org/programs.php.

——. "Types of Surgery." www.arthritis.org/types-surgery.php.

Arthritis National Research Foundation. "Studies May Yield New, Better Therapies." Press release. October 2007.

Arthritis Society of Canada. "Juvenile Arthritis." www.arthritis.ca/types%200f%20arthritis/childhood/defa ult.asp?s=1.

Arthritis Today. Flex-a-min ad. (January/February 2007): 3.

——. Medication Guide—Remicade (ad), Centocor Inc. (March/April 2008): 57–62.

——. Move Free ad, Schiff (January/February 2007): 82.

——. Patient Information Rituxan ad, Biogen Idec Inc. and Genentech, Inc. (January/February 2007): 18.

Callinan, Nancy. "Working with an Occupational Therapist." *Arthritis Self-Management* (March/April 2007): 15, 16, 19.

Centers for Education & Research on Therapeutics. "About CERTs." www.certs.hhs.gov/about_certs/index.html.

Chek Med Systems, Inc., and Jackson Siegelbaum Gastroenterology. "Gluten-Free Diet." www.gicare.com/pated/edtgs06.htm.

Childhood Arthritis and Rheumatology Research Alliance. "Current Studies." www.carragroup.org/content_dsp .do?pc=fact.

———. "Fact Sheet." www.carragroup.org/content_dsp.do ?pc=fact.

———. "Mission Statement." www.carragroup.org/content_dsp .do?pc=mission.

———. "Scientific Agenda." www.carragroup.org/content_dsp .do?pc=agenda.

Children's Hospital of Philadelphia. "Pain Management Program: Overview." www.chop.edu/consumer/jsp/ division/service.jsp?id=26662.

Cincinnati Children's Hospital Medical Center. "Mixed Connective Tissue Disease." Arthritis and Rheumatology Conditions and Diagnoses. www.cincinnatichildrens.org/ health/info/rheumatology/diagnose/mctd.htm.

Cohen, Stanley B. "Treatment of Arthritis/2008." *LoneStarthritis*. January 2008.

Consumer Health Information Network. "Juvenile Arthritis Symptoms." http://arthritis-symptom.com/Juvenile -Arthritis-Symptoms/index.htm.

Dinsmoor, Robert S. "When You're Considering Surgery." *Arthritis Self-Management* (March/April 2007): 20, 22–24.

Easter Seals. "The Story of Easter Seals." www.easterseals .com/site/PageServer?pagename=ntl_wwa_we_are&s_ esLocation=wwa.

Eustice, Carol, and Richard Eustice. "What Is Rheumatoid Factor?" About.com. arthritis.about.com/od/radiagnosis/ a/rheumfactor.htm.

Falco, Joyce L., Diane Veach Block, Mary Diane Vostrejs, and Karen M. Mergendahl. *JRA & Me: A Fun Workbook*. Denver, CO: Rocky Mountain Juvenile Arthritis Center at the National Jewish Center and the Arthritis Foundation. 1987.

Farrow, S. J. "Sir George Frederick Still (1868–1941)." *Rheumatology* (2006): 777–78.

Fibromyalgia Network. "Criteria for Diagnosis." www.fmnetnews.com/basics-symptoms.php.

———. "Symptoms." www.fmnetnews.com/basics-symptoms .php.

———. "Treatment." www.fmnetnews.com/basics-symptoms .php.

Gilbert, Tom. "New RA Therapy: Immune Reeducation vs. Immunosuppression." The Doctor Will See You Now. May 2004. www.thedoctorwillseeyounow.com/news/ arthritis/0504/ra.shtml.

Gott, Peter. "Home Remedies." *Sharon (PA) Herald*, April 24, 2007. www.sharonherald.com/community/local_story_ 113143138.html.

Greene, Alan. "Henoch-Schonlein Purpura." www.drgreene .org/body.cfm?id=21&action=detail&ref=842.

Heinrich Rizzo, Terrie. "On the Ball." *Arthritis Today* (March/ April 2008): 49–50.

Juvenile Scleroderma Network. "What Is Juvenile Scleroderma?" www.jsdn.org/whatisjsd.htm.

Lab Tests Online. "ESR." www.labtestsonline.org/ understanding/analytes/esr/glance.html.

———. "Rheumatoid Factor." www.labtestsonline.org/ understanding/analytes/rheumatoid/test.html.

Ludlam, Kerry. "A Hip, New Option." *Arthritis Today* (January/February 2007): 33.

Metroplex Clinical Research Center. "About Clinical Research." www.mcrcdallas.com/clinical_research_pt.aspx.

———. "Current Research." www.mcrcdallas.com/ current_reserach_pt.aspx.

———. "Site Qualifications." www.mcrcdallas.com/site_ qualifications_pf.aspx.

National Council on Independent Living. "Centers for Independent Living." www.ncil.org/about/ CentersforIndependentLiving.html.

National Heart Lung and Blood Institute. "What Is Sarcoidosis?" www.nhlbi.nih.gov/health/dci/ Diseases/sarc/sar_whatis.html.

National Highway Traffic Safety Administration, U.S. Department of Transportation. *Adapting Motor Vehicles for People with Disabilities.* Pamphlet, July 2002.

National Institute of Arthritis and Musculoskeletal Diseases. "Behçet's Disease." www.niams.nih.gov/Health_Info/ Behcets_Disease/behcets_disease_ff.asp.

———. "Mission Statement." www.niams.nih.gov/About_Us/ Mission_and_Purpose/mission.asp.

———. "NIH Pediatric Rheumatology Clinic." www.niams.nih .gov/Health_Info/Pediatric_Diseases/default.asp.

———. "Researchers Identify Genes That Increase Rheumatoid Arthritis Risk." Press release. October 4, 2007. www.niams .nih.gov/News_and_Events/Press_Releases/2007/10_04.asp.

National Osteoporosis Foundation. "Fast Facts on Osteoporosis." www.nof.org/osteoporosis/diseasefacts.htm.

Nemours Foundation. "About Anemia." KidsHealth. www.kidshealth.org/kid/health_problems/blood/ anemia.html.

———. "Inflammatory Bowel Disease." KidsHealth. www .kidshealth.org/kid/health_problems/stomach/IBD.html.

———. "Juvenile Rheumatoid Arthritis." KidsHealth. www.kidshealth.org/parent/medical/arthritis/jra.html.

———. "Kawasaki Disease." KidsHealth. www.kidshealth.org/ parent/medical/heart/kawasaki.html.

———. "Lyme Disease." KidsHealth. www.kidshealth.org/ parent/infections/bacterial_viral/lyme.html.

———. "Thyroid Disorders." KidsHealth. www.kidshealth.org/ kid/health_problems/glandshoromones/thyroid.html.

New Jersey Association of County Disability Services, Inc. Pamphlet, December 2007.

New Zealand Dermatological Society, Inc. "Cutaneous Polyarteritis Nodosa." www.dermnetnz.org/vascular/ polyarteritis-nodosa.html.

———. "Henoch-Schönlein Purpura." www.dermnetnz.org/ vascular/hsp.html.

———. "Kawasaki Disease." www.dermnetnz.org/vascular/polyarteritis-nodosa.html.

Penn State Children's Hospital. "Health & Disease Information: Juvenile Arthritis." www.hmc.psu.edu/childrens/healthinfo/jkl/juvenilearthritis.htm.

Roberts, Brandie J. "Conference Report: Highlights of the Society for Pediatric Dermatology Annual Meeting." *Medscape Dermatology*, 2005. www.medscape.com/viewarticle/512426_5.

Rosenfeld, Isadore. "Do Herbal Remedies Work?" *Parade*, March 16, 2008, 18, 21.

Shaklee Corp. "A Natural Approach to Arthritis." Doing Life Intentionally Together. www.healthyfiles.com.

Shomon, Mary. "Hashimoto's vs. Hypothyroidism: What's the Difference?" About.com. http://thyroid.about.com/cs/hypothyroidism/a/hashivshypo.htm.

Siegfried, Donna Rae. "2007 Drug Guide." *Arthritis Today* (January/February 2007): 38–56.

Simmons, Kenna. "Strong Advice." *Arthritis Today* (January/February 2007): 20.

Sports Fitness Advisor. "Resistance Band Exercises." www.sport-fitness-advisor.com/resistance-band-exercises.html.

State of New Jersey, Department of Labor and Workforce Development. "Services for Individuals for Disabilities." http://lwd.dol.state.nj.us/labor/dvrs/disabled/DisIndex.html.

Stone, John H. "Rheumatoid Arthritis Questions." *Arthritis Today*. June 2007. www.arthritis.org/rheumatoid-arthritis-questions.php.

Taylor, Michele. "Kid Power." *Arthritis Today*. July/August 1998.

UCLA Pediatric Pain Program. "Who We Are." www.mattel.ucla.edu/pedspain/whoweare.php.

University of Alabama at Birmingham Center for Education and Research on Therapeutics. "Musculoskeletal Center Wins $3.8 Million Research Grant." Press release. October 19, 2007.

University of Maryland Medical Center. "Omega-6 Fatty
   Acids." www.umm.edu/altmed/articles/omega-6–
   000317.htm.

University of Washington Department of Medicine
   Orthopaedics and Sports Medicine. "Fatigue."
   www.orthop.washington.edu/uw/livingwith/tabID__3376/
   ItemID__85/PageID__109/Articles/Default.aspx.

U.S. Department of Health and Human Services. *The
   Pediatric Rheumatology Workforce: A Study of the
   Supply and Demand for Pediatric Rheumatologists.*
   http://bhpr.hrsa.gov/healthworkforce/reports/ped_
   rheumatology/6.htm.

U.S. National Institutes of Health. "Understanding Clinical
   Trials." ClinicalTrials.gov. www.clinicaltrials.gov/ct2/
   info/understand.

U.S. National Library of Medicine & the National Institutes of
   Health. "Systemic Lupus Erythematosus." MedlinePlus.
   www.nlm.nih.gov/medlineplus/ency/article/000435.htm.

———. "Ventricular Tachycardia." MedlinePlus. www.nlm.nih
   .gov/medlineplus/ency/article/000187.htm.

———. "Wegener's Granulomatosis." MedlinePlus. www.nlm
   .nih.gov/medlineplus/ency/article/000135.htm.

Wedro, Benjamin C. "Pericarditis." MedicineNet.
   www.medicinenet.com/pericarditis/article.htm.

Who Named It? "Sir George Frederick Still."
   www.whonamedit.com/doctor.cfm/1671.html.

Wikimedia Foundation, Inc. "Autoantibody." Wikipedia.
   http://en.wikipedia.org/wiki/Autoantibody.

———. "National Institute of Arthritis and Musculoskeletal
   and Skin Diseases." Wikipedia. http://en.wikipedia.org/
   wiki/NIAMS.

———. "Intravenous immunoglobulin." Wikipedia. http://en
   .wikipedia.org/wiki/Intravenous_immunoglobulin.

WEB SITES

Aids for Arthritis. www.aidsforarthritis.com.
Arthritis Foundation. www.arthritis.org.

Centers for Education & Research on Therapeutics. www.certs
.hhs.gov.

Martha's Vineyard Holistic Retreat. www.mvholisticretreat.com.

Medscape. www.medscape.com.

Mercer County Office on Disability Services. www.state.nj.us/
counties/mercer/departments/hs/disability.html.

Metroplex Clinical Research Center. www.mcrcdallas.com/
mcrc/index_professional.aspx.

U.S. Department of Health and Human Services, Insure Kids
Now. www.insurekidsnow.gov.

Yoga Journal. www.yogajournal.com.

Index

Access Anything, LLC, 106, 124
accessible clothing, 144
acupuncture, 82–83
ADA. *See* Americans with
    Disabilities Act (ADA)
adaptive devices. *See* assistive
    devices
adaptive sports, 104–6, 253;
    adaptive sports centers,
    105–6, 124; Miracle League,
    104–5; Dance>Detour, 105
advocacy, 79–80, 178–80, 194,
    196–97, 205–6, 209–10, 214,
    217, 228
American Academy of Child and
    Adolescent Psychiatry, 191
American Academy of Pain
    Management, 191
American Autoimmune Related
    Diseases Association, Inc.
    (AARDA), 235–36, 244
American Board of Medical
    Specialties, 82
American College of
    Rheumatology (ACR), 228,
    238
American Occupational Therapy
    Association (AOTA), 140, 153

American Physical Therapy
    Association (APTA), 153
American Psychological
    Association, 191
American Self-Help Group
    Clearinghouse, 191
Americans with Disabilities Act
    (ADA), 206, 210, 213
anemia, 17, 20, 22, 37, 41,
    46–47, 165
ANRF. *See* Arthritis National
    Research Foundation
Arthritis Foundation, ix, x, 11,
    13, 22, 28, 32, 41, 62,
    115–16, 120, 125, 134,
    157–58, 160, 167–68, 171,
    173, 175, 177, 181, 191,
    206–8, 218, 234, 237–38,
    242, 244, 247–48, 255,
    264; exercise/exercise
    programs, 95, 97–100, 103,
    107–8, 124, 132; volunteer
    opportunities, 6, 16, 57,
    179–80, 194, 228
Arthritis National Research
    Foundation (ANRF), 58, 60,
    236–37, 243–44, 255–57,
    259–64, 270

assistive devices, 133, 139, 142–46, 164, 193, 211, 247–53

autoimmune, 28, 32, 40, 48, 61, 119, 125, 164, 235–36, 241, 260, 263–64, 267 .

biofeedback, 83

biologic agents, 59–60, 67–71, 256–57; Enbrel, 59, 67, 69–70, 76–77, 228, 270; Humira, 5, 59, 69–70; intravenous immunoglobulin (IVIG), 69–70; Kineret, 69–70; Orencia, 69–70, 76, 115; Remicade, 46, 59, 69–70; Rituxan, 69–70

biologic response modifiers (BRMs). *See* biologic agents

blood tests/blood work, 16–17, 20, 22, 37, 39–41, 49, 66, 188; antinuclear antibody (ANA), 16–17; complete blood count, 16–17; erythrocyte sedimentation rate (ESR), 16–17; rheumatoid factor, 16–17, 22

braces, 147–48

camps/camping, 173–74, 212

CARRA. *See* Childhood Arthritis & Rheumatology Research Alliance (CARRA)

Centers for Education and Research on Therapeutics (CERTs), 238–39, 267–68

Centers for Independent Living (CILs), 197, 209–10

Childhood Arthritis & Rheumatology Research Alliance (CARRA), 237–38, 242, 244, 264–67

chronic regional pain syndrome (CRPS), 44–45

clinical trials, 59, 61, 80, 86, 240–42, 256–57, 259, 266, 270

counseling, 34, 162, 165, 167, 169–70, 182; vocational counseling, 198–99

Crohn's disease, 35, 235, 256–57

CRPS. *See* chronic regional pain syndrome (CRPS)

dactylitis, 23

dancing, 103, 105

dating, 189–91

dentist, 74, 86–87

Division of Disability Services (DDS), 196, 205–6

documentaries: *Kids Get Arthritis Too*, 11; *Waking Up*, 233

driving: accessible vans and mobility, 201, 203, 205; driver training, 199–203; vehicle modification, 199, 201–5

Easter Seals, 210–13

endocrinologist, 72

fatigue, 16, 18, 24, 26, 32–34, 36–37, 39, 41, 44, 47–48, 65, 70, 99–100, 143, 145, 155, 162–65, 221, 252

Fernandez, Alexander, 56–57

fibromyalgia, 33–34, 44, 62, 72, 99, 162, 194

flares/flare-ups, 5, 26–27, 65, 73, 75, 77, 110, 113, 122–23, 130, 140, 141–42, 148, 150–51, 153, 155, 161, 216–17, 219–20, 226, 252, 269

Ginsberg, Seth, 79–80
Granger, Gale A., 60–61, 257, 259–60

health insurance, 82, 128, 195, 197–98, 205
heart conditions, 20, 24, 34, 36, 38, 41, 44, 47–48, 50–52; pericarditis, 50–51; supraventricular tachycardia, 51–52; ventricular tachycardia, 51–52
herbal remedies, 84, 86
HLA-B27, 19, 24–25
homeschooling, 220–22
human growth hormone (HGH), 72–73
hypnotherapy, 171

IBD. *See* inflammatory bowel disease
Individualized Education Program (IEP), 214–15, 218
Individuals with Disabilities Education Act (IDEA), 213–14, 217
inflammatory bowel disease (IBD), 24, 35–36
iritis. *See* uveitis
isometric exercises, 132
isotonic exercises, 132

juvenile arthritis, juvenile scleroderma, 42–44; localized, 42–43; systemic, 43–44
juvenile arthritis, juvenile spondyloarthropies (JSp), 10, 23–26, 79; enteropathogenic arthritis, 24; juvenile ankylosing spondylitis (AS), 24, 56, 62–65, 67, 256;

reactive arthritis, 24; seronegative enthesopathy and arthropathy (SEA) syndrome, 20, 24
juvenile arthritis, juvenile vasculitis, 10, 37–40, 157; Behçet's disease, 37, 39; cutaneous polyarteritis nodosa (PAN), 37–38; giant cell arteritis, 37, 64; Henoch-Schönlein purpura (HSP), 37–38; Kawasaki disease, 37–38, 67, 69, 270; Wegener's granulomatosis, 37, 39–40, 64, 66, 257
juvenile arthritis, types of: enthesitis-related arthritis, 20, 23–26; juvenile dermatomyositis, 10, 40, 44, 66, 119, 238, 267; juvenile idiopathic arthritis (JIA)/juvenile rheumatoid arthritis (JRA), 2, 10, 13–23, 32, 35, 44, 50, 56, 62–64, 67, 96–97, 99, 129, 130, 133, 144, 150, 166, 194, 202, 257, 264–65; juvenile psoriatic arthritis, 10, 20, 23, 63–64, 66–67, 256, 269; juvenile systemic lupus erythematosus, 10, 40–42, 263, 265–67; oligoarticular JIA, 19, 21; polyarticular JIA, 20–23; systemic JIA, 19–20

Lyme disease, 2–3, 10, 14, 21–22, 34–35
lymphocytes, 32, 260

MCTD. *See* mixed connective tissue disease (MCTD)

medicine, types of: analgesics, 62–63; anticonvulsants, 50, 71; antidepressants, 72; aspirin, 58, 63–64, 202; biologic response modifiers (BRMs) (*see* biologic agents); corticosteriods, 59, 64–65, 73; COX-2 inhibitors, 63, 118; disease-modifying antirheumatic drugs (DMARDs), 65–66, 71; Methotrexate, 5, 46, 59, 66–67, 69–71, 76–77, 86, 232, 257, 269; muscle relaxants, 71; Naprosyn/Naproxen, 58, 63, 69, 76–77; nerve blocks, 71–72; nonsteroidal anti-inflammatory drugs (NSAIDs), 63–64, 66; opioids, 71; Prednisone, 4, 64–65, 69, 71–73, 76–77, 121–22; salicylates, 63, 158

Medicaid, 195–98, 211, 213

Medicare, 196, 211

meditation, 183

Metroplex Clinical Research Center (MCRC), 58, 239–42, 268–69

mixed connective tissue disease (MCTD), 44

mobility devices: crutches, 104, 148–49; walker, 104, 106, 148, 205, 211; wheelchair, 104–6, 144, 148–50, 163, 187, 189, 194, 199, 202, 204–5, 215–16, 227, 249, 251, 253

National Center for Complementary and Alternative Medicine (NCCAM) Clearinghouse, 243

National Institute of Arthritis and Musculoskeletal and Skin Diseases (NIAMS), 232, 234–35, 242

National Institutes of Health (NIH) Pediatric Rheumatology Clinic, 240–41

National Mobility Equipment Dealers Association (NMEDA), 205

NMEDA. *See* National Mobility Equipment Dealers Association (NMEDA)

nodules, 15, 18, 48–49

occupational therapy, 34, 127, 138–53, 175, 211

ophthalmologist, 87

osteoporosis, 49–50, 64, 108, 239, 256, 268

pain management, 57, 146, 155–62; programs, 161–62

paraffin wax, 135–36, 157

pauciarticular JRA. *See* oligoarticular JIA *in* juvenile arthritis, types of

physical therapist assistant, 131, 152

physical therapy, 2, 5, 80, 127–39, 151–53, 161, 211, 240

rashes, 15–16, 20, 32, 39–41, 44, 66, 70, 257

remission, 19, 27, 59, 69, 226, 262

resistance bands, 107, 109, 133

rheumatoid factor, 17, 19–20, 22

rheumatologist, 2, 13, 18, 22, 28, 56, 58–59, 68, 70–71, 74–76, 78, 81, 87, 119, 161, 173, 175, 179, 182, 191, 193,

222–23, 225–28, 232, 237, 239–40, 242; pediatric rheumatologist, 2, 13, 161, 179, 225–27, 237, 240
Rizzo, Juliette, 99, 194
Rouba, Kelly, 96, 129, 144, 202, 227, 283–85

sacroiliac joints, 23–24
sarcoidosis, 36–37, 50
Section 504 Accommodation Plan, 214–15
self-help books, 167–68, 180
shoe lift, 148
Sjögren's syndrome, 32–33, 235
slow-acting antirheumatic drugs (SAARDs). *See* disease-modifying antirheumatic drugs (DMARDs) *in* medicine, types of
Social Security Disability Insurance (SSDI), 196
splints, 78, 141, 147–48, 150, 211
stability ball, 94, 133
Still, George Frederic, 13
Still's disease. *See* systemic JIA *in* juvenile arthritis, types of
stress, 43, 45, 83, 93, 103–4, 159, 162, 169, 176, 181–85, 191
Supplemental Security Income (SSI), 195–96
supplements, 83–86, 118–19, 122; calcium, 43, 50, 64, 84–85, 114, 125; fish oil, 117, 125; glucosamine and chondroitin, 83–84; Shaklee Corporation, 85; vitamin D3, 125, 164
support groups, 168–69, 180–81, 206, 210

surgery, 27, 49, 77–78, 80–82, 87, 148, 156; arthroscopy, 78; hip resurfacing, 81; joint fusion or arthrodesis, 78; joint replacement, 80; osteotomy, 78; resection, 80; soft tissue release, 78; synovectomy, 78
synovium, 11–12, 78

temporomandibular joint, 23
Thera-Bands. *See* resistance bands
thyroid disorders, 47–49; Hashimoto's thyroiditis, 48; hyperthyroidism, 47–48; hypothyroidism, 47–48
TNF. *See* tumor necrosis factor (TNF)
transcutaneous electrical nerve stimulation (TENS), 136
tumor necrosis factor (TNF), 59–61, 67, 70, 256, 259, 270; TNF inhibitor, 46, 59, 232, 256

ulcerative colitis, 35, 80
ultrasound, 49, 51, 136
uveitis, 21, 45–46, 87, 119, 235, 265

vocational rehabilitation, 198–201
volunteering, 6, 176–80, 236, 241–42, 244

walking aids. *See* mobility devices
weight gain, 64, 121–23
weight loss, 24, 36, 40, 48, 120–21
World Laughter Tour, 183

yoga, 92–93, 97, 138, 161, 176

About the Author and Illustrator

Kelly Rouba, who has juvenile rheumatoid arthritis, was only nineteen years old when she was thrown into the fast-paced world of news reporting. While still in college, Ms. Rouba took a position as a stringer for the *Trenton Times*, marking the start of her career in professional writing.

For the past few years, she has written for numerous magazines and Web sites. In addition, she is coproducer of mobilewomen.org and a member of the site's advisory committee. Ms. Rouba is also working for EAD & Associates, an emergency management firm, and she sits on the New Jersey Special Needs Advisory Panel.

Recently, Ms. Rouba had the pleasure of working for Assemblywoman Linda Greenstein. Prior to that, she worked as a special needs specialist for the Department of Homeland Security/FEMA Region II. Through this position, she handled emergency preparedness issues relating to special needs populations.

Previously, Ms. Rouba worked for the *Pennington Post* as an editorial assistant and freelance writer. She has also handled public relations projects for Robert Wood Johnson University Hospital at Hamilton and Deutsch Communications Group in Princeton on a freelance basis.

Throughout her career, Ms. Rouba has interviewed numerous notable personalities ranging from Dr. Ruth Westheimer (psychosexual therapist) to Duane Chapman (*Dog the Bounty Hunter*) to Elisabeth Hasselbeck (*The View*). In 2006, she was honored by the State of New Jersey's Department of Labor for her outstanding work ethic and success in the workplace as a local journalist and woman with a disability.

Ms. Rouba is also a 2008 Governor's Volunteerism Award recipient. She is a member of Project Freedom's Board of Trustees and Hamilton Township's Advisory Commission on the Status of Women. For several years, she has been the public relations chair for both the Central New Jersey Kappa Delta Alumnae Association and the Kappa Delta Chapter Advisory Board at The College of New Jersey. And, she recently began assisting with public relations for the Granville Academy, which has schools worldwide.

In addition, Ms. Rouba is a member of the Arthritis National Research Foundation's Advisory Board. She also has been publicity chair and a key organizer of the Arthritis Foundation's Mercer County Arthritis Walk for two years and the Middlesex County Arthritis Walk for one year. At last year's walk, Assemblywoman Greenstein presented Ms. Rouba with a proclamation recognizing her community service efforts and role as a journalist.

In the past, Ms. Rouba was publicity chair of the Trenton St. Patrick's Day Parade & Scholarship Committee. Last year, she served on the planning committee for the New Jersey Governor's Conference on Employment for People with Disabilities and was chair of the public relations sub-committee. She also served as emcee and a panelist at the conference.

From December 2006 through February 2008, Ms. Rouba held the title of Ms. Wheelchair New Jersey. She is now the state program coordinator. To date, Ms. Rouba has been featured in numerous publications and television programs, from NJN News to *Live with Regis and Kelly*. She was also interviewed on

ABC's Perspective New Jersey, WZBN News, and Disaboom Radio. In addition, she was featured in two commercials.

Presently, Ms. Rouba is being filmed by Agency New Jersey for two documentaries and she is hosting and writing for a new New Jersey–based television show called *Breaking Barriers*.

Ms. Rouba earned her BA from The College of New Jersey in 2002, where she majored in journalism/professional writing and minored in communications.

Geoffrey Trapp currently aids in action figure production for the entertainment collectibles company NECA. He has shown artwork in several galleries, including the Bill Maynes Gallery of New York. In 2005, Geoffrey graduated from the Rutgers Mason Gross School of the Arts. He is very grateful to his longtime friend Kelly Rouba for including his illustrations in her book.